T0303984

Volume 8

TAXATION BY POLITICAL INERTIA

TAXATION BY POLITICAL INERTIA
Financing the Growth of Government in Britain

RICHARD ROSE AND TERENCE KARRAN

Routledge
Taylor & Francis Group

LONDON AND NEW YORK

First published in 1987 by Allen & Unwin

This edition first published in 2019
by Routledge
2 Park Square, Milton Park, Abingdon, Oxon OX14 4RN

and by Routledge
711 Third Avenue, New York, NY 10017

Routledge is an imprint of the Taylor & Francis Group, an informa business

British Library Cataloguing in Publication Data
A catalogue record for this book is available from the British Library

ISBN: 978-1-138-56291-2 (Set)
ISBN: 978-0-429-48988-4 (Set) (ebk)
ISBN: 978-0-8153-4967-9 (Volume 8) (hbk)
ISBN: 978-1-351-10745-7 (Volume 8) (ebk)

Publisher's Note
The publisher has gone to great lengths to ensure the quality of this reprint but
points out that some imperfections in the original copies may be apparent.

Disclaimer
The publisher has made every effort to trace copyright holders and would welcome
correspondence from those they have been unable to trace.

TAXATION
BY
POLITICAL
INERTIA

Financing the Growth of
Government in Britain

Richard Rose

Terence Karran

London
ALLEN & UNWIN
Boston   Sydney   Wellington

Allen & Unwin, the academic imprint of

Unwin Hyman Ltd

PO Box 18, Park Lane, Hemel Hempstead, Herts HP2 4TE, UK
40 Museum Street, London WC1A 1LU, UK
37/39 Queen Elizabeth Street, London SE1 2QB, UK

Allen & Unwin Inc.,
8 Winchester Place, Winchester, Mass. 01890, USA

Allen & Unwin (Australia) Ltd,
8 Napier Street, North Sydney, NSW 2060, Australia

Allen & Unwin (New Zealand) Ltd in association with the Port
Nicholson Press Ltd,
60 Cambridge Terrace, Wellington, New Zealand

First published in 1987

British Library Cataloguing in Publication Data

Rose, Richard, *1933–*
 Taxation by political inertia: financing the growth
 of government in Britain.
1. Finance, Public——Great Britain
I. Title   II. Karran, Terence
336.41 HJ1023
ISBN 0-04-320197-0
ISBN 0-04-320198-9 Pbk

Library of Congress Cataloging in Publication Data

Rose, Richard, *1933–*
 Taxation by political inertia.
Bibliography: p.
Includes index.
1. Taxation——Great Britain.
I. Karran, Terence.   II. Title.
HJ2619.R68 1987   336.2'00941   87-11478
ISBN 0-04-320197-0 (alk. paper)
ISBN 0-04-320198-9 (pbk.: alk. paper)

Typeset in 10/12 point Palatino by MCL Computerset Ltd.
and printed in Great Britain by Billing & Sons Ltd., London & Worcester

Contents

iv

Figures and Tables

Acknowledgements

Anyone who has ever contemplated the national tax system as a whole is immediately struck by how *un*systematic it is. Different taxes appear to have been introduced for different reasons at different times, and each to have grown without plan or direction, more or less reflecting forces of political inertia. The more that critics of a tax system attack the alleged faults, the more it is made apparent that the forces accounting for this 'unsystematic' system must be strong, and only imperfectly understood.

In order to understand taxation, one must deal with taxes as they actually are, and with politicians as they actually are, rather than as one might like them to be. To understand taxes as they actually are requires a public-policy approach that draws upon knowledge from many different disciplines. At a time when social science and business schools have diverged, it is well for social scientists to remember why lawyers and accountants, as well as economists and political scientists, have a professional interest in taxation.

In developing ideas robust enough to be relevant across time and space, the first-named author benefited greatly from a period as a visiting scholar in the Fiscal Affairs Department of the International Monetary Fund, a group whose daily work raises problems that are best understood in the light of a millennium of fiscal history.

The Economic and Social Research Council (formerly, the Social Science Research Council) financed the work of the authors through a programme grant to study the Growth of Government in the United Kingdom (HR 7849/1). The grant made it possible to join together topics that can be set asunder by conventional academic boundaries: laws, taxation, public employment, political organizations and the big-spending programmes of the contemporary mixed-economy welfare state. As the citations in this book show, each of the topics is relevant to taxation, for all are part of a single system of government.

Helpful comments upon portions of the manuscript circulated in draft were received from Lord Barnett, Naomi Caiden, M. F. Cayley, David Heald, Arnold J. Heidenheimer, Edward C. Page, Joseph Pechman, Cedric Sandford, Douglas Todd and Jack Wiseman. A substantial portion of the comparative analysis was presented in a special issue on taxation of the *Journal of Public Policy*, 1985, 5, 3).

Responsibility for any errors of fact and interpretation remains with the authors.

Richard Rose
University of Strathclyde

Terence Karran
Leeds Polytechnic

CHAPTER ONE

Why Inertia? Taxation as a Political Problem

Politics is about power, and nowhere is this truism more important than in taxation. Whereas participating in elections or receiving social benefits enhances an individual's resources, taxation involves the surrender of money. Taxes are paid because laws compel people to do what they would not otherwise do, give money to government. Only a government with substantial authority – moral as well as organizational – has the power to extract money from citizens.

Power precedes taxation: without some form of power it is not possible to extract money. But the force of arms – whether belonging to bandits in a primitive society or to a mugger in a modern city – is not taxation as we know it. In a modern state, taxes are collected peacefully under the authority of law. The ability to collect taxes is a defining characteristic of a modern state (Rose, 1976).

The need for money is a constant of government. When the American bank robber Willie Sutton was asked 'Why do you rob banks?', he replied: 'Because that's where the money is.' A government levies taxes because it is a simple way to get money; unlike organizations trading in the market, government can enact laws to raise revenue. While taxation can be treated as a means to many different ends – managing the economy, redistributing income, or discouraging drinking or smoking – it is always the principal means of financing the costs of modern government.

Taxation precedes big government. The development of the

1

capacity to collect large and increasing sums of money in taxes has been a necessary condition of the growth of government. In order to spend two-fifths of the national product on public policies, government must collect upwards of two-fifths of the national product in taxation. A government that has not the institutional capacity to collect lots of money in taxation cannot be a big-spending government (Goode, 1984).

Public spending on education, health care, social security and other public policies provides tangible benefits of citizenship. Nearly every citizen benefits from programmes financed by public expenditure. When opinion polls ask whether people favour more spending on health, education and pensions, or spending being kept the same or cut, most of the electorate consistently endorse more spending (*Gallup Political Index* No. 315, 1986: 15).

Taxes represent the costs of citizenship; everyone must pay substantial taxes to finance the benefits of public expenditure. When the Gallup Poll asks people how important it is that government cut taxes across the board, about two-thirds consistently say this is important (Heald and Wybrow, 1986: 128). The dues of citizenship differ from the dues of a social club, for a club is a voluntary organization whereas citizens are compelled to pay taxes.

Many studies of contemporary government concentrate upon the friendly hand of government, the hand that pays for the many benefits of the welfare state. Yet it is also necessary to look at the unfriendly hand of government, the hand that collects the taxes to pay for these benefits. The bigger the size of government, the greater the importance of taxation. The power to tax is a double-edged sword. Imposing taxes gives politicians more money to spend on popular social programmes, but it also identifies politicians with the costs of government. In office politicians find that they need money to finance the popular programmes of government. Big tax cuts normally require big cuts in popular programmes, a big increase in the public deficit, or both. The practical issue is not that of deciding in the abstract how much a government ought to tax and spend; it is to pay for the long-established commitments of the mixed-economy welfare state.

Party principles are not a good guide to what politicians in office will do about taxation. A rightwing party may proclaim a desire to cut taxes, but when it learns that the price of doing so is cutting popular programmes, there is often a change of mind. For example, the Thatcher government has not produced a big reduction in total taxation, because it has not been prepared to accept the political obloquy of making radical cuts in costly but popular social programmes. The Reagan administration did reduce taxes without substantially cutting expenditure in 1981; it thus became responsible for a big boost in the federal deficit, and had to accept tax increases the following year.

Public-finance theories are not a sufficient guide to taxation when they treat the concerns of politicians as exogenous variables (Lindbeck, 1976), that is, influences outside the theoretical calculus of economic policy. Theoretical prescriptions about taxation are 'of little help in dealing with the everyday problems of the British tax system', conclude two experienced applied economists.

> The ways in which actual taxes differ from theoretical taxes are often of much greater economic significance than the ways in which theoretical taxes differ from each other. (Kay and King, 1983:1)

The concerns of politicians are immediately relevant in making public policy, including major economic decisions. Politics is about the articulation and resolution of conflicting opinions. There is no shortage of conflicting opinions about taxation among the general public, and among tax experts. Disagreements reflect conflicts between political values, not least between what politicians would like to do, and what they find it is necessary to do. In order to understand how politicians finance the costs of big government, we need a political theory of taxation.[1]

Maximizing Tax Revenue While Minimizing Political Costs

The political problem of taxation is easily stated but hard to resolve: how can elected politicians maximize spending on popular programmes while minimizing the political costs of paying for these programmes? Although the tasks of spending money and collecting revenue are logically complementary, there is no symmetry in the calculation of the political costs and benefits. The politics of avoiding blame are very different from the politics of credit-claiming (cf. Weaver, 1986; Mayhew, 1974: 49ff). For example, American Congressmen may support bills that they know will not become law in order to claim credit with the electorate for taking a popular stand.

Claiming credit for public expenditure is attractive, for most public spending goes on the goods of government, such popular programmes as pensions, health care and education. It is also easy, for no positive decision is required: the big programmes of big government are primarily the product of old laws, enacted decades or generations ago (Rose, 1986). A party newly installed in office is immediately responsible for millions of pensions, educating millions of young people and caring for the health of young and old. Without taking any positive actions, it can claim credit for all the continuing programmes of the welfare state.

Credit-claiming is an important political art. The newest recruit to Cabinet soon learns to match rhetoric to formal responsibilities. Since a minister is notionally responsible for everything a department does, when discussing popular spending programmes he tells the House of Commons: 'I have decided . . . ', even though the relevant actions were determined under his predecessors in that office. In taxation, credit may be claimed by introducing tax cuts. However, the simple desire to introduce tax cuts is no match for the necessity to collect large sums of public revenue. Margaret Thatcher – a committed opponent of big government, and by training a tax lawyer – is a spectacular example of the inadequacy of the politician's will to introduce big tax cuts when confronted by the government's need for big sums of money.

Taxation is a political orphan. No politician wants to claim paternity for unpopular tax increases. Yet annually raising vast and increasing sums of tax revenue is necessary to finance big government. The opportunities for cutting taxes are marginal. Moreover, a reduction in the rate of one particular tax is no promise of a reduction in total taxation; it may be counterbalanced by increased revenue from another tax, so that spending commitments are not reduced.

4

Non-Decision-making: Credit without Blame

Keeping out of trouble is one of the basic rules of politics – and being identified as the cause of increased taxation is likely to invite political trouble. Since government collects large and increasing sums of money each year, politicians cannot easily do what is superficially attractive, voting for tax cuts. The practical political problem is how to avoid blame for taxes that government *must* collect. The basic axiom of the politics of taxation is thus:

Non-decision-making is preferred to decision-making.

A decision is an identifiable political act that resolves a conflict about what government should do in a given context (Parry and Morriss, 1974: 324). A tax law is a decision identifying the method of calculating a tax that citizens must pay to government. Enacting a tax is a very visible political activity; a minister is responsible for introducing a bill to the House of Commons, and the governing party must accept full responsibility for it. While a government can fudge the specific content of decisions in foreign policy, or blur responsibility (for example by agreements with industry and unions about the economy), a tax law cannot be vague; it must prescribe in detail the means of calculating what citizens are obligated to pay. The paternity of a tax act is clear too: a party with a majority in the House of Commons cannot escape responsibility for introducing a tax.

Whether or not the existing tax structure is optimal in economic theory, from a politician's point of view it can be viewed as the least worst that is available. Compared to the alternative of taking responsibility for introducing new tax measures, a politician may decide that doing nothing and relying upon existing taxes is preferable. If keeping out of trouble is a basic law of politics, then not making decisions about taxes is one way to avoid trouble – in the short run at least.

Force of Politicial Inertia

How can government collect tens of billions in taxes each year if politicians avoid making decisions about taxation? The answer is: taxation by political inertia. Political inertia is the force that makes it possible for politicians to raise the maximum of tax revenue with the minimum of political costs.

Political inertia is not static; it represents the tendency of objects in motion to remain in motion. As long as tax revenue can be collected through the force of inertia, then no decisions are required of politicians. The tax laws, administration and economic activity that generate revenue remain in place. Only if government decides to alter the direction of inertia is action required. A significant change in taxation requires a political will strong enough to redirect a tax system that moves with great force from its own momentum, and to accept the resulting political criticism for introducing new tax measures.

Tax laws remain on the statute book from year to year. Upon entering office a government finds that it has inherited a host of tax laws as well as a host of statutes authorizing spending programmes.[2] Established laws authorize the collection of billions of pounds in income tax, social security, sales, excise, property and other taxes. The statute book does more than give authority to the government of the day to collect tax revenue. It also leaves the political responsibility for enacting tax laws with governments of past decades, generations or centuries.

The administrative apparatus for tax collection is also sustained by political inertia. Tax-collecting agencies are mammoth bureaucracies; they are not created overnight. Being staffed by personnel trained to carry out laws routinely, tax agencies can continue by their own inertia without any decisions by politicians. A decision to introduce a novel tax is likely to be met with resistance by tax administrators. Known taxes are preferred to unknown taxes, for they are predictable sources of revenue that can be administered by established routines.

Economic activity is continuous too. Even if there is nil growth in the national product, the economy will still produce another year's tax revenue from the recurring activities of a steady-state economy. When the economy grows, the application of established laws to a bigger tax base produces more tax revenue. As

6

long as tax legislation remains the same, taxpayers as well as tax collectors can draw upon lots of experience in calculating and paying large sums in taxation.

By sustaining familiar taxes, inertia tends to make taxation politically acceptable, or at least less unacceptable. Proposals for new taxes can induce anxiety by their unfamiliarity, whereas an existing tax has been approved by Parliament and is familiar to citizens. Familiarity tends to increase acceptance, if only by a process of resignation. British taxpayers are so inured to existing levels of taxation that consistently more people are likely to expect taxes to rise than to fall (see Figure 8.1).

Because politicians are risk-averse, they want to avoid being blamed for increasing taxes. Politicians rarely make substantial changes in tax law, notwithstanding the recurrent clamour to do something about taxation, and the assumption in many writings about taxation that choices are frequent (cf. Roskamp and Forte, 1981; Robinson and Sandford, 1983; Alt, 1983). When the status quo is attacked, strong pressures are mobilized in its defence, for the simple reason that it is there. Those who dislike existing tax laws may be less intense in political activity than those who fear adverse effects from new tax legislation. In the short term, the theory of political inertia prescribes: Do nothing.

Non-decision-making is not equivalent to defaulting on tax collection; it means enforcing past laws to provide current revenue. Nor does it mean that tax revenue does not increase; seemingly small annual changes in the economy, in conjunction with established laws, can gradually compound into big increases in revenue (Rose and Karran, 1984). Thus, the force of political inertia is consistent with the growth of government.

Routines Rather Than Decisions

If government were to start afresh after every election, then the national tax system could conceivably be decided by the government of the day. But in fact government is continuing; the great bulk of public programmes is carried forward by the force of political inertia: this is true of spending as well as taxing, and of public agencies as well as of public employees, and it is also true of public laws (Rose, 1984).

The theory of political inertia does not deny that political

7

decisions are made. What it does is to emphasize that most decisions determining taxes today were in fact taken by governments in the more or less distant past. Because most British taxes have their origins in the time of Queen Victoria, George III, Elizabeth I, or that of medieval kings, the blame for their introduction can be placed on politicians who died long ago. Even in a country such as France, where constitutions can change with some frequency, most tax laws endure from regime to regime.

Once a law is enacted and implemented, its administration is carried out by routine, rather than by decisions of the politicians who constitute the government of the day (Rose, forthcoming). Routines rely upon bureaucratic adherence to formal laws and regulations, which are particularly numerous and significant in tax administration, and upon informal standard operating procedures that constitute the expertise of tax officials. Routines are also important for what they exclude: they are 'substitutes for the rational calculations' posited by theories of frequent and active decision-making (Sharkansky, 1970: 5).

In any given year, most taxation is administered rather than decided – that is, the great bulk of tax revenue is collected by permanent officials who routinely carry out established laws that antedate the entry to office of the government of the day. Only a very small proportion of revenue will be collected according to laws enacted during the relatively brief term of the government of the day. By relying upon the inertia of existing taxes, the governing party avoids the blame of introducing new taxes, while claiming credit for the benefits financed by the revenue thus gained.

Because the organized routines that sustain inertia are directly observable, they provide an empirically verifiable basis for explaining taxation. The absence of a decision is most parsioniously explained by the uncalculated maintenance of routines. However, public choice theories, assuming that politicians 'must' constantly be calculating the net present utility of their activities, cite the absence of a decision as evidence that a positive decision to do nothing 'must have been' taken. Whether or not such an inference is valid can only be proven by studying the behaviour of decision-makers. A decision-making approach does not depend upon inference concerning the motivations of politicians: it starts from empirical observation of whether current taxation is authorized by current decisions, or by decisions from the distant past.

The 'free policy choice' about taxation that Musgrave (1969: 147) thought available in a country with a large and increasing national product is not available today – and perhaps it never was. A decision to introduce a major new tax today would stimulate controversies about raising a large and visible sum of money in a novel way. A decision to repeal a major tax would threaten substantial and visible spending cuts to balance the resulting shortfall in revenue.

To Govern Is to Inherit

Government today is not so much an opportunity for politicians to exercise their will: it is an inheritance. The legacy that a new government receives consists of a great collection of taxing and spending decisions taken and modified by politicians in the past. A government's taxes and spending programmes are no more the result of a decision taken at one point in time than a cathedral is the result of a single plan. A cathedral typically grows by additions; what is added by the current incumbent of a bishopric is less than what has gone before.

In budgeting, the inheritance of newcomers to office is described as the base; as Webber and Wildavsky emphasize (1986: 31), 'the base is non-discretionary', being mandated by law. Insofar as it reflects 'social agreement on essentials', it is not an object of political conflict, and no decisions are required to maintain the base. The budget base has two elements, one which is central to its structure, and one which is marginal. To alter central features of a national tax system requires restructuring the base. By contrast, marginal modifications can be made at the periphery of the structure. The base tends not to be susceptible to change, because it provides a tolerable means of securing a large amount of revenue without decision-making. At the periphery of the budget, where there is scope for decision *because* the sums of money are relatively small, there are many opportunities for political controversy.

The fundamental problem facing politicians is whether to seek office. Holding office requires two very different types of decision. The first consists of calculations about the measures

9

that the party must put forward (or avoid mentioning) in order to win an election. A leftwing party is likely to balance pressures within the party to increase spending against a fear that competitors will attack it for planning big tax increases. For a rightwing party, pressures for tax cuts from activists must be balanced against fear of an accusation that the party is planning big expenditure cuts. The opposition party always has the momentary advantage, for it can be relatively optimistic about the margin available for spending increases without tax increases, or tax cuts without spending cuts. After an election is won, politicians accept office – with all this means in terms of accepting the base laid down by decisions of previous governments. Office is invariably accepted, whatever the terms. Victorious leaders have only a momentary sense of omnipotence. In an era of big government, they immediately learn that to govern is not to choose but to inherit.

An incoming government of the right would not choose to inherit the spending obligations that require it to sustain historically high levels of taxation, or risk the instant loss of popularity by financing tax cuts through repealing programmes that it had pledged to maintain during its election campaign. A leftwing government would not choose to inherit an economy in which tax revenues were inadequate to finance its spending promises. Nor would it welcome introducing tax increases to finance new programmes, if this would result in a cut in the take-home pay of its supporters.

No election winner has ever turned down the opportunity to hold office because of the taxing and spending obligations that it would inherit. Politicians enter office determined to do the best they can – given the situation that they inherit. This is a far cry from that view that sees government actions as directed by the brute force of political will, or by the rational calculation of precise trade-offs between competing preferences (cf. Deutsch, 1963: 105ff.; Mueller, 1979).

A newly elected government accepts – or surrenders to – the force of political inertia. The first thing that leaders must do is swear to uphold the laws of the land. The good news is that spending laws incorporate many popular public benefits for which they can take credit. The bad news is that these spending programmes must be paid for. If a newly elected government decided that the existing tax system should be replaced by a new system that would raise the same amount of money in different ways, it would receive all the blame for the new taxes. But it would not be able to claim any credit for additional spending programmes. If old tax laws routinely continue, the political costs are minimized.

Recognizing the strength of the status quo, Bachrach and Baratz (1970) have argued that this is more a reflection of the continued dominance of rightwing political interests than a product of forces that could benefit a variety of interests. Non-decision-making is said to occur because established interests prevent changes from being debated or put into effect that would be harmful to their material wellbeing. Nothing appears to happen, because the dominant interests consciously and continuously assert their preferences in government, and keep alternatives off the agenda for decision-making.

However, taxation in major industrial nations does not support the view that non-decision-making favours the political right. Whereas Bachrach and Baratz presume that non-decision-making elites are against high taxation, in every advanced industrial nation taxation is near or at its highest level in history – and has risen substantially in the period since the two authors propounded their arguments (OECD, 1986). Moreover, upper-income groups tend to pay more in taxation (OECD, 1980). The great bulk of the money raised from the high level of taxation is spent on programmes that provide major benefits to low- and middle-income groups: social security, health and education (OECD, 1985). As long as nothing is done to change contemporary governments, the state's taxing powers will continue to finance wide-ranging social benefits for the mass of the population.

Unintended and Intended Change

Decisions have consequences in the long term as well as in the short, and unintended consequences are often as important as the things that politicians immediately intend. The long-term consequences of particular decisions about taxation are the primary concern here, for their effect is felt for decades or

11

generations, whereas short-term effects are usually registered by the time of the next budget, or the next election.

Calculating the effects ten, twenty or fifty years ahead of a particular tax change is not so much difficult as it is absurd. Lloyd George did not think about the level to which the social security tax that he introduced would rise long after he had left Parliament. Nor could Mr Gladstone have contemplated the level to which income tax had risen a century after its enactment by the House of Commons in 1842. Nor is it necessary for a politician to look far ahead. Warnings to President Reagan that his 1981 tax cuts threatened the problem of a big federal deficit in the 1990s could be met with the White House rejoinder: 'That is not our problem; Ronald Reagan will not be President in 1990.'

Non-Decision-Making Can Cumulatively Have Big Consequences

Anyone who has ever been responsible for looking after a house or garden knows that doing nothing will sooner or later have big consequences. If grass is not cut and a garden not weeded, it will soon become an overgrown jungle. And if a house is not painted, the woodwork will gradually rot. The immediate consequence of doing nothing is to maintain the status quo; this preserves, by intention or default, the established distribution of advantages and disadvantages in the tax system (cf. Schattschneider, 1960). If married women are taxed less favourably than single women or vice versa, this continues. If there are tax advantages for home-owners, these continue too. Whatever the bias in tax laws today, it is more a reflection of the nation's past than of its current configuration of political interests. While current interests may push for change, these interests are usually not strong enough to deflect the force of political inertia.

A model of decision-making in a crisis, for example a decision about the Falklands War, is inappropriate for taxation. There is never an 'all-or-nothing' decision about taxation, as in choices between war or peace. Decisions about taxation concern changes at the margin. Even when a substantial alteration occurs at the margin, the basic structure of a tax immediately remains intact.

Changes in the structure of taxation are most likely to occur by the compounding of seemingly small rates of change. While

12

an increase of 2 or 5 per cent in tax revenue will not appear large in a single year, if such an increase is compounded for ten, twenty or thirty years, it will cumulatively become very large. While the government of the day may view their marginal decisions as small in terms of an immediate impact, history places more weight on the cumulation of long-term consequences. The absence of political decisions about taxation has consequences too, for 'big events are not necessarily produced by big causes' (Parry and Morriss, 1974: 324). If laws for calculating taxation remain constant while changes occur in the economy, then total tax revenue will change. Most of the apparent increase in tax revenue has not been a consequence of conscious decisions to push up tax rates, but because inflation has greatly increased the nominal value of wages and expenditure subject to tax.

The national tax structure can be destabilized in the long run by the combined consequences of decisions and non-decisions. It is impossible for the government of the day to have a realistic expectation of the net effect upon tax revenue two decades later of changes in the national and international economy, and of decisions taken or avoided by its successors as well as by itself. Nor is there any reason why it should do so. Political morality follows the Biblical injunction 'Take therefore no thought for the morrow ... Sufficient unto the day is the evil thereof.' It is assumed that the evil will come the day after the next election, not the day before.

Limits of Intentional Change

Given that political inertia accounts for most tax revenue, conscious political decisions to change taxes must be treated as deviant. If the existing system and level of taxes is regarded as unpopular, it is only natural for politicians to search for alternatives that could be put in place of the status quo. As taxes claim more and more money, the pressure increases to 'do something' about taxation. Because they are exceptions, new taxes are news. But newsworthiness may reflect novelty, rather than a substantial contribution to the fisc, which receives the nation's tax revenue.

Talk is vague; discussions of tax reform do not distinguish between changes that reduce total taxation, as against a revenue-neutral change that simply shifts revenue collection from one tax to another, leaving total revenue the same as before. Revenue-neutral changes are frequently discussed by experts, because they focus attention upon a search for more efficient means of raising a given sum of revenue, rather than raising a debate about how much tax is enough (or 'too much') tax. However, tax cuts are more appealing to voters, because they *do* reduce the revenue going to the fisc.

Talk is cheap; decisions that change taxation can cost money, and also votes. Decisions to reduce rates or repeal existing taxes cost the fisc billions of pounds. It will cost citizens billions of pounds if decisions lead to an increase in tax revenue. Even if changes are revenue-neutral, they need not be politically neutral. Politicians will have to pay the costs of defending their proposals to increase taxes against those who will be hurt by the neutralizing increase, and those gaining from tax cuts may not provide compensating electoral benefits.

'Reform' as a Political Symbol

There are far more incentives for politicians to enunciate views about tax reform than there are to take action. In opposition, a party can easily voice a general desire to do something about taxation. As long as propositions remain at a high level of generality, for example with a call for greater 'fairness' or more 'realistic' tax rates, such statements cause no countervailing difficulties. They are in the realm of speculation or hypothesis; no specific action need be proposed.

When politicians try to spell out in detail what their reforms would do, they immediately run into trouble. For example, in 1979 Margaret Thatcher campaigned on a manifesto declaring that the state's share of the nation's income 'must be steadily reduced'. But Mrs Thatcher explicitly rejected assertions that a Conservative government would finance tax cuts by introducing big changes in welfare services, for instance by 'privatizing' health care or education. Hence, public expenditure as a proportion of the national product has remained as high as under Labour, and so too has tax effort (Cm. 14, 1986: table 2.2). The promise in the 1979 Conservative manifesto to cut income-tax rates was carried out – but taxpayers learned that the promise to 'simplify taxes like VAT' meant that the income-tax cut was financed by the Conservatives nearly doubling the rate of VAT.

The opposition to the Thatcher government has also faced a dilemma. Any statement that more should be spent on fighting unemployment, helping pensioners, expanding the health service or other programmes prompts a government challenge: how are you going to pay for it? A vague reply leaves opposition parties vulnerable to a Conservative charge that Labour policies would add 5p, 10p or 20p to the standard rate of income tax. In 1986, Conservative charges about the risk of a high-spend, high-tax Labour government so concerned Labour that the Shadow Chancellor, Roy Hattersley, preferred to damp down expectations about increased expenditure by placing low limits on the extent of Labour's plans for tax increases. But as this frustrated Labour politicians who wanted to increase public expenditure, by January 1987 Hattersley was prepared to accept that a Labour government introduce tax increases or, as he preferred to put it, reverse tax cuts made by the Conservatives since 1979 (cf. *The Times*, 12 September 1986; 16 January 1987).

A Social Democratic Party working party sought to resolve the dilemma by publishing, prior to its 1986 party conference, a detailed description of how it would raise more money to finance its policies (Taverne, 1986). A document entitled *Attacking Poverty: Merging Tax and Benefits* indicated that measures increasing income-maintenance benefits and the income of those with below-average earnings would result in higher taxes for some families earning £10,000 a year or above, and for most taxpayers earning more than £17,000 a year. Liberal and SDP leaders quickly distanced themselves from detailed proposals of the SDP working group, which identified a third of the electorate as losers, and thus risked alienating many Alliance supporters. A *New Society* editorial drew the appropriate moral:

> The incident illustrates a fundamental difficulty in democratic politics. No politician is thanked for what he gives, for the recipient always believes it to be his birthright. Every politician is cursed for what he tries to take away, for the targets of taxation believe what they have to be their inalienable birthright too. (*New Society*, 12 September 1986)

Alternative Forms of Change in Tax Revenue

Given the need for more revenue to finance the growth of government, changes in taxation are here evaluated in terms of the amount of money that they add or subtract from the fisc. As subsequent chapters will demonstrate, most intentional changes in taxation have a very limited effect upon total tax revenue.

Because total tax revenue aggregates money raised by a great variety of taxes, it is important to consider tax changes in *systemic* terms – that is, to ask about any tax, or proposed change in tax: what proportion of money does this add (or subtract) from total tax revenue? Only in this way can we appreciate that a tax that raises what appears to be a large sum of money, say £1b, contributes much less than 1 per cent to total tax revenue, and a tax 'cut' of £250m reduces total taxation by only 18/100ths of 1 per cent.[3]

When changes in the whole of the tax system are considered together, it is important to distinguish between gross and net changes in revenue. It is far easier for the fisc to countenance a loss of revenue from one tax if it is simultaneously benefiting from an increase in another tax. Even when decisions produce a noteworthy gross effect on tax revenue, if increases and decreases in different parts of the system cancel each other out, the net effect will be nil. Changes in tax revenue must therefore be classified according to two criteria: i) a big or small gross impact upon total tax revenue; ii) a big or small net impact upon total tax revenue. Together they produce a fourfold classification of changes in a national tax system. (Figure 1.1)

Figure 1.1 Impact of decisions upon total tax revenue

Gross Impact	Net impact	
	Large	Small
Large	Radical reform	Neutral change
Small	Inertia change	Fringe tuning

Fringe tuning (small gross, small net impact) On an annual

16

basis, the changes most consistent with the theory of political inertia involve fringe tuning. The structure of the tax system is unaltered; the only changes that occur are strictly marginal, involving small amounts of tax revenue.

Inertia change (small gross, large net impact) Cumulatively, a series of small-scale decisions about revenue can have a large net impact. For example, if voters tended not to notice small annual increases in a tax, then each year the government might make a small upward adjustment that at the end of the decade involved a large change.

Neutral change (large gross, small net impact) Revenue-neutral changes offer great fiscal scope for altering the sums raised by particular taxes, for the value of all tax decreases must be offset by increases of an equal value. Politically, there is a risk that tax increases will incur more political costs than tax cuts provide benefits.

Radical reform (large gross, large net impact) Politically, radical reform means a big change in total revenue, whether down or up. This could follow the repeal of taxes, or a cut in the rate of such major sources of revenue as income tax and VAT, without any offsetting tax increases. A radical reform could alternatively introduce a big new tax or steeply increase the revenue yield from an existing tax, thus providing much more money for public expenditure.

While four different types of changes could logically be made, the theory of political inertia predicts that most decisions will be confined to one category, fringe tuning. Politicians will be averse to imposing big tax increases and also to paying the price of big tax cuts, namely big cuts in popular programmes. Hence, a risk-averse politician will only take responsibility for measures that only make small changes in total tax revenue.

Radical reform can occur but rarely, and then in response to a crisis, or *a*typical circumstances. The two biggest innovations in taxation in Britain in the past half century – the introduction of the Pay As You Earn (PAYE) method of collecting income tax and the introduction of the Value Added Tax (VAT) – were both

17

stimulated by international events. The PAYE system of collecting tax revenue from employers through weekly deductions from wages was introduced to help finance the Second World War. VAT was introduced when Britain joined the European Community in 1973, in order to meet an obligation of Community membership.

Revenue-neutral reform is a relatively rare event, for political benefits are not easily gained by a great deal of recycling of revenue between taxes with no net change in total revenue. Exceptionally, in 1979 the Thatcher government introduced a relatively large revenue-neutral reform, swapping a 3p in the pound reduction in the rate of income tax for an increase in VAT from 8 to 15 per cent. It was strongly attacked for thus pushing up the price of goods in the shops. It has not made a big revenue-neutral tax change since. The revenue-neutral 1986 tax act in the United States was not only substantial in the amount of money affected, but also unique in the postwar history of American tax legislation (cf. Witte, 1985).

Inertia change can produce the most additional revenue at the lowest political cost to the government of the day – but it can only do so in the course of decades, far beyond the time-scale of a government's current problems. Moreover, the effect of small annual changes can only add up to a big sum in total if successive governments, regardless of party, tend to make the same annual marginal change. Cumulatively, changes can have nil effect, if the pattern of change is cyclical, with increases offsetting decreases.

Politicians wanting to have a big impact upon tax revenue face a dilemma. The bigger the immediate benefits of their decision, the bigger the costs. A measure that might at first glance appear superficially popular, a radical reform that cut taxes, would also require cutting expenditure on popular social programmes. The more reasonable political course is to avoid big decisions about taxation. If a few decisions about taxation turn out in retrospect to have big consequences for revenue (for example, the initial introduction of income tax at low rates in 1799), they are not apparent until long after their authors are in political retirement or dead.

Taxation as It Actually Is

The starting point for public policy research is the world of government as it actually is. Following the injunction of Kay and King, we want to concentrate upon the world of actual tax revenue – and the way in which taxes differ from each other.

Taxation as Public Policy

Taxation is specially suitable for public policy analysis, because revenue is the result of the interaction of laws, administration and economic activities; it is thus intrinsically interdisciplinary. Tax revenue is far too important to government to be valued exclusively in terms of political vote maximization, or solely in terms of economic efficiency. The principle of avoiding political blame for introducing new taxes is matched by the need to maintain a flow of revenue sufficient to finance the programmes of the welfare state.

By contrast with studies that concentrate exclusively upon prescriptions for the future, this book seeks to understand future trends as the outcome of a long historical process described by a group of French historians as the *longue dureé*. The analysis commences shortly after the end of the Second World War, when British government had raised its capacity to collect taxes to new heights. Examining the decades since 1945 makes it possible to understand the significance of the little by little compounding of changes through the years.[4] A study confined to a single bill, a single Parliament or the term of a single Prime Minister would miss all that is significant in the *longue dureé*.

By contrast with studies of particular taxes, actual or hypothetical, this book is comprehensive, examining the whole of the tax system. It emphasizes the variety of ways in which taxes are levied, and the very different sums that particular taxes contribute to the fisc. Within a given revenue total, an infinity of combinations of taxes can be employed. For example, total taxation in France is similar to Britain, but the French have a much lower income tax and a much higher social security tax (Rose, 1984: fig. 4.1).

By contrast with insider accounts purporting to describe what goes on within Downing Street and Whitehall, this book directs attention at the public side of taxation, that is, the money that is collected nationwide. Private discussions between the Chancellor of the Exchequer and senior Treasury officials dominate descriptions of the closed world of high politics, but public policy is about public affairs too. As Chapter 7 demonstrates, the private discussions leading up to the Chancellor's budget have very little impact upon the total amount of tax paid by ordinary households at the end of the year.

Concentration upon the revenue raised by taxation follows logically from an interest in the growth of government: without more money, government cannot grow. While raising revenue is a major motive for taxation, fringe tuning of the tax system may be undertaken for other reasons. Taxation can be considered in terms of effects upon such macro-economic conditions as growth, inflation, and employment, and upon investment. Taxation can also be examined in relation to such social values as the distribution of the tax burden according to the ability to pay, or the disincentive effect upon behaviour of high taxes on goods deemed injurious to health, such as whisky and tobacco. Purely political concerns, such as altering taxes to improve a party's chances of re-election, can also be examined (cf. Musgrave and Musgrave, 1980: ch.1; Pechman, 1985; Atkinson and Stiglitz, 1980; Alt, 1983; Webber and Wildavsky, 1986: ch. 1).

Taxation is a universal problem of government, and economic theories emphasize what is generic in taxation. An income tax or a sales tax is expected to demonstrate similar properties, whatever the nation using it. By contrast, many historians and political scientists emphasize that which is distinctive in a national culture. Britain is expected to differ from France or Germany, and America from all three countries, because of differences in political institutions and culture.

A public-policy analysis of taxation should combine both general and specific knowledge. This book is broad in conception, for the theory of political inertia is relevant across national boundaries, and to the spending as well as the taxing side of government (see Rose and Karran, 1984). This book concentrates upon Britain, for only by examining the way in which government maintains or alters revenue from many different taxes over a period of time is it possible to understand the pervasive effects of inertia upon a tax system as a whole.

Britain is particularly suitable for analysis in terms of political inertia because its system of government has continued for many centuries. The concentration of tax powers in central government and within Whitehall in the hands of a single ministry, the Treasury, gives great opportunity for politicians to make decisions with a big impact on the national tax system. Insofar as any tax system is representative, Britain's tax system is relatively close to the average of advanced industrial nations both in terms of the use made of particular taxes, and total tax as a proportion of the national product (Rose, 1985).

Plan of the Book

The opening chapters concentrate upon practical questions that any theory must address. The next chapter sets out the link between taxing and spending; the great identity in the budget requires public expenditure and public revenue to be equal, whether the sums of money involved are a small or large proportion of the national product. When spending goes up, revenue must increase too. It also demonstrates that while tax revenue has increased by thousands of per cent in value in the postwar era, so too has the national product. Hence, total public effort (that is, taxation as a proportion of the national product) has hardly increased.

Analysing disparate properties of taxation requires a model identifying the principal determinants of taxation, and how their changes alter tax revenue. A public policy model of taxation must incorporate three different elements: laws, administration, and the economy. Chapter 3 sets out a general model of tax revenue. Laws define the tax rate and the tax base; public administration organizes the collection of revenue from individuals and organizations; and economic activities produce the money that is collected.

Total tax revenue is the sum of disparate activities affecting a multiplicity of different taxes. Chapter 4 shows that the laws authorizing taxes do not constitute a uniform code, chosen and enacted at one time; tax laws accumulate through the centuries. While British government is unitary, the institutions for administering tax collection are several. Taxes are levied upon a multiplicity of economic activities, upon expenditure as well

21

as income, and on corporations as well as individuals. Everyone pays taxes and everyone receives benefits from government. But everyone does not pay the same amount of tax or receive the same amount in public benefits.

While a model can show how taxes are raised, it cannot explain why taxation takes the form it does. Chapter 5 explains why political inertia is the theory that best explains taxation. Rather than constantly making decisions about large or small increments in revenue, politicians can rely upon the persistence of taxes authorized by old laws and established institutions. The similarities and differences between the inertia theory and that of incremental decision-making are set out in detail. The inertia theory is more appropriate for understanding the long-term dynamics of government, whereas incrementalism is a description of the short-term behaviour of politicians.

The assertion that taxes are always increasing is often false. Chapter 6 shows how the force of inertia causes some taxes to lessen their contribution to the national tax system and their claim upon the national product, while others increase in significance. When taxes are compared, we have to explain why some taxes grow, others contract, and a third group shows little change. Two different types of explanation are offered for contrasting directions of change in taxation. Economic theories emphasize the impact of economic growth, inflation and structural changes within the economy. Political theories offer explanations emphasizing the right- or leftwing character of the government of the day, or the proximity of a general election.

Because the theory of political inertia places so much emphasis upon the continuity of tax laws and administration, a political decision that changes tax revenue is the exception rather than the rule. In order to measure by how much political decisions actually alter tax revenue, we must consider decisions taken by the Chancellor of the Exchequer, by officials responsible for administering taxes, and by individual citizens interested in minimizing their contribution to the fisc.

Comparing the revenue raised by the inertia of established laws with that produced by the Chancellor's annual budget decisions challenges the conventional journalistic view of the Chancellor of the Exchequer as the person who determines taxation from his lofty position in the Treasury. Chapter 7 analyses official Treasury estimates of the impact upon revenue of every year's budget since 1953. It shows that the Chancellor's budget-day speech is an exercise in fringe tuning. The political effect of the budget is easily exaggerated; a government cannot hope to turn around its electoral fortunes simply by introducing a 'giveaway' budget.

Confronted with demands to pay increased taxes, can ordinary citizens decide to pay less? Whereas tax evasion was once thought by Anglo-Saxons to be an activity confined to Latin cultures, today journalistic reports suggest that 'everybody is doing it' (that is, evading taxes), not least Britons. But the capacity of government to collect great amounts of tax revenue suggests that taxes with strong tax-handles can deny taxpayers the opportunity of large-scale tax evasion. Chapter 8 shows that the major decisions that individuals are able to make about paying taxes are at the margin, and more often rely upon reducing tax liabilities through legal tax avoidance than upon illegal evasion.

Given the persisting influence of past decisions, Chapter 9 considers the scope for decisions that can positively change taxation in future. Notwithstanding the vulnerability of Britain to trends in the open international economy, the future direction of the country's tax system is likely to be determined by nation-specific characteristics, maintaining substantial differences between the British system and those of most advanced industrial nations. Within Britain, political constraints are of paramount importance; proposals for changing taxes must be arrayed on a dimension from those that are currently politically impossible to those that are 'not impossible'. In pursuit of more revenue a government may seek to turn to non-tax sources, such as privatization, the sale of state-owned assets such as oil, and profitable nationalized industries. However, such measures are a limited source of money. The crucial political question for the future is the extent to which the views of the electorate impose both a floor and a ceiling upon taxation, because of a broad acceptance of the present mixture of costs and benefits of government.

Notes

1   Applying political concepts to taxation, conventionally considered an economic problem, thus complements the public choice approach, which emphasizes 'the application of economics to political science' (Mueller, 1979 : 1).
2   Due to conventions dating back to the time when the monarch was the effective head of government, Parliament must formally renew tax legislation each year, that is, grant supply after the redress of grievances.
3   Billion (a thousand million) is abbreviated b; million is abbreviated m.
4   It also focuses on a period without war, by contrast with the pioneering study by Peacock and Wiseman (1961) of the growth of public expenditure in Britain, 1890–1955.

CHAPTER TWO

The Great Identity:
Revenue Equals Expenditure

Taxation is not an end in itself; it is a means to other ends. Politicians do not extract thousands of pounds in taxation from ordinary households because they want to do so, but because they must do so in order to achieve other goals. Taxation cannot be understood in isolation from other activities of government. In order to understand the purpose of taxation, we must understand the purpose of government. The budget combines the benefits and costs of government. Responsibility for spending money is much more congenial to politicians than is responsibility for collecting taxes.

'Budgeting is translating financial resources into human purposes' (Wildavsky, 1975: 3). The fact that both sides of the budget are expressed in money terms is a disadvantage as well as an advantage. Insofar as it implies that money is the measuring rod of all public purposes, it is a half-truth. The classic purposes of government are 'priceless' intangibles: liberty, public order and national security. To think of the purposes of government as requiring large sums of money to be spent on social programmes is a relatively recent idea (Rose, 1976).

Because the budget represents taxing and spending in terms of a common denominator, it can enforce a truth of fundamental political importance, what Crecine (1971) calls *the great identity*: *expenditure must equal revenue*. If spending is to be increased, the great identity can be satisfied only if revenue is increased. Metaphorically speaking, the budget represents both the pleasure and the pain principle. Politicians can ease the constraint of the great identity by raising a little money from non-tax sources of revenue. Borrowing is the chief non-tax source. Government borrows because it does not want to raise taxes to meet all of the cost of public expenditure, to finance such long-term benefits as roads, hospital buildings and schools, and because, under certain circumstances, borrowing is deemed helpful for its macro-economic policy. Government also receives revenue from charges, fees and royalties, for example council house rents and North Sea oil.

This book concentrates upon tax revenue.[1] Taxation accounts for the great bulk of total government revenue. Furthermore, non-tax sources of revenue also generate claims on the spending side of the budget. This is most evident in the case of borrowing; the annual interest that must now be paid on past borrowing is more than double the amount of money that government raises by current borrowing (Cm. 14, 1986: tables 1.10, 1.12).

However public spending is financed and whatever its level, the great identity remains true. It held for a Victorian government intent upon reducing expenditure by saving candle ends, as well as for a Thatcher government wanting to cut spending when there are no longer candle ends to save. It is true for a Reagan administration that found that if it cut taxes without cutting spending it had to increase public borrowing. It also holds for any party promising to spend more money in hopes that this will promote an election victory. In opposition, politicians must be careful to limit promises of increased spending in order to avoid being attacked for threatening big tax increases to finance big spending increases.

Comparisons with the past show that many different levels of taxing and spending can satisfy the great identity. From Japan to Sweden, nations differ greatly in their level of taxing and spending. Economics cannot provide a scientific answer to the crucial practical questions: how much is enough public expenditure? How much is too much taxation? Answers to these questions can be given only in the light of political values (Heald, 1983). The institutions determining the relation between taxation and public expenditure are political institutions.

Even though the two sides of the budget must be equal in money terms, they are not the same politically. The first part of this chapter reviews the amount of money collected in taxes and how the costs of politics have been rising in the postwar era. Higher taxes will not require greater tax effort, if national income is increasing at the same rate. In order to evaluate whether taxes are high, or higher than formerly, we must compare tax effort in Britain with other advanced industrial nations, and present and past levels of tax effort in Britain. The spending side of the budget is examined too, in order to identify the public benefits financed by the costs of taxation.

How Much Tax?

While money is the common denominator of tax revenue, there is more than one way to answer the simple question: how much tax does the British government collect? An answer must involve billions of pounds. But given continuing inflation, sometimes at high rates, money values change their meaning from year to year; this too must be taken into account.

A Lot of £ from a Few Taxes

The cash flow of government is bigger than that of any business, for government provides services for everyone in society, and in one way or another taxes every citizen. In the latest year for which full figures are published, 1985, British government collected £134,970,000,000 in tax revenue.[2]

Total tax revenue is the sum of money raised by dozens of different taxes. An exhaustive catalogue of taxes levied by British government is a very long list. But taxes are unequal in the amount of money that they contribute to the revenue. To understand how government raises the great bulk of tax revenue it is only necessary to understand a few big taxes. More than two-thirds of total tax revenue is raised from four taxes: income tax, national insurance, value added tax (VAT) and local authority rates. Each tax raises more than £10b a year. On its own, each tax raises more money for the fisc than a combination of familiar taxes on motor cars, beer, wines and spirits, tobacco, and a number of miscellaneous other taxes. Altogether, the four largest taxes accounted for £91b in revenue in 1985, 68 per cent of total taxation (Table 2.1).

Table 2.1 Major Sources of Tax Revenue

Tax	£m 1985	% total
Income tax	35,448	26.3
National insurance	21,468	15.9
Value added tax (VAT)	20,962	15.5
Local authority rates	13,580	10.1
Corporation tax	9,128	6.8
Petroleum revenue tax (PRT)	7,369	5.5
Hydrocarbon oil duty	6,260	4.6
Tobacco	4,342	3.2
Motor vehicle duty	2,389	1.8
Wines and spirits	2,212	1.6
National health	2,019	1.5
Beer	1,935	1.4
Customs	1,304	1.0
Stamp duty	1,160	0.9
Capital gains	1,209	0.9
Other taxes	4,185	3.1
Total	£134,970	100

Source: United Kingdom National Accounts 1986, tables 7.2, 7.5, 8.2, 9.6.

Taxes can raise big sums of money in very different ways. Income tax is a tax financing general expenditure, whereas national insurance contributions are a payment for social security benefits. Income tax is a deduction from gross earnings, whereas national insurance revenue consists of payments made by employers additional to wages, as well as deductions from wages. Value added tax is a tax upon expenditure rather than income. From the perspective of an ordinary individual, VAT can be conceived as additional to income tax, for when VAT is charged on household purchases it must be paid from earnings in hand after income tax. Local authority rates are levied on yet another basis; they are a tax on the occupation of property.

Taxes that account for only a small percentage of total revenue are less important to the fisc, but the sums raised are not small in absolute terms. A tax claiming £1,000,000,000 a year appears small to government – it contributes only 0.7 per cent of total taxation – but this sum is large in almost any other context.

Among the smaller sources of revenue, corporation tax can contribute more than £9b in a year, and petroleum revenue tax duty on North Sea oil, £7b. Many historically important taxes, such as customs, nowadays contribute relatively small sums to the fisc.

In the management of the public budget, changes in lesser taxes are easier to make because they alter revenue less. A 1p increase or reduction in the income tax is worth more than £1.4b in a full year, and a 1 per cent change in the rate of VAT is worth £1.1b. By contrast, a 1p change in the tax on beer is worth £90m, and a 10p increase on a bottle of spirits only £15m (Cm. 14, 1986: tables 4.5–6). Hence, the Treasury's evaluation of tax increases or cuts is very much contingent upon the tax at issue. It is easier for the Treasury to accept political arguments for a large cut in the rate of a tax that does not raise much money than to accept a seemingly small reduction in a tax that accounts for a large amount of public revenue.

Calculating the cost of taxation on a per head basis brings total tax revenue down to a human scale. Indirectly if not directly, taxation falls upon every citizen. In 1985 taxation was equivalent to £2,410 for every man, woman and child in the United Kingdom, or £46 a week. For the proverbial married couple with two children, total taxation was equivalent to £9,640 a year or £185 a week. In fact, the average family is not required to hand over nearly ten thousand pounds a year to government. Nor could it do so, when the average wage is less than that. As Chapter 3 explains, there is no need for individuals to pay into the fisc all the money that government raises. Most taxes are paid by intermediary organizations – employers, manufacturers and retailers. Most money collected in taxation has never been in the hands of the people on whom the ultimate cost of taxation falls.

Changes in Tax Revenue

When the amount of money collected in taxes is viewed in historical perspective, a simple (some would argue too simple) picture emerges: tax revenue is continuously rising. The further back in time the comparison is extended, the greater the increase appears. This book covers four decades of the postwar era, in which Britain's political and economic conditions altered greatly.

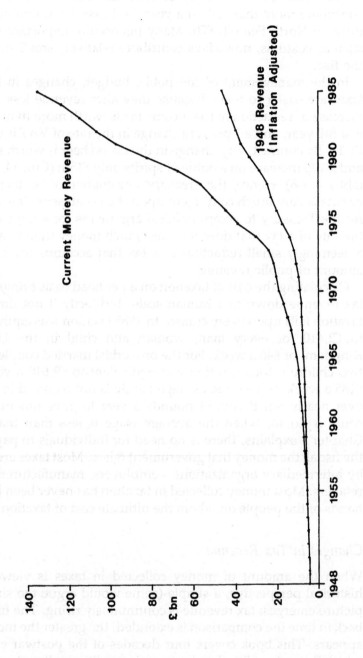

Figure 2.1 Total tax revenue in current money terms since 1948

The year 1948 is taken as the starting point, since that was the first full year after the end of the Second World War when taxation was no longer on a wartime basis.

The money collected in taxation has increased by more than 3,200 per cent in the postwar era. In 1948 total tax revenue was £4.1b; in 1985 it was £135b (Figure 2.1). Since the population of the United Kingdom has remained very stable, the amount of taxation collected annually per person has therefore risen by more than 30 times in the period.

The amount of money collected in taxes has been increasing at an accelerating rate. In the decade from 1948 to 1958, tax revenue increased by £2.6b, whereas in the next decade it increased by £7.3b, and from 1968 to 1978 by £41b. In the following seven years, taxation has increased by an additional £78b. The acceleration is illustrated by the number of years required to double the amount of revenue. Starting from 1948, it took 14 years to double tax revenue. It took 8 years to double tax revenue from 1962 to 1970. As the rate of inflation rose in the 1970s, there was a further acceleration; tax revenue doubled from 1970 to 1975, and it doubled again in the 5 years up to 1980. Since then taxation has 'only' increased by about two-thirds; from 1980 to 1985 revenue in cash terms increased by £53b.

When total tax revenue increases greatly, the amount of money collected by particular taxes is virtually bound to increase too. Taxes only differ in the amount by which their contribution to the fisc has gone up. In absolute terms, income tax has gone up the most, by £34b. National insurance contributions have been second in the amount of increase, £21b. The only taxes that have decreased the amount of money raised for the fisc are the few that have been repealed, for example purchase tax which raised £300m in 1948.

Inflation

Because a pound paid in taxes does not have the same value today as it did a few decades ago, a significant portion of the increase in taxation since 1948 can be attributed to inflation. But it does not follow that the whole of the tax increase can be explained away by inflation. The retail price index is the conventional measure of the extent of inflation. This price index rose by almost 1,200 per cent from 1948 to the end of 1985. If tax revenue had simply risen in line with inflation, it too would have increased 12 times. In fact, it increased more than 32 times. There was thus a difference of £85b between tax revenue actually collected in 1985 and what would have been paid if 1948 taxes had simply risen with inflation.

Inflation directly accounts for less than half the total increase in tax revenue in the postwar era. While the retail price index and tax revenue have both gone up together, they have not risen at the same rate. Tax revenue has normally risen at a much faster rate than inflation. Figure 2.1 illustrates the relationship. The area below the 'inflation-adjusted' line indicates the amount of revenue that would have been raised if taxes had just increased at the rate of the retail price index. The greater area between that line and the line tracing actual tax revenue emphasizes the extent to which taxation has risen by much more than inflation.

The difference between what government collects in taxes today and what it collected in 1948 reflects many influences in addition to the rise in the retail price index. There is an indirect effect of inflation. By making incomes buoyant, a larger portion of earnings are liable to income tax, after the deduction of personal allowances, and more persons become liable to higher rates of income tax. The net effect of this fiscal drag is that income tax rises at a faster rate than inflation. Taxes levied in terms of specific sums of money, such as tobacco and beer, rise at a lower rate than inflation (see Karran, 1985: table 1). Real growth in the economy and political decisions about tax policy affect revenue too (see Chapter 6).

In principle, there are good reasons for discounting *some* of the increase in taxation as an artefact of inflation. But in practice no formula can adequately adjust figures of the revenue flowing into the fisc. Taxes cannot be measured in volume terms as can the notional constant basket of goods used to calculate the retail price index. The money value of a tax *is* its volume. Even though £10 paid in tax will have a different subjective significance to taxpayers in 1948 than in 1985, it still remains £10 collected by the fisc. In the words of a senior Treasury official, taxes belong to 'the actual world of calculations in money' (Clarke, 1973: 159).

A further complication is that the government's own cost of living grows at a different rate from the overall retail price index.

While the retail price index is appropriate to measure changes in the value of money to an average consumer, it is not appropriate for measuring the cost of the goods and services that government buys. From a budgeting perspective, changes in the price of goods and services purchased by government are the best measure of its need for more revenue. Over the postwar era, the cost of final public consumption has risen much more than the retail price index (Rose and Karran, 1983: table 2.2). Hence, government has needed to push up taxes faster than the national rate of inflation, because its costs have been rising at a substantially faster rate than prices overall.

Moreover, ordinary people do not calculate the value of money with the same precision and standards as economists accustomed to constructing indicators of inflation. Empirical studies in economic psychology emphasize that popular perceptions of taxing and spending are often misperceptions (Rose, 1980; Furnham and Lewis, 1986; Lewis, 1982). Age is important as an influence upon what a person thinks of as a 'normal' level of taxation. A person who first went out to work in 1935, earning £1 to £2 *a week*, is likely to have a very different view of the value of money today than a 40-year-old who first went to work in 1960, or a 22-year-old who first went to work in the 1980s. A sum that was a good weekly wage before the war would have been a daily wage in the 1950s and an hourly wage in the 1980s. There is no way in which the Treasury can adjust taxes for differences between taxpayers in the psychological significance of money.

How Much Tax Effort?

Taxes are significant not only in terms of what they buy for government, but also in terms of what they cost citizens. While the cost of taxation is measured in money terms, the effort required to pay taxes is assessed in relation to the ease or difficulty of earning the money needed to pay taxes. If taxation increases by £100 a year and average gross earnings increase by £200 a year, then there is double affluence. A person's take-home pay increases, and so too does the revenue of the fisc for expenditure on public goods and services. But in a no-growth economy if taxes increase by £200 a year per worker and earnings

33

remain static, political trouble is likely to result, for growth in public spending will then be financed by a cut in post-tax earnings.

The tax effort of a country is expressed as the proportion of the gross domestic product that is claimed by all levels of government taxation. In 1985, total tax revenue equalled 38.6 per cent of the British national product.[3] While the claims of taxation are large, the bulk of the national product is *not* transferred to the fisc; it remains in the hands of those who produce it.

Politically, the impact of taxation is cushioned by the fact that more than one-third of the money collected in taxes is subsequently paid out as cash transfer benefits for pensioners, the unemployed and other categories of individuals eligible for social security benefits. In addition, tax revenues are used to pay the wages of millions of public employees, and to buy goods and services from private-sector firms, some of which, such as civil engineering firms, depend heavily upon the government as a customer.

While inflation pushes up the money value of taxation, it also pushes up the value of the national product. If the two rise at the same rate, then tax effort will remain constant; the fisc will have more money in hand to spend, and so too will the average taxpayer. If the effects of economic growth cause the national product to grow faster than taxation, then tax effort will be reduced. Alternatively, if taxation grows faster than the economy as a whole, tax effort will increase.

No Steady Increase

In the postwar era, tax effort in Britain has been relatively stable (Figure 2.2). In 1948 taxation claimed 35.5 per cent of the national product. By 1985 taxation had increased its share of the national economy by only 2.5 per cent. While it is correct to say that tax effort has increased in the postwar era, on average it has increased by rather less than one-tenth of 1 per cent a year. In a parliament lasting four years, the average government will only increase tax effort by one-quarter of 1 per cent of the national product. It has taken an average of 15 years for tax effort to increase by 1 per cent of the national product.

Contrary to popular beliefs and academic theories about the

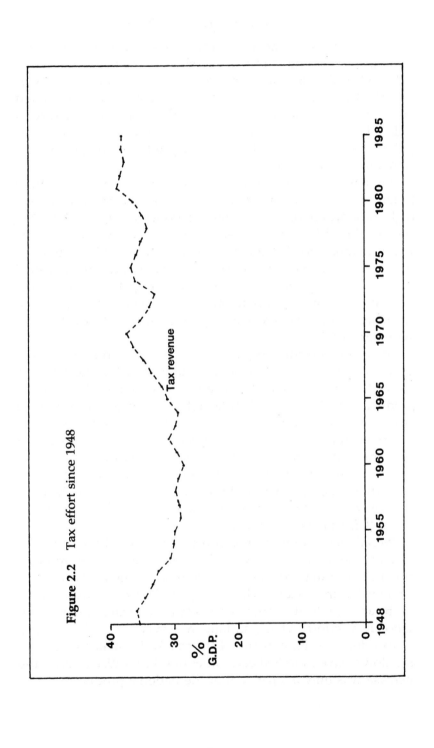

Figure 2.2 Tax effort since 1948

Tax revenue

% G.D.P.

inevitable growth of government, tax effort has *not* been continuously increasing. Taxation as a share of the national product fell in 11 of the 16 years from 1948 to 1964, reaching a postwar low of 28.4 per cent in 1960. In the early 1960s taxation claimed one-sixth less of the national product than had been the case in 1948.[4] Less tax effort nonetheless produced more money for public spending, since the national product had grown substantially in the intervening period.

One reason why tax effort has not risen so much in postwar Britain is that government was already mobilizing a relatively high proportion of the national product at the end of the Second World War. From 1940 to 1945 Britain experienced five years of total mobilization for the war effort; this required a high level of taxation. The Labour government returned in 1945 inherited a tax system demanding a very high level of tax effort from its citizens; it drew upon this to finance the peacetime expansion of welfare-state programmes (Peacock and Wiseman, 1961).

Taxing and spending began to show an upward trend following the return of a Labour government in 1964. Tax effort passed the 1948 level in 1969, and reached 37.5 per cent of the national product in 1970. In the 1970s tax effort fluctuated from year to year – but not in accordance with party. The postwar high has occurred under the Thatcher administration, which claimed 38.9 per cent of the national product in taxes in 1981. According to Treasury forecasts, if Mrs Thatcher's policies were continued for more than a decade this would not reduce tax effort to the level of 1978, the last full year of the Labour government, until the 1990s! (Cf. Cm. 14, 1986: table 2.2.)

Overall the pattern of tax effort in postwar Britain can be described as cyclical, showing downturns as well as upturns, rather than as an inexorable upward trend. In the 1970s tax effort actually fell in 6 years, while rising in 4. It is meaningful for politicians to talk about the possibility of reducing or increasing national tax effort. What is striking, however, is that the changes in tax effort are slight; many of the relatively small changes up and down have cancelled each other out. From 1970 to 1985, the increase was only 0.5 per cent of the national product.[5]

Comparative Decline

In the postwar era, tax effort in Britain has actually *fallen* relative to other advanced industrial nations. In 1950, the first year for which comparable OECD statistics are available, British taxes claimed 33 per cent of the national product, the highest level of tax effort among OECD nations, where the average tax effort was 24 per cent (OECD, 1971). In the decades since, European countries have enjoyed the benefits of national economic growth at a higher rate than Britain, and have had a high level of growth in public spending and taxation (Rose and Karran, 1984: table 2.6).

By comparison with most European nations, the British pattern of taxing and spending has been distinctive for nearly half a century. Under threat from a foreign enemy, in the Second World War the British government successfully imposed very high taxes to finance the war effort. By contrast, Continental European regimes had their taxing capacity shattered by invasion and military defeat. In the 1950s British tax revenue increased with economic growth but tax effort decreased, as most of the dividend of economic growth was devoted to increasing take-home pay. In the 1960s public expenditure in Britain rose – but not as much as in most Western nations. Had Britain retained its high rank in tax effort among OECD nations, today tax effort would be 53.0 per cent of the national product, more than one-third higher than it actually is.

Among twenty-two advanced industrial nations in the Organization of Economic Cooperation and Development (OECD) Britain is average in tax effort. By comparison with Sweden, which is first, British government asks one-quarter less tax effort from citizens. Governments throughout Northern Europe, from Scandinavia to France, make a bigger effort to raise taxes than does Her Majesty's Government. Less tax effort is usually found among historically poorer Mediterranean countries and in countries distant from the European welfare states model, such as America and Japan (Rose, 1985a).

Since all advanced industrial nations, and particularly European countries, collect a substantial portion of the national product in taxation, current levels of taxation cannot be explained in terms of characteristics unique to Britain. Complaints that individual British citizens might voice about taxation should not so much be addressed to specific actions of British government as to the general conditions causing OECD nations to claim a substantial proportion of the national product in taxation.

Table 2.2 Tax Effort in Advanced Industrial Nations

	Taxes as % GDP	Tax Revenue in Dollars Per Capita
Sweden	50.5	5,760
Denmark	48.0	5,079
Belgium	46.7	3,682
Norway	46.4	6,133
Netherlands	45.5	3,886
France	45.5	4,057
Austria	41.9	3,581
Luxembourg	41.4	4,456
Italy	41.2	2,530
Ireland	39.5	1,968
UNITED KINGDOM	38.2	2,886
Germany	37.7	3,783
Finland	36.0	3,783
Greece	35.2	1,190
Canada	33.7	4,598
Switzerland	32.2	4,505
Portugal	32.0	609
Australia	31.2	3,697
New Zealand	31.0	2,222
USA	29.0	4,356
Spain	28.4	1,190
Japan	27.4	2,906
Mean	38.1	3,493

Source: Revenue Statistics of OECD Member Countries 1965–85 (OECD: Paris, 1986): table 1, p. 82; table 34, p. 99, for 1984.

Everything else being equal, countries making less tax effort will have less money to spend on public programmes. A high national product per capita can, however, provide substantial public revenue even with a not so high level of public effort. For example, America has a relatively low tax effort, but a high national product; its government can thus spend more while making less effort to collect money from its citizens. Sweden stands out because it combines a high tax effort and a high national product.

When the absolute value of taxing and spending in Britain is compared with other OECD nations, Britain is in the bottom quarter in the amount of money that is actually raised in taxes, because the per capita national product of Britain is in the bottom third of OECD nations. Asking an average amount of tax effort from citizens whose income is below average results in Britain being below average in the amount of money that government can spend to provide benefits for its citizens.

Postwar Britain embodies a political paradox: tax *revenue* has been rising by thousands of per cent, yet tax *effort* has been relatively steady. Those who believe that taxes are increasing so much that they must be out of control can cite as evidence the rising claims for money shown in Figure 2.1. But those who favour maintaining high taxes to finance high levels of public spending can cite evidence to show that tax effort has hardly risen within Britain, and has fallen relative to other nations (Figure 2.2, Table 2.2). Statistics of taxation do not end the political debate: they are the fuel that sustains it.

The Spending Side of the Budget

When attention is turned to the spending side of the budget, we see the friendly face of government – that is, government as a provider of a multitude of benefits for individuals, such as health care; for families, such as education for children; and public goods for society collectively, such as defence. Because most taxes go into the general fund of the treasury, it is not possible to earmark particular tax payments for particular spending benefits. But the great identity requires that what is spent on public programmes must be matched by public revenue from all sources.

Spending by Programme

The biggest single programme is social security; it dispenses £46b, nearly one-third of revenue (Table 2.3). The great bulk is

39

in cash benefits paid to the elderly and others entitled to receive weekly income-maintenance or income-supplement grants. Four other programmes account for £17b to £20b each. Two of these programmes – health and education – provide popular services directly benefiting millions of individuals. The other two – defence and debt interest – provide for collective concerns of government. Together, these five very big programmes spend more than three-quarters of total public revenue.

Table 2.3   Distribution of Public Spending

Programme	£m 1985	% total
Social security	45,894	29.2
Defence, external affairs	20,971	13.4
Health	17,837	11.4
Debt interest	17,526	11.2
Education	17,508	11.1
Police, fire, public order	6,166	3.9
Transport, communication	5,545	3.5
Tax collection, general public services	5,164	3.3
Community: water, sewage, refuse, etc.	5,014	3.2
Housing	4,553	2.9
Employment	3,769	2.4
Agriculture, fishing, food	2,824	1.8
Fuel and energy	2,332	1.5
Trade and industry	1,874	1.2
Other	55	0.0
Total	£157,032m	100

Source: United Kingdom National Accounts 1986 (London: HMSO, 1986): table 9.4.

To say that the other spending programmes make less claim on public expenditure is not to imply that they make small claims. The smallest (*sic*) programme in 1985, trade and industry, claimed £1,874,000,000 from the fisc. The largest programme in this category, police, fire and public order, claimed more than £6.1b, and transport and communications £5.5b. The programmes accounting for less than one-quarter of public revenue collectively spent £27b in total. The multiplicity of big spending public programmes means there is something for everybody, and often many things.

Public expenditure has grown enormously in money terms in the past four decades. Whereas social security payments only claimed £674m in 1950, by 1985 spending on social security had multiplied by 66 times to £45,894m. In the general rise in public expenditure, every programme except agriculture and fishing has increased spending by 12 times or more. The biggest percentage increase in spending is for debt interest; it has gone up by 21,537 per cent since 1950.

While the growth in expenditure is unprecedented by comparison with Britain's historical past, it is very much in keeping with the pattern of OECD nations in the postwar era. Everywhere spending on health, social security and education has risen much more than spending on other programmes, and faster than the growth of the national product (OECD, 1985; Rose, 1985b). The growth in spending on social welfare programmes has been a principal cause of the growth in taxation, and in tax effort.

In the course of 35 years, major shifts have occurred in the relative significance of public programmes. Social security has increased its share of public revenue by 12.6 per cent, thus moving from second to first, passing defence, which has reduced its share of public expenditure by 12.4 per cent. Debt interest has shown the second-biggest increase in claims on the fisc, rising by 9.2 per cent. The claims of health on public funds have risen by 7.0 per cent, whereas education spending in 1985 is only 0.2 per cent higher than in 1950. Major decreases in spending have occurred in agriculture, fishing and food subsidies (-7.7 per cent) and in housing (-5.5 per cent).

The conjoint effect of changes is to concentrate more public spending under fewer headings. The five biggest programmes in 1950 accounted for 60 per cent, today they account for 76 per cent of public spending, an increase of one-quarter. If any substantial reductions are to be achieved in taxation, substantial cuts must be made in spending on three popular social programmes, social security, health and education, or on two necessary collective obligations, defence and debt interest.

Filling the Gap

While taxing and spending are necessarily correlated, the correspondence is not complete. Each year there is normally a gap between the total sum raised by government in tax revenue, and the total sum that it spends. The size of the gap has been growing gradually through the years, as successive governments have found it easier to accept increased spending commitments than to impose increased taxation. The gap is filled by a variety of non-tax sources of revenue available to government.[6]

Politically, borrowing is the most attractive way of claiming the benefits of spending without the costs of taxation – at least in the short term. Borrowing is important in managing fiscal affairs, and particularly in satisfying the great identity within each fiscal year. At the start of a year, a budget is only an estimate of the flows of money in and out of the fisc. As the year progresses, unexpected increases in spending (for example a rise in health or education costs due to a wage increase) or shortfalls in revenue (for example a fall in income tax receipts because of increased unemployment) may be financed by borrowing rather than by an abrupt increase in taxation.

The annual borrowing requirement of government today goes well beyond what is necessary to accommodate the uncertainties of expenditure claims and revenue receipts. In the past, economic theories tended to regard borrowing to finance general expenditure as undesirable, except to finance major capital investments and such emergencies as war (cf. Skidelsky, 1970; Buchanan and Wagner, 1977). The Keynesian revolution in economic theory prescribed that government should increase its deficit in times of recession in order to stimulate demand; the deficit is financed by borrowing. Borrowing has continued, even when governments did not want to stimulate demand; it can be regarded as a lesser evil than cutting expenditure or increasing taxation (Rose and Peters, 1978: 135ff.). In theory, the Thatcher government has rejected Keynesian priorities in favour of a supply-side monetarist approach to economic problems. In practice, it has simply reduced public sector borrowing to a lower share of the national product than in the 1970s.

Public corporations (familiarly known as nationalized industries) generate more than £60b in gross revenues in a year.

Because they are trading enterprises, they must also spend tens of billions of pounds annually on current operating costs and capital investments. Among the diverse public corporations, some generate a trading surplus (electricity, for example) and others (such as coal) a loss; the calculations of net revenue and loss are complex (cf. Cmnd 9702–II, 1986: ch. 5). The Treasury gains revenue from nationalized industries with a net surplus, and must spend revenue where there is a deficit. On balance, public corporations tend to claim more money from the fisc than they contribute to it (cf. Cm. 14, 1986: tables 2.3, 2.3A).

Charges are imposed upon the recipients of a variety of goods and services. Some, such as patent fees, are intended to make a profit; others, such as charges for school meals, cover only a portion of the total cost. The largest single source of revenue from charges, rent for local authority council housing, is not adequate to cover the full costs of council housing, and the rent of those who lack the income to meet the charge is often paid by supplementary benefit grants financed by the fisc. Charging raises significant issues of political and economic principle (cf. Seldon, 1977; Judge, 1980). Politicians tend to be as averse to imposing new charges or substantially raising charges as they are to increasing taxes.

Government can also raise money by selling assets, for example, licensing to profit-making companies the right to drill for oil in the North Sea, a source of more than £1b a year in revenue when high oil prices encouraged exploration there. A distinctive feature of the Thatcher government has been the privatization of public corporations such as British Telecom and British Gas (Steel and Heald, 1985). Privatization has been justified on grounds of political principle; it also provides substantial sums that effectively reduce the Chancellor's need for tax revenue. In 1982, privatization proceeds netted £488m, in 1983 £1.1b, and the Treasury is now counting on up to £5b a year for three years (Cmnd 9702–II, 1986: table 2.23; Cm. 14, 1986: 34).

Many of the devices employed for avoiding an increase in taxation or a decrease in public expenditure only delay the need for increased tax revenue. Borrowing generates annual interest charges that must be financed from future tax revenue; each year's public-sector borrowing involves the addition of £500m a year (or more) to debt interest payments. The once-for-all sale of capital assets is also very much a temporary expedient. When government no longer has assets to sell, then it will either have to cut public spending by £5b, substantially increase public sector borrowing (itself a temporary expedient), or put up the income tax rate by 3.5p in the pound or the VAT rate from 15 to 20 per cent.

No Escape

The great identity requires that when public spending goes up, then public revenue must also go up. Government cannot escape from this fundamental constraint. An increase in tax revenue is the normal way to satisfy the cumulative demands of the great identity. While this principle is easy to state in accounting terms, it is difficult to satisfy politically, for politicians are as averse to increasing taxes as they are predisposed to claim credit for expanding popular but costly programmes.

Notes

1   In this book the word revenue normally refers to tax revenue unless it is clearly in a more general context.
2   For details of the sources used for tax revenue, see the list of sources in the Appendix.
3   All calculations in this book referring to the national product use the gross domestic product, unless otherwise noted.
4   Fitting a least square regression line to the data from 1948 to 1964 in Figure 2.2 shows an annual trend decline in tax effort of 0.38 per cent of the national product; the goodness of fit (r^2) is 0.64.
5   Fitting a least square regression trend line to taxation as a proportion of the national product from 1964 to 1984 shows an increase of 0.33 per cent a year; the r^2 goodness of fit is 0.68.
6   For a more detailed analysis of the potential – and political costs – of raising revenue by non-tax means, see Chapter 9.

CHAPTER THREE

Exercising the Taxing Power: A Public-Policy Model

Like the points of the compass, the principal determinants of tax revenue are few but diverse: laws, public administration and the economy. Because they are few, they are easy to state in the abstract. Because the ramifications of each is different, most discussion of taxation is specialized, concentrating upon one element only. Yet to look solely at tax legislation, or the administration of tax collection, or the relation between taxes and the economy, is to lose sight of their necessary interdependence. Tax revenue is not determined solely by any one element; it results from the interaction of tax laws, administration and economic activity.

As a classic function of government, the procedures for taxation have evolved through the centuries; they have been routinized by public officials responsible for collecting the billions of pounds that government needs. The accretion of detail and the development of specialist concepts and procedures creates barriers to understanding the underlying principles of this basic activity of government.

A public-policy model can bring together what is separated by the barriers imposed by specialization among the professionals of tax administration, and by the division of labour in the social sciences. Taxation combines elements of politics, administration, economics, law and accountancy – including the history of each of these subjects. A public-policy model can focus upon all that is necessarily involved in collecting taxes. Examining only tax laws ignores the influence of the economy in determining how much money such laws can actually raise. Focusing exclusively upon the state of the economy ignores the political considerations that affect how much money the government seeks in taxes, and how it goes about collecting revenue.

To understand taxation, we must understand generic properties of revenue-raising. Tax revenue (TR) is a function of Laws (L), Administration (A), and Economic Activity (E).

$$TR = f (L, A, E)$$

The clarity of the model provides a guide to what we need to know about raising tax revenue. Anyone who has ever looked in a tax manual designed for accountants or lawyers, or in publications of the Inland Revenue, knows that detail can often obfuscate.

The dynamics of taxation are produced by changes in any of the terms in the public-policy model. An economic boom will increase revenue by increasing the base of taxation; a deterioration in administration can lead to increased tax evasion; and alterations in law can raise or lower the rate at which taxes are levied. If laws and economic activity change simultaneously, the resulting interaction multiplies the effect. Alternatively, modifications may be designed to cancel each other out, so that revenue can remain relatively constant, as in a revenue-neutral set of changes.

Law as the Foundation of Taxation

Citizens do not voluntarily make gifts of money to government; taxes are paid because they are required by Acts of Parliament. Whatever moral solidarity may exist in a society (cf. Titmuss, 1970), altruism cannot generate sufficient voluntary contributions to finance the programmes of contemporary big government. Laws also give authority to organizations to act as intermediaries in tax collection. Employers could not deduct money from wages or shopkeepers add on VAT charges without the legal authority to do so. Nor could tax officials present claims for payment without the sanction of an Act of Parliament to justify their demands. If a government took money from people

46

without any legal sanction, we would describe it as levying tribute. Law is the foundation of taxation.

Because tax legislation is enacted by Parliament, political responsibility for taxation is clear. Like it or not, politicians cannot deny their responsibility for taxation, particularly in the British system of government, which makes the governing party responsible for everything that is done. In the United States, by contrast, the division of powers as between the President and Congress, and the multiplicity of Congressional committees and subcommittees, fragments responsibility.

A tax law stipulates two essentials, the tax base and the tax rate. The base defines the particular economic activity subject to taxation. For example, VAT can have its base so defined that it is levied on the sale of all goods and services, or exemption from VAT can be allowed for some goods deemed essentials, such as food. The rate is the formula for determining how much tax must be paid for a given base. The rate may be a constant, as in tobacco tax, or it may vary, as in taxes on wine and spirits, which increase with alcoholic content of the drink. Each term is independently important in determining the revenue yield of a given tax, and there is great scope for variability in how each term is defined (cf. OECD, 1986a: ch. 2).

Tax base

The base of a tax is a variable – and because it is defined by statutes, a *political* variable. It is not defined by economic theory, conventional business accounting practices or, for that matter, by common sense. The Acts of Parliament defining the tax base are measures that particular politicians had to introduce to a potentially hostile House of Commons, and for which a governing party has had to accept responsibility. To determine which economic activities are or are not subject to a particular tax, one must turn to the law, and to interpretations of tax laws.

The law of the land expresses general political norms. Actions that have been proposed by a popularly elected government and duly approved by Parliament have the strongest claim to be legitimate. The fact that the laws are not simple statements of principle but complex statements of inclusions and exclusions does not detract frrom their binding character. Whether or not one understands tax laws, in a democracy they must be accepted as authoritative.

Tax laws allocate the burden of taxation between two groups of people, those who pay a tax, and those who do not. For example, the base of income tax may be so defined as to exempt from taxation those with small amounts of casual or part-time earnings, and taxing the income of those whose earnings are above a stated threshold. Laws also discriminate between different types of economic activity by the same person, that which is liable to the tax, and that which is not. A sum of money given to a youthful baby-sitter is not subject to income tax, but a payment to a registered child-minder normally is.

A historical process of legislation and the accumulation of judicial and administrative interpretations defines the base of a tax. Whereas an economist can start with a *tabula rasa* to produce a logical and coherent definition of a tax base, such as income, the government of the day must start with laws inherited from its predecessors; eighty-nine different measures qualify the base of Inland Revenue tax collections (Cmnd 9702, 1986–II:30).

A tax base is usually the outcome of a process of accretion rather than of logical deduction. No Act of Parliament gives a comprehensive answer to the question: what is income? According to a standard manual of taxation (*Butterworths UK Tax Guide, 1984–85*: 54): 'Income is taxable if it falls within one or other of the Schedules of the Taxes Act 1970.' This Act consolidates a series of previous Acts, some dating back to the Napoleonic wars. The six schedules each define a particular form of income as liable to tax: Schedule A (rent and land); B (commercial woodlands); C (public revenue dividends); D (principally, profits of self-employed persons); E (wages and salaries); and F (company dividends). No tax is liable on any income derived from a source not enumerated in a schedule.

Taxpayers have a vested interest in narrowing the definition of the tax base. The narrower the base then, for any given rate, the less the tax that is due. The governing party's effective control of the House of Commons prevents interest groups from slipping into a tax bill clauses narrowing the tax base in favour of a particular activity or industry. By contrast, in Washington interest groups regularly lobby Congressional committees in efforts to insert into pending legislation clauses that limit the proportion of their economic activities included within the tax base.

The interpretation of a tax law can be challenged by the taxpayer. The assessment of the rateable value of a house or commercial property allows grounds for differences of opinion. A householder who disagrees with the initial assessment of rateable value can challenge the assessment in hopes of lowering the assessed base for rates, and thus lowering his or her tax. Even more debatable is the assessment of legitimate and necessary business expenses to set against income. A rock star may argue that a private airplane or giving expensive parties at a nightclub are business expenses necessary to maintain his celebrity, rather than pleasures to be financed from post-tax income.

Because the definition of the tax base is a political act, it is also the subject of contention. Particular types of exclusions from the tax base are sometimes described as tax expenditures, that is, statutory allowances that reduce the tax base and thus payments due for particular taxes. These may include deductions from income for married and single persons, the treatment of pension schemes, interest paid on mortgages, and corporation tax relief. Tax expenditures are usually evaluated as departures from the 'generally accepted' or 'normal' base for levying taxes (cf. Surrey, 1973: 16; Surrey and McDaniel, 1985). It is argued that when government narrows the tax base and thus the amount of tax due (for example by exempting from taxation the first £6,600 of capital gains) it is putting money in the hands of citizens just as surely as it would by making a social security transfer payment.

Estimates of the revenue foregone by the fisc because of tax expenditures can only be approximate, because they rest upon what the Treasury regards as 'very uncertain' assumptions about how taxpayers would have behaved had the laws been different. Of the many Treasury estimates of the likely revenue effect of laws narrowing the tax base, forty-two are characterized as 'particularly tentative and subject to a wide margin of error', because of uncertainties about the extent to which economic behaviour would alter if tax allowances were repealed. (Cmnd 9702–II, 1986: 32; OECD, 1984: 18ff.).

Insofar as the concept of tax expenditures calls attention to the importance of varying the definition of the tax base, the point made is indisputable. But when the claim is made that tax expenditures are distortions from a normal tax, then the idea is disputable, for it assumes political consensus – that is, that there can be a generally accepted standard for defining what a tax base ought to be normally. The concept of tax expenditures implies that public-finance experts can define what is a normal tax, and that when public laws deviate from such standards there is something deficient in Acts of Parliament. In fact, there is no generally agreed standard among OECD nations about what are and are not normal allowances to reduce the tax base (cf. OECD, 1986a: 20ff.).

The literature about tax expenditure has succeeded in increasing public awareness of the political importance of the tax base. But it has not succeeded in resolving political disputes. Wildavsky (1985:414) challenges the basic assumption that tax expenditures involve government giving away money to which the fisc has first claim. 'Whose money is this anyway?' he asks, arguing that the first claim on money earned is that of the wage-earner rather than the government.

Insofar as the definition of the tax base is the subject of dispute, disputes will be resolved by political means. For example, most tax experts consider that the relief from taxation of mortgage interest payments is an undesirable subsidy to home-owners and should be repealed. But political parties take a very different view: they believe that it is a means of encouraging a socially desirable goal, home-ownership, and to repeal this tax advantage would be electoral suicide (Kay and King, 1983: 57; Rose and McAllister, 1986: 60ff.).

In a book concerned with the chief means of financing the growth of government, the primary concern must be with what is actually collected as public revenue in order to satisfy the great identity. Hypothesizing what revenue could have been raised if tax laws were written differently will not meet the demands of this year's budget.

Tax rates are of fundamental importance too, for the rate determines how much money is due to the government from a particular base. A tax levied at a rate of 30 per cent will generate twice as much revenue from a given base as a tax levied at a rate of 15 per cent. A change of 1 per cent in the rate of income tax will have a substantial impact on the fisc. The reduction of the standard rate of income tax from 29 to 27 per cent in the 1987 budget cost the Treasury more than £25b in revenue, more than half the public sector borrowing requirement.

Historically, objections to taxation were often voiced as matters of principle. Opposition to the re-introduction of income tax in 1842 did not focus upon the rate, less than 3 per cent, or the base, a minority of middle-class incomes, but upon the principle. Today, nobody doubts the need of government to levy substantial taxes to finance the costs of big government. The main issue is a matter of degree: how much? Many complaints about taxes are not so much about taxation in principle as about the rate of tax levied.

The history of VAT provides a simple and striking example of the importance of tax rates. Members of the European Community are obliged to levy a Value Added Tax; thus, the tax had to be introduced when Britain joined the Community in 1973. But each nation is free to choose the rate at which VAT is levied. The standard rate differs among Community nations from a low of 12 per cent in Spain and Luxembourg to 22 per cent in Denmark and 25 per cent in Ireland. (The effects of these differences in rates are modified by differences in defining the transactions subject to VAT.) In 1973 the British government set the rate of VAT at 10 per cent; the Labour government reduced this rate to 8 per cent in 1974, but also brought in a higher rate of 25 per cent for certain scheduled goods. In 1979 the newly elected Conservative government raised the rate of VAT to 15 per cent to finance an income tax cut. The variation in the rate of VAT appears as a matter of only a few per cent, but given the broad base of the tax, seemingly small percentages can involve big sums of money. At current Treasury calculations (Cm. 14, 1986: table 4.7) the difference in revenue between VAT at 8 and 10 per cent is £2.2b a year, and the difference between VAT at 8 and 15 per cent is nearly £8b.

Tax rates can be set in two contrasting ways. Either the rate can be stated in terms of a fixed sum of money for a given unit of a commodity (for example 88p per gallon of petrol, or 18.6p per pint of beer), or it can be an *ad valorem* tax, levied as a percentage of a particular base (for example, 15 per cent of sales subject to value added tax). A fixed-money tax upon commodities achieves certainty. But in an era of inflation, such a tax is of declining revenue importance, because the money it raises remains constant, while the value of the commodities taxed rises with the cost of living.

An *ad valorem* tax is buoyant in its revenue yield, raising more revenue when the value of the tax base goes up, because it is levied as a percentage of the current money value of the tax base. Much of the increase in revenue from income tax and national insurance contributions over the years has been the result of an increase in money wages due to inflation. While an *ad valorem* tax is better adapted to inflation, it presupposes that the value of the goods being taxed can easily be assessed. While this is true of retail sales, it is much more difficult to value an estate for death duties, if some goods (for example the family home and other household possessions) are not sold.

Tax revenues reflect the combined effect of laws defining the tax base and tax rates. In determining liability for income tax it is necessary to identify the unit (a family, or an individual) to be taxed, the total amount of income subject to taxation, and the relief to be granted by various allowances in order to establish the tax base. The rate of income tax due increases progressively with the amount of taxable income; the rate rises progressively with income by six steps, from 27p to 60p. British practices are similar to those in other OECD nations. Two-thirds have a larger number of steps in their income tax rate, and every OECD nation has a similarly complicated set of allowances to subtract in calculating a tax base (OECD, 1986a). The total tax due is thus the result of a variety of clauses in the tax law, and rulings about the application of these clauses to particular circumstances.

No Taxation Without Administration

The effective administration of tax laws is a necessary condition of financing contemporary government. This point is well understood by fiscal and political historians (see for example Ardant, 1975; Braun, 1975; Webber and Wildavsky, 1986), and by persons concerned with taxation in Third World countries that often lack effective institutions of tax administration (Goode, 1984; Hinrichs, 1966; Radian, 1980). The historic effectiveness of tax administration in Britain means that one takes for granted a *sine qua non* of public revenue.

52

The inertia of tax legislation is paralleled by the inertia of administrative institutions. Tax administration can be handled routinely in Britain, since the institutions responsible, such as the Inland Revenue and Customs and Excise, have had more than a century in which to accumulate experience in administering taxes (Dowell, 1888). Critics of tax administration complain that the routines of tax officials are too well established, causing administrators to be excessively sceptical about the difficulties of implementing novel taxes and thus encouraging politicians to be even more averse to innovation in taxation (cf. Kay, 1986; Cmnd 8822, 1983).

Tax officials are professionals who tend to view existing and proposed changes in legislation in terms of the ease and effectiveness with which a tax can be administered. Ease of administration is important in reducing friction with taxpayers, and in promoting administrative efficiency. Effectiveness in administration is important to tax officials, for not only does it assure a steady flow of revenue to the fisc; it also avoids criticisms that tax officials are not collecting all the money that is due to the fisc.

Tax-collecting agencies are unique among government departments in being highly 'profitable'. For every pound spent in administration, the institutions yield 10–80 times more in revenue, a very high rate of return by the conventional criteria of the business world. But the more money that is collected, the greater the political costs.

Tax Handles

From an administrative point of view, the crucial feature of any tax is its tax handle, that is, the mechanism by which money legally due from the taxpayer is turned into money in the hands of the fisc. A good tax handle assures both ease and effectiveness of revenue collection. Important properties of tax handles include whether or not the transactions to be taxed are monetized (a money wage) or not (payments in kind); are recorded or not (payment by cheque or payment in cash); and readily accessible to tax collectors and inspectors (a transaction by a large firm, or by a housewife). In a modern economy there are many tax handles, for economic transactions are usually carried out in money rather than barter, and most transactions leave a paper trail, being recorded by the payer, the recipient and/or a third party, such as a bank or credit agency. Tax officials in advanced industrial nations have a much wider choice of tax handles than in a poor Third World nation in which barter is a normal means of exchange, and few records are kept accessible to a tax inspector.

The importance of designing a tax with a good handle can be illustrated by reviewing alternative ways of imposing a tax on gambling. To tax the proceeds of winners would be difficult administratively and limited in effectiveness, for the crowd of people frequenting a bookmaker's shop or bingo parlour is transient, and money changes hands quickly over the counter. To enforce such a tax, government officials would have to be present in each shop and claim the money due as successful punters collected their winnings. It would be difficult to trace winners a day later, let alone at the end of the tax year, and winners could gamble away the winnings liable to tax. By contrast, a tax on the proceeds of bookmakers is easy to enforce, for tax officials need only inspect periodic returns from bookmakers to ensure that the payments are reasonable. If a return is not filed, a tax inspector can visit the bookmaker's premises to demand payment, and a bookie who refuses to comply with the tax law can lose his licence.

From an administrative point of view, organizations provide better tax handles than do individuals. An organization is readily accessible at a registered address; its size as well as its legal form compel it to keep copious records; and it normally has assets that can easily be attached if taxes due are not paid. Organizations are far better equipped than individuals to deal routinely with tax officials, and there are millions fewer organizations than there are individual taxpayers.

Taxing Organizations Not Individuals

To speak of taxation as a burden on the individual taxpayer is to state a half-truth. In economic theory, the burden of taxation is ultimately assumed to fall upon individuals. However, in administrative reality very little money is collected directly from individual taxpayers. The tax collector does not normally put his hand in the taxpayer's pocket. It is far easier and more effective to collect money *before* it is disbursed among tens of millions of people.

Nine-tenths of tax revenue is collected from organizations. In some instances the organization pays the tax on its own activities, for example in the case of corporation tax, or the duty that a whisky distiller must pay on spirits distilled. Sometimes the tax is paid on behalf of individuals; the PAYE (Pay As You Earn) system of income tax depends upon the employer making payments for the Schedule E tax liabilities of named individuals.

Employers Income tax is easily and effectively collected from some 20 million wage-earners each week because the law obliges employers to make a weekly PAYE return for employees. National insurance contributions are similarly easy to collect, for the employer is liable to pay a portion of tax and must also withhold the employee's contribution from wages, forwarding both to the Inland Revenue.

Trading firms Value added tax is due every time goods or services liable to VAT change hands. The seller must charge VAT, and issue a receipt to the purchaser that identifies the VAT payment made. In the course of a series of transactions from the suppliers of raw materials to the seller of the finished product, value is added at each stage, and VAT is payable. A firm not only pays VAT on the inputs of its products but can also collect VAT when it sells goods. Thus, the effective tax on its activities is only on the value added by its activities, the difference between the VAT it pays and the VAT it collects. The Customs and Excise collects VAT payments regularly from trading firms, but does not have to collect a separate payment each time a transaction occurs.[1]

Producers and importers In an island nation imports have historically been good tax handles because they enter through a limited number of ports which customs officials can watch. By contrast, in European countries with long land frontiers, it is more difficult to monitor the movement of goods. Tax can be collected from the importer when goods arrive in Britain, and payment of tax can be a condition of clearing goods through customs. When goods are produced within Britain, such as beer, gin or whisky, the Customs and Excise regularly inspects production records in breweries and distilleries in order to keep track of quantities in stock. Its analysis of production records, including allowances for the evaporation of spirits kept for years in cask, is the basis for determining the exact amount of money that must be paid in duty.

Most organizations, including many public sector organizations, are routinely engaged in paying three sets of taxes to the fisc: income tax, national insurance contributions and VAT. In addition, firms may be liable to corporation tax on profits, rates on property that they own, and customs or excise duties.

Collecting taxes from organizations rather than individuals effectively insulates most people from needing to think about the taxes paid on their earnings and expenditure. An individual who reads the fine print on his or her pay slip would know how much was deducted in income tax and national insurance before net wages were in hand. But it would require an enormous and unwarranted amount of paperwork to calculate how much was paid in VAT or excise taxes on a household's purchases during a year, and substantial (and contestable) assumptions to impute a value to corporation taxes levied directly upon impersonal bodies.

Of the one-tenth of tax revenue collected directly from individuals, domestic rates are the most significant. Real estate is a good tax handle because, unlike diamond rings, it is a form of property impossible to conceal from the assessor. Home-owners pay rates directly to their local authority. Tenants often have their rate payment included in their weekly or monthly rent bill; the landlord makes the actual payment to the local taxing authority. Motor-vehicle licence tax is a second source of direct payments from individuals to government. The tax is easily administered: a car-owner receives a computerized reminder of renewal and the tax can be paid at a post office. It is effective insofar as a car is constantly in use in public places, where the absence of an up-to-date licence need only be noticed once by a passing policeman or traffic warden to create difficulties. The motor-vehicle tax is easier to enforce than a television licence fee, for a TV set is normally used in the privacy of a home.

Self-employed people are deviant taxpayers because they actually pay their own income tax. The Inland Revenue lacks a convenient tax handle since by definition there is no organization to pay tax for the self-employed. Whereas income tax due from a firm with 1,000 employees can be quickly calculated by computer and paid as a single cheque, the calculation of the tax due from a single self-employed person is done one case at a time. It is thus much less easy and certain to collect tax from the self-employed (Cmnd 8822, 1983: ch. 3).

A high standard of routine tax administration is not an accident. Tax laws are written so that the revenue can be collected from readily accessible sources that have every incentive to discharge honestly their obligations, both as corporate taxpayers, and as corporate collectors of taxes from individuals.

As the Economy Goes

The state of the economy is a major determinant of tax revenue: 'You can't tax it if it isn't there.' The point is most obvious in a comparison of First and Third World economies, for a country with a low national product has a much smaller tax base per capita than does a rich country. It is also evident in comparisons between Britain today and Britain a generation or two ago, for economic growth has greatly increased the tax base and thus the revenue of British government.

The Size of the Pie

It is attractive for politicians averse to raising tax rates and broadening the tax base to rely upon economic growth rather than increased tax effort to produce more tax revenue. Each increase in tax effort induces a disproportionate decrease in take-home pay. If a government claims 40 per cent of the national product in taxation, an increase in tax effort to 45 per cent will reduce the private-sector share by 8.3 per cent (that is, from 60 to 55 per cent).

The reasons why government favours economic growth are multiple: in a booming economy there is a lot more money to spend, and fewer political difficulties. Moreover, as economic growth is cumulative, in the course of a five-year Parliament an annual growth rate of 2.5 per cent will, by a process of compounding, increase the national product by 16 per cent, and total tax revenue with it.

Viewing the economy as a source of tax revenue imposes a one-dimensional perspective upon a multi-dimensional set of activities. Models of the economy designed to illustrate processes important in economic theory often give very little attention to taxation. From a broad economic perspective, issues of prices and wages, investment and growth and foreign exchange rates appear of pervasive importance. Taxation appears only as an intervening variable in the economic system as a whole (Wallis *et al.*, 1984). In many contexts, taxation can be seen as a fiscal instrument used for ulterior, non-revenue ends. Economic activities are reduced by tax laws to such categories as taxable income, or goods liable to value added tax. The flow of income and expenditure through the economy is not the concern of tax authorities, whose primary job is to divert a portion of that flow to the fisc through appropriate administrative means.

Certainty and Predictability

Government is concerned with the certainty of revenue and, because budgets are statements about future taxing and spending, about the predictability of revenue. A good tax is not only easy to collect but also will yield an amount of revenue that can be predicted when forecasts are required for the budget in the year ahead. Otherwise the Treasury may make policies based upon misleading assumptions about the public-sector borrowing requirement, the difference between the forecast total expenditure and total revenue.

A good tax is a tax that is not only certain of collection but also unlikely to fluctuate greatly from year to year. One advantage of taxing habits such as smoking and drinking is that they do not fluctuate much on a year-to-year basis. While petroleum revenue in a good year can provide more tax revenue, it is vulnerable to fluctuations arising from actions by OPEC nations that are outside the capacity of the Treasury to predict, let alone control. Even the best of taxes cannot be 100 per cent predictable, because of the effects upon tax bases of short-term fluctuations in the economy. An increase in unemployment will reduce the number on whose behalf income tax and national insurance contributions are paid, and a spending boom will affect the turnover of goods and services on which VAT is levied.

While the economy is always in flux, there is a high degree of continuity in economic activities on a year-to-year basis. A rise of 2 per cent in unemployment still leaves 98 per cent of taxpayers paying taxes. Errors in forecasting tax revenue, which depend upon activity in the economy as a whole, tend to be less than errors in forecasting public expenditure, nominally within the control of the Treasury.

A long-term review of the accuracy of taxes (Table 3.1) shows that the average error in estimating revenue from a tax is usually· only a few per cent. Among major taxes it is as low as 2.3 per cent for income tax, and up to 6.5 per cent for VAT and 7.4 per cent for the national insurance surcharge on employers. Corporation tax and capital gains taxes are subject to relatively high error rates, because profits are not so easy to forecast from year to year, and this is even more true of decisions of investors to realize capital gains. These taxes are not large sources of revenue, nor could they be when they are so unreliable as revenue sources.

Table 3.1 Accuracy of Forecasts of Tax Revenue, 1951–81

Tax	Period 1981	£ revenue %	Average error
Income tax	1951–81	27,734	2.3
National insurance surcharge	1977–81	3,787	7.4
VAT	1973–81	13,710	6.5
Corporation tax	1967–81	4,194	8.3
Hydrocarbon oil	1961–81	4,450	2.5
Tobacco	1961–81	3,200	2.1
Alcohol	1961–81	3,020	3.8
Capital gains	1967–81	753	26.9
Motor vehicle	1951–81	1,510	3.4
Total taxation	1951–81	95,380	2.1

Source: Derived from Mosley (1985), table 4. Average error is the mean percentage difference between the money collected and the estimated revenue for the tax.

Altogether, unanticipated fluctuations in economic activity cause an average error of 2.1 per cent in estimating total tax revenue each year. The error for the aggregate is low in part because errors in estimating particular taxes often cancel out. While such a figure is small in relative terms, it represents more than £3.5b in current tax revenue, and can have a significant impact upon official plans for the economy (Treasury, 1984: 24). Because the budget deficit expresses the difference between total revenue and total expenditure, a revenue error can be compounded by an error in estimating expenditure; together, these estimating errors can be large in relation to a public-sector borrowing requirement of £5b–£10b.

A government seeking to fine tune its management of the economy, as the Treasury has characteristically sought to do in the postwar era, must have fine-tuned forecasts of revenue. The 98 per cent degree of accuracy in forecasting total tax revenue is of limited avail, insofar as official policy judgements require accuracy of 99 or even 99.9 per cent in estimating the major terms of the economy (Mosley, 1985).

Taxation as a System

Tax revenue is the result of a system of relationships; it is not the result of a single tax, or a single attribute of the political or economic system. No one tax is the dominant source of total revenue. Because of the interaction of laws, administration and economic activity, there is never a simple answer to the basic question: How much money can this tax raise? The amount of money that a tax can raise is a variable, not a constant.

Changes in the revenue produced by a particular tax, if administration is relatively constant, will reflect changes in tax legislation or in the economy, or both. Within the economy, economic growth and inflation can both make revenue increase. By contrast, in tax legislation the crucial variables of tax rate and tax base can be altered so that the revenue is decreased, or a given amount is produced in different ways.

The systemic character of taxation is even more evident when one considers total tax revenue. It is the sum of the revenues yielded by many different taxes, each of which has its own particular way of raising money through the interaction of laws, administration and the economy. Even though a few taxes raise a lot of money, at the margin fluctuations in less important taxes can alter total revenue.

The Parts and the Whole

There is a dissociation between the sums raised by particular taxes and the spending side of the budget. Taxes are not earmarked – that is, the revenue raised is not assigned to a particular spending programme. The revenue raised by each tax is normally paid into the general revenue fund. In Britain the general revenue fund is very general indeed, for nine-tenths of tax revenue flows into central government, where it is in principle available for allocation in many different ways. Local authorities, though raising much less revenue, are multi-purpose agencies, and in theory also have substantial discretion in determining what to do with their tax revenues. By contrast, in the United States the large number of single-purpose agencies, such as school districts and sewer districts, are much more limited in the purposes on which they can spend their revenues.

Tax experts favour the pooling of tax revenues in a general fund, because the government then retains the right in theory to decide what is the best use to make of total revenue (Musgrave and Musgrave, 1980: 241ff.). Moreover, it avoids the problem of particular spending claims growing faster than particular sources of revenue; for example, social security benefits no longer depend solely upon national insurance contributions.

Politically, the dissociation of taxing and spending lines in the budget means that proponents of specific programmes do not have to identify the specific source of tax revenue that will finance it. The absence of a tax price makes the benefits of public spending appear relatively more attractive. In a complementary fashion, the absence of a policy price makes the benefits of reducing taxes appear more attractive. In each instance, the benefits are specifically visible, and the costs are as diffuse as the general revenue fund. As long as attention is focused upon one particular tax, it is relatively straightforward to argue a case for its reduction. The increase in retail prices caused by VAT can be cited as an argument for reducing the VAT rate. The disincentive

61

to employment in the employer's national insurance contribution can be argued as a justification for its reduction. But however valid the criticism of a particular tax, it cannot be accepted in isolation.

In the budget the whole is different from as well as greater than the sum of the parts – and the whole constrains the parts. Because the bottom line of the budget is about total revenue and expenditure, the reduction of any one tax must be matched by an increase in another tax, if total tax revenue is to remain constant. A Chancellor of the Exchequer does not need to confront the argument for reducing a particular tax. He can oppose changes by posing a related question: What tax should be raised or what programme cut to replace the revenue lost by a proposed tax cut?

Whilst the proponents of tax cuts are many, the proponents of tax increases and programme cuts are few. Most Cabinet ministers are spending ministers, and they will not casually volunteer to reduce the programmes in their own department. Most Cabinet ministers are also elected politicians, and they represent to the Chancellor the view that any significant tax increase will be electorally unpopular.

The public-policy model does not prescribe what a Chancellor should do, but it does show how tight are the constraints when tax reductions are mooted. Any legislation introduced to lower tax rates or broaden the tax base will result in a fall in total tax revenue unless something is done to improve tax administration, or the economy expands. While tax cuts are formally within the Chancellor's hands, the power to make the economy grow is not. Moreover, tax administration involves such a great volume of activity and so large a staff that any improvements in that field are likely to come slowly, if at all.

When a model of public expenditure is aligned with a model of tax revenue the differences between them are more striking. Increases in public expenditure tend to reflect more or less 'uncontrollable' demands on established programmes, for example an increase in the number of elderly entitled to a pension. Influences on the major spending programmes, and thus on the total of public expenditure, are not identical with the determinants of tax revenue (OECD, 1985; Rose, 1984: ch. 2).

When the initial estimates of total revenue and total expenditure are brought together in the annual budget cycle, the effects of political inertia upon public expenditure usually generate a different revenue requirement from that produced by the inertia of taxation. The revenue requirement is invariably higher than estimated revenue when the extra cost of fresh proposals from spending ministers is included. At this point, politicians are confronted with the opportunity to make (or try to avoid) marginal but politically unattractive decisions: whether to spend less in delivering public benefits, or to raise the costs of taxation.

Note

1 On the complexities created by zero-rating and exemption from VAT for certain types of trading activities, see the relevant sections of the annual report of the Customs and Excise, for example Cmnd 9655 (1985), 21ff., 36ff.

CHAPTER FOUR

Taxation in Practice

Although a public-policy model can outline the chief determinants of taxation, filling in the practical details is a laborious task, for taxation involves complex calculations specific to given circumstances. Because the purpose of this book is to explain the role of taxation in government, it would be inappropriate to linger in the labyrinthine ways familiar to accountants and tax inspectors. But it is desirable to set out, succinctly and clearly, details important in influencing how tax revenue is collected in practice.

Variety is the pervasive characteristic of taxation. There are dozens of different taxes, hundreds of tax laws, a multiplicity of tax collection agencies, and major differences between the economic activities subject to tax. Most generalizations about taxation require qualification, for even when they are usually true, it is easy to find exceptions. The greatest difference is that between the perspective of the Chancellor of the Exchequer, who is concerned with total tax revenue, and the view of the ordinary taxpayer, who is concerned with his or her tax payments. Taxes that look large in a household's budget contribute only a mite to total tax revenue.

Viewing taxation as a means of raising revenue concentrates attention upon one particular aspect of a tax: how much money does it raise? This introduces a sense of proportion. From a revenue perspective, one tax that raises a large sum of money is worth more attention than dozens of taxes that contribute very small sums to the fisc. The first section of this chapter examines the multiplicity of taxes. The three succeeding sections review in detail the multiplicity of laws that define taxes; the administrative institutions that collect taxes; and the different types of economic activity subject to taxation. The chapter concludes by comparing the sums contributed to the fisc by millions of taxpayers with the benefits that ordinary citizens receive from programmes financed by taxation.

Many Taxes

Defining Taxes

In generic terms taxes are 'compulsory, unrequited payments to general government' (OECD, 1984a: 39). The first distinguishing feature of a tax is that it is compulsory. Only government can levy taxes, because only the state can compel people to do what they would not voluntarily do. The second feature of taxes is that they are unrequited – that is, the payments are not exchanged for particular goods or services. In the market, a person paying money receives something specific in return but nothing specific is given in exchange for the payment of a particular tax. Benefits of public policy are normally not contingent upon the payment of particular taxes.

There are hundreds of different ways of collecting money. The International Monetary Fund (1983: 284f., 77f.) reports forty-eight different taxes in use in Britain, and 137 different taxes in France, including three different taxes on *pari-mutuel* betting. The more taxes that are enumerated the smaller the proportion of money that the average tax can contribute to the fisc. In the case of France, eighty-two of the taxes each produce less than 0.01 per cent of revenue.

The most comprehensive single catalogue of British taxes is that contained in the National Accounts, which lists taxes under thirty-eight different headings that vary enormously in money value. The criterion used for selecting a tax as suitable for analysis here is that it accounted for at least 1 per cent of total tax revenue in at least one year since 1948. So low a threshold ensures the inclusion of taxes that may have interesting attributes, even though (or because) they are relatively small in money raised. Taxes that contribute less than this amount, such as a variety of customs and excise taxes, are aggregated under a single heading

65

(for further details, see Appendix A, and Rose and Karran, 1983:10ff.).

In Britain today total tax revenue is the sum of fifteen different categories of taxes, plus a residual category; they are very unequal in their contribution to the fisc. No one tax is dominant – the largest single source of revenue, income tax, contributes one-quarter of total tax revenue. Four taxes – income tax, national insurance, value added tax and local authority rates – are major taxes, for each contributes at least 10 per cent to total tax revenue. Together these major taxes account for more than two-thirds of total tax revenue. Four more taxes – corporation tax, petroleum revenue, hydrocarbon oil duty and tobacco – account for an additional 20 per cent of revenue. These eight taxes generate 88 per cent of total tax revenue (Table 1.1). The remaining 12 per cent is produced by dozens of taxes each having a very low revenue yield.

Why Have So Many Different Taxes?

On *a priori* grounds it can be argued that the more taxes a government levies the greater its total tax revenue (cf. Brennan and Buchanan, 1980). This assumes that while individuals will notice the high rates of a small number of taxes they will be less likely to notice or object to less high rates spread over a large number of taxes, even though these raise more money in aggregate. In fact, this is not the case: there is no significant correlation between the number of taxes that are levied in a country and the proportion of the national product claimed by taxation (Rose, 1985: 296).

Each tax can be justified by particular analytic and historical characteristics. Since the national tax system was not created at a single point in time, it is reasonable to justify particular taxes on different grounds. The less revenue a tax contributes to the fisc, the more likely it is that a non-revenue justification can be given for it. Yet taxes that contribute large sums to the fisc can have non-revenue justifications too.

The income tax, the largest single tax, can be justified as a tax based upon the ability to pay, since the rate rises progressively with income. The progressive character of the rate also makes it a potential means of income redistribution, insofar as a well-to-do person is left with a lower proportion of post-tax income than a person who is poorly paid. Persons with very large incomes may pay as much as 60p in the pound on the top portion of their income, more than double the standard rate of 27p. But because the highest rate affects only a small portion of total income, even wealthy Britons usually pay less than half their income in tax. The element of progressivity in the British income tax is small (cf. Kay and King, 1983: 19ff.; Prest and Barr, 1979: ch. 13). Insofar as income tax does contribute to the redistribution of income, it is principally through the spending programmes that it helps to finance.

The historical justification for a separate national insurance contribution was that workers should not get something for nothing; they were expected to make a contribution to their own social security, albeit the contribution was only a fraction of the total cost. Today social security payments are financed by a combination of deductions from employees' wages, employers' contributions and contributions from general revenue funds. Political inertia explains the maintenance of a separate national insurance contribution. To abolish this tax and replace the revenue lost by an increased income tax would raise income tax by more than half.

A variety of theoretical arguments can be adduced in support of value added tax, for it is a tax on amount of expenditure. Doing so may encourage people to save money, and thus encourage investment in the economy. The exemption of export sales from VAT may encourage sales abroad. As a matter of historical fact, VAT was introduced in 1973 because it was a political obligation of Britain's entry to the European Community. In the period since, politicians have shown no inclination to innovate further by levying a general expenditure tax (cf. Kay and King, 1983: 68ff., 117ff.; Kaldor, 1955).

Taxes may be levied in ways intended to encourage economic activities regarded as desirable. For example, capital gains realized by the sale of shares or other assets are not taxed as income, which would then be subject to a levy as high as 60 per cent for a well-to-do investor. Instead, such gains are subject to a flat-rate tax of 30 per cent, and the first £6,600 of gains realized by an individual are exempt. The lower rate of tax on capital gains as against income is an encouragement to people with the means to invest in ways that will create capital appreciation. Allowing the deduction of the interest paid on a mortgage from income subject to tax encourages home-ownership.

Taxes may also be justified as measures designed to discourage lawful activities regarded as anti-social. High rates of tax on whisky, gin and other spirits and on tobacco are meant to discourage heavy consumption of these products deemed injurious to health. If these goods were taxed at the VAT rate rather than at 93p for a packet of kingsize cigarettes and £4.73 for a bottle of whisky, then retail prices would fall dramatically and consumption would rise of goods likely to damage the health of heavy consumers.

A logical justification of a tax is not necessarily a historically accurate explanation. To be logical, an explanation must be internally consistent in reasoning from premises to conclusion. But contemporary logical justifications are likely to be *ex post facto* justifications, when applied to taxes that are a century or more old. A reasoned justification of a tax is not to be confused with a historically determined sequence of events resulting from political inertia.

Politics as Explanation and Justification

Every tax requires a political explanation, since it derives from actions by politicians. The divergence between explanation by the analysis of historical political events and an *ex post facto* rationale is likely to be greatest with old taxes. Rates on property were attractive as a source of revenue in the seventeenth century because a large portion of economic activity was then outside the money economy. The historical reason why Pitt introduced the income tax was to finance the war with Napoleon; it was not to redistribute wealth in accord with doctrines of Fabian Socialism, expounded centuries later. Lloyd George was won over to the idea of employee contributions to national insurance as a means of guaranteeing the political acceptability of what was then a radical social policy (Bunbury, 1957).

The critical test of political as against fiscal explanations of taxation arises when political inertia favours doing nothing whereas strong logical arguments can justify a significant alteration in taxes. The benefits of making a decision will be in fiscal policy; the cost will be political. By contrast, the benefits for letting inertia maintain the tax system as it is are political; the costs are in fiscal efficiency.

Given a choice between acting according to a political or fiscal logic, politicians have no difficulty in following their political instincts and accepting the inertia of established taxes, whatever the logical arguments for making other decisions. If the political circumstances make inaction intolerable (Rose, 1972), then any policy – logical or contradictory – may appear acceptable to end an intolerable situation. If fiscal, social and other arguments imply major political benefits from a positive change in taxation, then action may follow. But this does not detract from the essential point, that the rationale must be political. As Richard Neustadt once remarked: 'No President can have an economic policy; all his policies must be political.'

Many Laws

Laws, like taxes, are plural not singular. Just as a summary statistic of total tax revenue masks the variety of activities involved in collecting particular taxes, so a reference to tax law or the statutory basis of taxation makes tax legislation appear simpler than it is.

Many Laws for Each Tax

A tax is not normally calculated solely according to a single Act of Parliament; every tax is usually subject to conditions scattered among dozens of different laws. The official *Index to the Statutes* lists forty-six different Acts of Parliament affecting income and corporation taxes; thirty-four Acts for national insurance; and twenty-nine Acts for rates in England and Wales. Even taxes that raise relatively little money can be the subject of much legislation; 147 different Acts of Parliament affect the calculation of stamp duties, and eighty-six Acts concern death duties (Table 4. 1).

In order to come to grips with tax legislation, one must survey hundreds of Acts of Parliament. A one-volume reference book for tax lawyers and accountants, *Butterworths UK Tax Guide 1984–85*, devotes twenty-nine double-column pages to an index of tax laws cited therein, each column containing dozens of different references. While tracing out the legislative history of a tax created centuries ago does not make it appear logical, at least it will explain why illogical elements now exist.

Table 4.1 Complexity of Tax Legislation

Tax	Number of Acts	Number of Topics
Income and corporation	46	708
Social security	34	304
Rates[a]	29	151
VAT	18	59
Petroleum revenue tax	6	23
Customs and Excise[b]	91	538
Alcohol		110
Hydrocarbon oil		30
Tobacco		13
Other		377
Death duties	94	193
Stamp duties	147	278
Vehicle excises	13	40

a For Scotland, twenty-nine Acts, oldest 1845, and ninety-seven topics referenced.
b Includes Customs and Excise management.

Source: Index to the Statutes (1982). The tax identified is the principal index entry; the number of topics refers to sub-entries under the principal entry. The taxation categories do not exactly match those reported in Table 3.1 because of differences in categorization as between the national income accounts and statutory publications.

Time and effort permitting, obsolescence can be reduced by repealing antique laws. For example, Section 85 of the 1985 Finance Act abolished thirteen different stamp duties at rates of from 5 to 50p; five of the duties were peculiar to Scotland, and the Inland Revenue could not even find out what one duty, on a deed of procuration, was meant to apply to! The consolidation of legislation, as many old Acts are replaced by a single, more easily accessible statute, reduces the multiplication of laws and provides occasion for updating. The income tax, initially introduced at the end of the eighteenth century, is today governed by Acts which at their oldest date from 1931.

In the course of a few decades or generations, legislation

about a particular tax will proliferate in several ways. First of all, new Acts will be adopted that deal principally with the tax. Secondly, the tax will be affected by legislation about related subjects, e.g. income and corporation taxes are affected by Acts of a single Parliament concerning Merchant Shipping (1970), National Savings Bank (1971), Parliamentary and Other Pensions (1972), Local Government (1972), National Health Service Reorganization (1973) and Fair Trading (1973). Thirdly, each year's Finance Bill can contain a clause or two that affects a particular tax.

Because the average Act has many clauses to deal with a wide variety of contingencies, tax legislation tends to be complex. Complexity can be approximately indicated by the number of topics given as sub-headings under the chief entry for a tax in the *Index to the Statutes* (Table 4.1). Under income tax there are forty-six different laws referenced, and 708 different topics are separately listed. For example, under a heading concerning supplemental charging for Schedule E taxation there are separate topical references to laws concerning voluntary pensions; the scope of charges, and the meaning of emoluments received in the United Kingdom; living accommodation provided by an employer; the exemption of the occupation of Chevening House by the royal family; share option and incentive schemes; payments on retirement; workers supplied by agencies; and miscellaneous exemptions and reliefs.

In order to come to grips with all the legal ramifications of a tax, it is normally necessary to consider the way in which dozens of different Acts affect hundreds of different topics in the *Index to the Statutes*. The tax on tobacco is atypical in dealing with only thirteen different topics. At the other extreme, income and corporation tax is subdivided into 708 separately indexed topics. The host of Customs and Excise taxes collectively cover 538 topics, albeit many readily grouped under specific headings such as alcohol. National insurance taxes are related to 304 topics.

Resolving Ambiguities and Disagreements

Since even the most carefully drafted statute cannot anticipate all eventualities, the revenue authorities issue statements of practice intended to clarify the interpretation of ambiguous or

71

unclear tax laws without the delays and expense of court cases (*Butterworths* , 1984: 15). Statements of practice occasionally take the form of written quasi-binding concessions, or rulings in advance of particular problems coming before the revenue authorities.

For non-routine calculations of tax, a taxpayer may need to consult more than one official form, and to take professional opinions from an accountant and, upon occasion, a lawyer. Professional tax advisers interpret statements of practice by tax collection authorities, the informal operating routines for processing tax returns, and the law itself. Since a non-routine problem may not point to a single unambiguous conclusion, once a tax is paid Inland Revenue staff can review the relevant statutes, judicial opinions, and statements of practice and may arrive at a different interpretation of the tax due.

When disagreement persists between the tax collector and a taxpayer, disputes about the facts of income and corporation tax and VAT are usually referred to independent expert tribunals. Most disagreements between taxing authorities and taxpayers are resolved at this level, if not before. A court case may be launched to arrive at a judicial interpretation of the tax law governing an issue of particular concern to tax officials, or a large amount of taxpayer's money. The court's interpretation of a statute is the ultimate authority binding both tax authorities and taxpayers.

Because the tax laws at a given moment reflect the outcome of a historical process extending over centuries, it is misleading to think of it as a system, with the unity that the word 'system' implies. Two economists describe the result thus:

> The present state of the British tax system is the product of a series of unsystematic and ad hoc measures, many undertaken for excellent reasons – for administrative convenience or to encourage deserving groups and worthy activities – but whose over-all effect has been to deprive the system of any consistent rationale or coherent structure. (Kay and King, 1983: 18)

A standard reference manual for accountants and lawyers is more outspoken and succinct:

The result might be described as a patchwork were it not for the overtones of antique cosiness that go with that word; it is better described as a shambles. (*Butterworths*, 1984: 11)

The laws against which these complaints are directed were not decided by one particular government. They are the unintended consequences of past decisions remaining in force. The harshness with which the consequences are evaluated today is a grudging admission of the importance of political inertia.

Many Administrators

The theory of the Crown in Parliament is unitary – there is only one authority within British government – and this is particularly true in taxation. Whereas in federal systems taxing powers are dispersed among several different tiers of government, in unitary states such as Britain the centre is likely to control nine-tenths of taxation (OECD, 1984a: table 135). The political structure of Britain centralizes responsibility for taxation to a very high degree. The Treasury is the ministry responsible for determining the taxes of central government. Local authorities are subject to a variety of central government constraints upon the one tax they levy, the rates. The Thatcher administration's desire to control the totality of public finance has further restricted the limited discretion of local authorities (Cmnd 9714, 1986; cf. Jones and Stewart, 1983).

Decentralized Administration

There is a political administrative rationale for separating the administration of taxes from the Treasury. The political rationale is that taking tax collection out of the hands of politicians frees it from pressure by elected officeholders, and from the suspicion of corruption. It also enables politicians to avoid responsibility for any particular tax assessment that causes a taxpayer to complain: all complaints can be passed to separate authorities responsible for tax collection. Administratively, the task of tax collection involves many millions of detailed transactions. It is thus very much larger than the task of superintending the economy, which requires only a few thousand Treasury staff. The separation of tax collection frees the Treasury from involvement in details of tax administration. The Chancellor retains the overall authority for tax policy, on which he is advised by the revenue authorities who carry the responsibility for the routine and not-so-routine administration of tax collection.

The administration of taxation in Britain today reflects the gradual amalgamation through the centuries of many separate revenue authorities. In the distant past, authority for collecting particular taxes was vested in many different agencies. In 1780 the administration of taxes was described as 'a great swarm of Collectors and Receivers-General working in conjunction with seven Boards of Commissioners' (Binney, 1958: 1). The seven boards were responsible for customs; excise; stamps; salt; hackney coach and chair licences; hawkers and pedlars; and one general tax board for such things as the land tax, the window tax and inhabited-house duty. In addition, there were two agencies that collected money for both tax and non-tax purposes: the Office of Woods, Forests and Land Revenues, primarily concerned with royal resources, and the Post Office (Chester, 1981: 224–34).

In Victorian times tax agencies began to be amalgamated. In 1849 the Board of Inland Revenue was created by combining the Board of Stamps and Taxes and the Board of Excise. In 1909 responsibility for excise duties was transferred to what became the present Board of Customs and Excise. Lowell (1912, Vol.I:28) noted that while there were proposals to merge the two departments this was thought inadvisable. The dyarchy created in 1912 remains in effect today. Customs and excise taxes date back almost a millennium: Magna Carta of 1215 includes a pledge by the King not to levy 'evil tolls' upon merchants, as distinct from customary taxes upon wine, fish, salt and the export of wool and leather. Customs duties upon imports and exports were gradually identified by state rather than royal prerogative, and consolidated by Acts of 1660 and 1787. Excise duties on the consumption of articles produced within England, such as beer, were introduced in the seventeenth-century Commonwealth under Cromwell. The repeal of the Corn Laws in 1846 reduced the significance of customs as a restraint on trade. The merger of Customs and Excise in one administrative organization in 1909 followed the logic of centralizing responsibility for taxes upon the sale of goods and services (Anson, 1908, Vol. II:ii: 113–22; Smith, 1980).

Today, the *Customs and Excise* is responsible for collecting £35b in revenue from a very wide variety of products (Table 4.2). Half of the revenue collected comes from the value added tax, which is broad in its economic incidence but concentrated administratively upon traders required to register for VAT. In 1985 1,458,900 traders were subject to VAT; the burden of keeping track of each transaction subject to VAT falls on the traders. The Customs and Excise is only required to evaluate the accuracy of their records, and collect the tax due. Excise duties specific to three different industries – tobacco, alcoholic drinks and hydrocarbon oil – each produced more than £1b of revenue, and motor-car taxes and betting and gaming taxes more than £0.5b of revenue. A tax on matches, subsequently extended to mechanical lighters, is a historical relic producing very little revenue.

Table 4.2 Revenue Raised by the Customs and Excise

Function	Staff	Cost £m	Revenue £m	Cost as % Revenue
VAT	12,544	191	18,535	1.0
Hydrocarbon oil	529	9	6,198	0.1
Tobacco	241	4	4,140	0.1
Alcohol	2,056	29	3,760	0.8
Customs duties[a]	4,519	69	1,476)	
Preventive	3,693	65	n.a.)	10.3
Trade statistics	1,052	13	n.a.)	
Other	387	6	n.a.)	
Vehicle tax	112	2	744	0.2
Betting and gaming	411	6	660	1.0
Matches and lighters	13	0.2	19	1.0
Totals	25,557	394	35,536	1.11

a. Includes 416 staff and £152m collected for European Community levies under the Common Agricultural Policy.
Source: Derived from Customs and Excise *Report*, Cmnd 9655, 1985: 11.

The collection of customs combines revenue and non-revenue responsibilities, for the Board is responsible for inspecting all movements in and out of Britain of aircraft (384,000 in 1984), and boats and ships (162,000). Whereas smuggling once involved evading taxes on the importation of goods that could legally be sold (tobacco, for example), today the most serious smuggling offences involve the importation of heroin, cocaine and other illegal drugs (Cmnd 9655, 1985: 25). The Customs and Excise also deals with the European Community, as Britain's payment to the Community is based upon a proportion of money allocated in VAT and excise duties and levies.

The Board of Customs and Excise is extremely cost-effective: of every £100 collected, only £1.11 is spent on the cost of administration. Administrative costs differ substantially from tax to tax. Customs is the most expensive, because it involves the labour-intensive checking of the movement of hundreds of thousands of carriers, and millions of people and parcels. Moreover, the amount of money collected in customs duties is no longer substantial. By contrast, VAT involves less inspection of goods and persons, and the tax rate for VAT is high. Tobacco and oil are even cheaper to administer, for the importation and production of both products is highly centralized. These taxes yield £1,000 in revenue for each £1 spent in administration.

The Board of Inland Revenue is a relatively recent creation by the standard of many British institutions, and is centuries newer than many of the taxes that it collects. Stamp duties were introduced into England in 1694, estate duty in 1780 and the first income tax in 1799.

The Board was originally created in 1849 by the amalgamation of the Board of Excise and the Board of Stamps and Taxes in order to collect domestic taxes, as distinct from customs. At that time revenue from excise taxes was far more important than revenue from the recently reintroduced income tax. In 1909 the Board lost its responsibility for excise taxes to the Board of Customs. When a system of income-related graduated contributions to national insurance came into force in 1961, the Board became responsible for collecting national insurance contributions, and thus assumed its present range of responsibilities (Johnston, 1965), and its present rationale, concentrating upon taxes that are related to income or profits.

76

Income tax is the principal tax collected by the Inland Revenue, raising more than £32b in a year from more than 20 million taxpayers (Table 4.3). The laborious system of estimating the tax liabilities of individual taxpayers results in a relatively high administrative cost, equivalent to 2.2 per cent of total revenue. In absolute terms, income tax remains very profitable, for revenue exceeds direct administrative costs by more than £31.7b.

Table 4.3 Revenue Raised by the Inland Revenue

Tax	Staff	Cost £m	Revenue £m	Cost as % Revenue	Taxpayers
Income tax	50,137	730	32,508	2.2	20,300,000
National insurance	3,312	40	22,033	0.2	n.a.
Petroleum revenue	44	0.9	7,177	0.01	81
Corporation	3,354	60	8,341	0.7	646,000
Capital gains	573	14	730	1.9	124,000
Estate and capital transfer	1,070	19	664	2.9	24,000
Other (stamp, land, etc.)	930	14	992	1.4	n.a.
Administration	6,259	94	n.a.	n.a.	n.a.
Totals	65,679	972	72,445	1.3	n.a.

Source: Compiled from Board of Inland Revenue *Report* (Cmnd 9831, 1986), 46. Tax revenue is for the financial year 1984/6, and thus will vary slightly from calendar year figures normally used in this book.

The collection of national insurance contributions is piggybacked on the collection of income tax, for these are paid by employers at the same time as PAYE payments. This results in a very low administrative cost for this tax, less than 0.2 per cent. A political consequence of centralizing collection of national insurance contributions, as against the old system of having employees affix a weekly stamp in token of their contribution, is that the connection between benefits paid and the cost of payment by the employee is less evident.

The most cost-effective levy is the petroleum revenue tax levied on oil companies. It can produce a yield of more than £7.1b a year with only 44 employees. The reason is simple: there are only 81 taxpayers. Each oil company pays an average of £88m to the fisc. Petroleum revenue tax on a few dozen firms thus produces almost as much revenue as corporation taxes levied on 646,000 firms. The average firm's corporation tax payment is less than £13,000 a year.

Ease of tax administration is not proportionate to the money collected. Capital gains taxes and estate and capital transfer taxes are comparatively costly to administer, because there are often difficulties in assessing the base to which these tax rates should apply. Each case must usually be assessed from scratch, and there are almost 150,000 cases a year to assess.

Local authority rates are administered by a combination of central and local government institutions. The Inland Revenue is responsible for assessing the value of properties subject to local authority rates (Cmnd 9831, 1986: 11ff.). In law, the rateable value of a house is meant to be the annual rental value of the property. However, only a limited portion of housing is rented today, and the market for rental property is very much distorted by the fact that most tenancies are council houses. Hence assessed rental is often a notional figure. Moreover, only two nationwide assessments have been carried out in England since 1945, the latest in 1973, so the assessed value of a house is much lower than its current market value.

While the statutory authorization for rating is laid down in Acts of Parliament, the rate payable on a given property is the responsibility of the local authority (e.g. the shire county and local district) in which the property is situated. Since 1979 the Thatcher government has taken steps, by ministry advice and by statute, to limit the extent to which local authorities could increase their rates (cf. Newton and Karran, 1985; Cmnd 9714, 1986).

Increasing controversy about central government's responsibility for assessing property and the amount of rates levied by local authorities led the Thatcher administration in 1986 to propose the introduction of a flat-rate community charge – that is, a poll tax on all adults residing in a local area – as a replacement for domestic rates. The legislation is designed so that the Conservative government at Westminster can claim credit for abolishing domestic rates. Local authorities will bear the burden of administering the collection of a novel and potentially unpopular head tax (cf. Cmnd 9714; Annex G).

While the details are complex, taxes are designed so that the cost of administration is low: for every pound spent in tax collection, central government collects more than £80 from the taxpayer. There are perennial concerns about making the tax collection system more efficient, that is, costing the revenue authorities less to administer, and imposing less of a burden of paperwork and effort upon taxpayers (cf. Cmnd 8822, 9183). Notwithstanding divisions in organizational responsibility, the money required to finance the day-to-day running costs of government is collected in very large sums.

Making Taxes Invisible?

While taxes are matters of public record, there is political appeal in attempting to collect taxes in ways that are invisible rather than visible (Wilensky, 1976). A tax may be said to be invisible if an individual is not aware of it, for example corporation tax or an import duty paid by the importer and absorbed in the price before goods are retailed. A tax may be described as visible if an individual is likely to be aware of it, for example income tax or national insurance contributions.

In economic theory, a similar distinction is often made between direct taxes, which are imposed directly upon the individuals or households bearing the burden (income tax, for example), and indirect taxes, imposed upon intermediate economic activities, such as sales or corporation taxes. Although this terminology is familiar it is increasingly rejected by public finance experts. Musgrave and Musgrave (1980: 234) regard the distinction as at best 'ambiguous'. Kay and King (1983:7ff.) emphasize that it confuses the formal incidence of a tax base with the effective impact of the tax upon the ultimate payer. Brown and Jackson (1978:179) describe the distinction as 'misleading, because it is based on the assumption that we know the answer before we start', that is, that we know who actually bears the burden of the tax.

Insofar as taxes are invisible, then individuals may pay taxes without even knowing that they are taxpayers. Tax administration does remove from individuals the responsibility for paying upwards of nine-tenths of total tax revenue (Chapter 3). But the way in which economic transactions are administered is about

79

as likely to provide information to individuals about invisible as about visible taxes. Many shops and firms specially display the VAT charge, so that the customer understands that a sales tax is being paid, adding 15 per cent to the price of goods. On the other hand, excise taxes on such goods as automobiles, alcohol and tobacco are usually absorbed in the sale price without specific publicity. An employee receives with each wages payment a slip indicating how much money has been deducted as income tax and national insurance contributions. But no information is given about how much the employer has had to pay as the firm's contribution to national insurance, or pay in other taxes.

Individuals receive a substantial amount of information about taxes being paid, but the information may not be accurately perceived and popular perceptions of taxes may not match the records of taxes actually paid (Lewis, 1982). Thus we lack empirical justification for regarding some taxes as specially visible and others as invisible. A survey of attitudes toward taxation in Sweden (Hadenius, 1983:353ff.) hypothesized that if the distinction were meaningful, there would be much more discontent with so-called visible taxes than with invisible taxes. Not only was there little agreement among economists about which taxes would be expected to be most visible, but also citizens' complaints were chiefly about one direct tax, income tax, and one indirect tax, VAT.

Many Economic Activities

From a panoramic perspective, the economy is a great hubbub of continuous activity, all of which is (or could be) subject to tax. In the course of a year there are more than a billion payments of wages and salaries, and tens of billions of sales of goods and services. Summary statistics such as the gross domestic product simplify almost to vanishing point the activities of a contemporary economy.

The economic activities that can be taxed may be grouped under three broad headings: income, expenditure and wealth. Because each of these elements is the subject of a number of taxes, the tax base is not a simple entity but rather a collective noun labelling aspects of the economy subject to taxation. The tax base is not a picture of the economy in the round; it is a distorted representation, selectively including activities identified by legislation as a basis of taxation.

The structure of the economy is a variable, not a constant. Structural differences are most evident in cross-national comparisons. A country with a high proportion of peasants, self-employed artisans and shopkeepers, such as France, will not have tax handles of the same character as Britain, where the labour force consists principally of employees of organizations from whom tax revenues can easily be collected. Some changes are cyclical, such as periods of boom generating more tax revenue by increasing the value of the tax base, and recession, reducing economic growth and, incidentally, growth in the tax base.

Income

Changes in income immediately affect tax revenue. Wage increases, whether due to economic growth, inflation or a mixture of the two, will increase revenue from income tax and national insurance contributions. However, the two taxes do not increase revenue by the same extent. An increase in income produces a disproportionate increase in tax revenue. Insofar as personal allowances reducing the tax base have already been used up, the whole of the increase will be taxed at the standard rate or at a higher marginal rate.

By contrast, national insurance contributions are a flat-rate tax on earnings from a minimum of £38 a week to a maximum of £285. As with income tax, casual earnings of part-time workers can be exempt from national insurance contributions. Unlike income tax, no payment is due on earnings above a ceiling equivalent to £14,820 a year. The rationale for this ceiling is that social security benefits are limited to sums well below average earnings. Politicians have been averse to making the revenue side of social security redistributive, as the spending side is, because that would mean increased deductions from earnings. In 1985 the Thatcher government, in pursuit of more revenue, increased the contribution that employers make by removing the ceiling on the base of the tax; employers (but not employees) must now pay a national insurance contribution on the whole of an employee's salary, however high it is.

81

An increase or decrease in the number of people in work immediately alters the number of incomes that can be taxed. Whereas the British labour force was slowly expanding for the first three decades after the Second World War, in the past decade it has been contracting. The rise in unemployment removes people from the ranks of those paying social security taxes; simultaneously it adds their names to the list of those receiving social security benefits. Thus, revenue falls and expenditure simultaneously rises. When a person is unemployed for part of a year, the fisc suffers a disproportionately large loss of revenue, for the income foregone through unemployment is that portion of annual earnings that will be taxed at the standard rate or higher.

An increase in the number of women in work does not benefit national insurance revenue so much, for women are more likely to take part-time jobs that are below its tax threshold. Furthermore, the income of married couples is subject to a different set of tax allowances than that of single persons, or two persons in the same household, such as a brother and sister or a couple living together. The difference between these three groups in tax paid can be more than £1,000 (Cmnd 9756, 1986).

Expenditure

Taxation on expenditure can take two different forms: particular goods and services (tobacco, for example, or all consumption objects subject to VAT) can be taxed, or the total expenditure of an individual could be subject to tax. Whilst a general tax on individual expenditure is discussed in theory, it is not utilized in Britain (cf. Kaldor, 1955; Meade, 1978; Kay and King, 1983: chs 5–6,8).

Because VAT is a broad-based tax, covering the majority of forms of expenditure, the revenue it generates is sensitive to broad changes in the economy, whether a slowing down of expenditure in times of recession, or a boost in sales revenue due to inflation and/or economic expansion. Because VAT is remitted on goods that are exported, an increase in exports has the side effect of causing a relative decrease in VAT revenue.

A variety of expenditure taxes apply only to particular goods, such as alcohol, tobacco, oil or motor vehicles. Long-term changes in the economy can increase revenue, for example the increase in the number and use of motor cars in the postwar era. Changes in taste also affect revenue. If drinkers switch from spirits to wine, then the revenue of the fisc is likely to fall, because wines are taxed at a much lower rate than spirits. Government's policy towards smoking is ambiguous. The fisc has a direct interest in more people smoking, because this generates more tax revenue, whereas the health service has an interest in discouraging smoking, which increases the need for expensive health care.

Because most taxes on expenditure are fixed in terms of so many pence per unit of a commodity, price increases due to inflation will *not* increase revenue from such sources. Because the government's cost of living rises with inflation, the relative value of fixed-money expenditure taxes has declined by comparison with VAT and with income taxes, which are buoyant with inflation.

Wealth

Wealth is more difficult to tax than income or expenditure because wealth can exist without being involved in any market transaction during a year. In the absence of any transaction, there is no current record of value. Whereas a tax on income or sales is levied upon an identifiable current market value, the value of many forms of wealth can only be estimated.

Local authority rates provide a familiar example of the problems of imputing a money value to wealth. During the years in which a family lives in a home, its economic value, as expressed in the notional rent it would command, will rise with the inflation of house prices. But British government has been averse to the revaluation necessary to increase the tax base for fear of the political reaction from individuals who find that the value of their house has gone up, and thus fear that taxes will rise because a local authority does not need to reduce the rate to fully offset the increase in the base.

Housing is not the only form of wealth difficult to tax. Duties on the estates of deceased persons present problems of valuation, for the purchase price of goods accumulated in a lifetime is no guide to their current value. Some goods depreciate in value, such as a motor car, whereas others increase, such as a house, or some family heirlooms. Moreover, the value of an estate is not always in a form that is easily realized as cash, such as an old master painting, whereas inheritance taxes must be paid in cash.

Even when wealth is realized through the sale of assets, the nominal capital gain, which serves as the basis of the capital gains tax, can be misleading as a guide to the real gain, because of inflation. A taxable gain in nominal terms may involve a loss in real terms. For example, if a person buys shares for £10,000 and sells them for £20,000, he can be subject to a tax on the £10,000 capital gain. However, if inflation has been 100 per cent, no gain has been realized in purchasing power.

Growth in the economy, whether through inflation or expansion in the real national product, is an important condition of taxation by non-decision-making. As long as economic activity in aggregate does not contract, government can count on collecting nearly all its tax revenue from the inertia of established taxes. While some may not increase their contribution to the fisc as much as others, the net effect will leave government as well or better off than before, for the buoyant taxes – income tax, national insurance and VAT – are big, broadly based sources of revenue.

Many Taxpayers

In a democracy, participation is a double-edged sword. A democratic political system not only gives each adult a vote for the nation's government, but also presents tax bills to meet the costs of government. Directly or indirectly, every citizen receives tax bills. In a mixed economy welfare state, the tax bills, like the benefits, are substantial, and they are multiple.

Millions of Taxpayers

A tax that falls on only a small proportion of the electorate, such as capital gains tax, is likely to upset fewer voters than a tax that falls on many, such as rates or income tax. While there is an important administrative difference between a tax paid from an individual's own pocket as against a tax paid on behalf of a person by an employer or a shop, individuals are affected by a reduction in net earnings or by an increase in total price.

Most Britons are taxpayers in half a dozen different ways (Table 4.4). Value added tax is the most comprehensive tax, for it affects everyone who spends money each week. While the Customs and Excise collects the tax from traders, most shopkeepers identify the VAT element of a bill separately. Moreover, while trading firms can offset VAT payments that they make against money collected as VAT, an individual taxpayer cannot do this. In addition more than nine-tenths of persons in paid employment are subject to income tax and national insurance contributions. Only a portion of part-time and intermittent workers are not liable to such taxes. The spread of motor-car ownership, subject to motor-vehicle taxes and fuel oil taxes, causes the 70 per cent of households owning a car to pay an annual tax to license it for road use, and to pay tax every time the petrol tank is filled to run the car. Anyone who drinks beer, wine or spirits also pays a tax. The amount paid depends upon how frequently people drink and what they drink, for the extent of tax varies with alcoholic content.

Table 4.4 Number of Taxpayers and the Taxes Paid

Tax	Revenue £b	Number of Payers million	%
VAT	21.0	43.0	100
Income tax	35.4	23.8	93
National insurance	21.4	23.4	92
Beer, wines, spirits	4.1	31.8	74
Motor vehicles	2.4	13.6	70
Hydrocarbon oils	6.3	13.6	70
Rates	13.6	12.8	60
Tobacco	4.3	14.6	34
Capital gains	1.2	0.1	0.4
Death duties and capital transfer tax	0.8	0.028	0.1

Note: The base of potential taxpayers differs from tax to tax: all adults (VAT, beer, wines, spirits, tobacco); adults in work (income tax, national insurance, capital gains); households (motor vehicles, hydrocarbon oils, rates, death duties).

Sources: As in Tables 1.1, 4.3; incidence of motor vehicle, oil, alcohol and tobacco taxes estimated from General Household Survey data, and rates as paid by home-owners.

Local authority rates are levied on all occupied residences, whether they are owner-occupied or rented. Thus, it may be argued that everyone pays rates, either in their own name, through the head of the household or by a regular payment to a landlord, a part of which is passed on to the local authority as rates. Today most tenants live in council houses, where a weekly bill is due for rent and rates together; persons in bed-sitters normally do not pay rates directly to local authorities. If the term rate-payers is confined to home-owners, who are invariably responsible for paying rates directly to a local authority, then three-fifths of households identify themselves as rate-payers, and the proportion is rising with the extension of home-ownership.

Three taxes raising noteworthy sums of money are paid by a minority. Tobacco taxes are paid only by smokers, a third of the population. Capital gains taxes are paid only by less than 1 per cent of the adult population, individuals who realize thousands of pounds of wealth during the course of a year. Death duties are paid only on the estates of individuals who die in a year, and who leave a sum of money above the minimum exempt from tax, £90,000.

The taxes with the most taxpayers are those that yield the most revenue to the fisc: income tax, national insurance and VAT. Nor is this an accident. A tax that affected only the wealthy few, no matter how high its rate, could only yield a limited amount of public revenue, because of its narrow base. A not so high rate on a broad base of economic activity can yield more revenue in total than a high rate on a narrow base. Moreover, a small increase in the rate of a broad-based tax, or an increase in the base itself, can generate a substantial absolute increase in the revenue of the fisc.

An Increasing Number of Taxpayers

The growth of government has greatly increased the proportion of Britons paying taxes since the prewar era, and the number of taxes that people pay. As the income of households has increased due to economic growth, more and more people become eligible to pay taxes that once affected only the well-to-do minority, such as income tax and motor-vehicle taxes.

86

Income tax spectacularly demonstrates the effect of broadening the tax base. In 1938 there were only 3.8m people paying income tax, less than one-fifth of people in work. Some middle-class persons as well as nearly all manual workers did not earn enough to be subject to income tax, which commenced at a threshold higher than the average industrial worker's wage. The need for revenue in wartime led to a lowering of the threshold so that by 1948 the number subject to tax had risen to 14.5m, but it was still less than two-thirds of all persons in work (Inland Revenue, 1985: table 1.5).

In the postwar era the threshold for income tax has been effectively lowered by rising real wages. The married man's tax allowance has stayed virtually constant in money terms, while the average manual worker's earnings have risen. Hence, the proportion of the work force paying taxes has increased until now more than 90 per cent of people in work pay income tax. Whereas in 1938 a married man became subject to income tax when his earnings were 20 per cent greater than the average manual worker's wage, since the 1960s income tax has been due at between one-third and two-fifths of the average earnings of a manual worker. (Cmnd 9576, 1985: 12). When the welfare state was launched, most workers did not pay income tax. Today, four-fifths of those on below-average earnings as well as all on above-average earnings pay income tax. The number paying national insurance contributions has increased less, a rise of 50 per cent, because coverage for social security benefits was already broad before the Second World War.

The introduction of the broad-based value added tax has not only increased the number of people paying taxes on household expenditures; it has increased the frequency of payments. Before the Second World War, the average household's expenditure was concentrated upon basic necessities, such as food and clothing, which were usually not subject to tax. Only when common luxuries such as beer, whisky or tobacco were consumed was an excise tax paid. In the postwar era, rising incomes have increased disposable cash for expenditure on a wide range of goods, and VAT is imposed on the purchase of many goods and services that are now taken for granted within every household.

The expansion of home-ownership, and the great increase in

the rateable value of the average house, has made the direct payment of local authority rates important to millions more. In 1938, one-quarter of the population were home-owners. The proportion of households owning their own home did not reach 50 per cent until 1970, and is now passing 60 per cent. Concurrently, the value of housing has increased greatly, both in real terms and in nominal money terms. Hence, even if people were aware of rate demands when they were tenants, the rate demands that they receive as home-owners today are much larger.

Motoring taxes have increased their coverage most dramatically, rising by more than 600 per cent. In the prewar era, a motor car was a luxury vehicle, not a mass consumption product. In the years shortly after the war, the ownership of motor cars remained restricted by income limitations to less than one-tenth of the population. Since the purchase of a car was a major feature of the shift to mass consumption in the 1950s and 1960s, today most households pay tax on at least one car, and on the purchase of petrol to run the car.

Millions of Beneficiaries

To focus solely upon what government extracts in taxes is to tell only half the story of big government; it is equally important to attend to the benefits that government provides. Everyone benefits just as everyone pays. That is why substantial taxation is needed, and why it is acceptable politically.

The contemporary welfare state offers something for almost everybody. In the course of a year, government is engaged in a massive fiscal exchange, collecting taxes with one hand and making payments with the other. Some payments go directly to taxpayers (for example, pensions); others go to public employees who provide services from which taxpayers benefit (such as teachers or health service workers).

The Central Statistical Office annually calculates the position of households in terms of the benefits they receive in return for taxes paid. This does not imply that taxpayers should get back benefits equal to the taxes they pay; the calculation is analytic rather than political in intent. Moreover, a substantial proportion of taxing and spending *cannot* be attributed to households. The tax-benefit calculation of the Treasury excludes that 50 per cent of public expenditure that finances measures that are not deemed the private benefits of identifiable households, such as defence spending and payments of debt interest. It also excludes 41 per cent of taxation as not attributed to individuals, including employers' national insurance contributions, and corporation and petroleum revenue tax (*Economic Trends*, 1985).

The amount of benefits received varies greatly according to the family circumstances of a household. A family with two children will consume more education services, and an elderly couple will make more use of the health service. A high-income family will pay more taxes than a low-income family, but a high-income family with children is also likely to consume more public services. Here, there is only scope to examine the median taxpaying group, the middle fifth of the population. But in taxing and spending, there remain substantial differences between households according to their position in the life-cycle, and their level of income (*Economic Trends*, 1985; *Social Trends*, 1986: table 5.19).

The starting point (but not the finishing point) is the original income of the median household, £6,880 as of 1983. The net income is less, but the extent to which it is less depends upon the measure used. In the first instance, it is appropriate to subtract taxes on income, which reduce earnings by 21 per cent (table 4.5).

If the measure is cash in hand – that is, disposable income after taxes and the receipt of cash benefits from the welfare state – the picture appears different. The median household pays £1,410 in taxes on income, but it receives back £1,100 in a variety of cash benefits. The effect of taking and giving money is that the net cash disposable income of the median household becomes £6,570, only 5 per cent less than original gross income.

However, the money that a family spends is subject to a variety of expenditure taxes. VAT, rates, tobacco, drink and other consumption taxes on average claim £1,860 a year. This reduces the effective purchasing power of household income to £4,710, one-third less than original gross income.

The cycle of exchanges is not yet complete, for the average household also receives tax-financed public services without charge. If health care, education and income security in old age

Table 4.5 Collection and Disbursement of Money to the Median Family

	Tax £	Benefit £	Net £	% Original
Original income, median household			£6,880	100%
Income tax and national insurancecontributions[a]	1,410	-	5,470	
Cash benefits[b]	-	1,100	-	
Total cash income			6,570	95
Taxes on expenditures				
VAT	490			
Net rates	310			
Tobacco, drink	360			
Other	700			
Total	1,860			
Cash income net of all taxes			4,710	68
Benefits in kind				
Health		660		
Education		650		
Housing, travel, other		160		
Total		1,470		
Cash income plus benefits in kind			6,180	90

a. Employee's contribution only.
b. Age, child, income-related and other payments.

Source: Social Trends No. 16, 1986 (London: HMSO), table 5.19. Median quintile household described as 2 adults, 1.3 employed persons, 0.9 children and 0.2 retired persons.

were not provided by public expenditure, then a family would have to spend money in the private sector to maintain such services. To receive a tax reduction of £660 because of the abolition of the national health service and the next day receive a private health insurance bill for £660 would be no saving in itself. The official evaluation of these benefits in kind is that they add £1,470 to the consumption of the median household.

The accounts of the tax-benefit position of the median family can be interpreted in a variety of ways. Within the terms of a cost–benefit calculation, more than half of households receive less back in direct benefits, including benefits in kind, than they pay in taxes. However, the difference is limited for the average household to a 10 per cent charge upon family income for the benefits of living in an orderly modern society. However, if a free market perspective is adopted, then the average family is deprived of the right to determine how almost one-third of its income is spent, since the benefits received in kind are determined by public (and producer-oriented) organizations, not by consumer choice.

Another way to look at the same set of figures is to emphasize the amount of churning that occurs, that is, the circulation of money back and forth between the family and the fisc. Between original gross income and final income there are many inter-mediate steps. In the course of a year £3,270 is collected in taxes, £1,100 paid out in cash benefits, and £1,470 spent on benefits in kind. The gross exchange of £5,840 between the fisc and the family produces a net change of only £700 in a household.

A third important point is that most families are *not* average. In a trivial sense, this is true by definition, for half the families are above the median and the other half below. The circumstances of the middle-income group analysed by the Central Statistical Office are unusual. This family is deemed to have one child and a one in five chance of having an elderly person in residence. In median-income families without a pensioner or without children, benefits would be more than a £1,000 less. Family circumstances differ greatly through the life cycle. Large families will do better than average in claiming in-kind benefits, and pay less taxes because children reduce taxable income. Elderly families have less original income and do well from public benefits, making heavy claims on pensions and the health service. Well-to-do families make the most use of education, but they also pay the highest proportion of their income in taxes (*Social Trends*, 1986: table 5.19).

The average figures that the Central Statistical Office presents are reasonable statistically but not conclusive politically. The cries of the losers on the roundabouts and the demands of beneficiaries on the swings (often the same family at different stages of the life-cycle) create much of the political conflict about the budget.

91

A fundamental point, easily overlooked in a simple calculation of individual payments and benefits, is that government is about collective goods as well as private benefits. Government was not created to provide education or health care, but to maintain public order, to defend the country in relation to foreign nations, and to sustain conditions of lawful economic activity. These priceless collective goods cannot be included in a narrow cost–benefit analysis. There is no way in which the money value to an individual of freedom and security can be calculated, because these goods cannot be bought in the market place. The ultimate assessment of the value of government is political.

In the thinking of an ordinary person, subjective perceptions of taxing and spending are critical. Insofar as citizens do not think about benefits received when they think about taxes, then the amount of benefits is not relevant to their perception of the 'burden' of taxation. Insofar as citizens think about their standard of living in terms of disposable cash in hand, then expenditure taxes will be more appealing than taxes on income. Lacking familiarity with statistical data, the judgements that people make about their overall tax-benefit position is subjective: they select, from a repertoire of taxes and benefits, the few that each individual deems most important.

From a politician's perspective, the critical task is not that of fine tuning the distribution of taxes and benefits by deciding to lower taxes on some groups and raise taxes on others, or to raise spending and taxes substantially, or to cut both at the margin. Given an inheritance of popular spending programmes and not so popular taxes, the politician's task is to make sure to gain credit for the popular programmes, and avoid blame for unpopular taxes.

CHAPTER FIVE

The Force of Inertia

Government is always in motion, and often changes as it moves. The intentions of politicians need not be the causes of change. Change can be unintentional, reflecting forces independent of the wants of voters or politicians. This is particularly likely in the case of taxation, since high taxes are not what politicians like to take responsibility for; they prefer that the impersonal force of inertia, rather than their own decisions, cause taxes to go up.

Many theories of democratic politics treat decision-making as central in government. The demands of voters and groups are not effective of themselves; popular pressures become significant only insofar as they influence the decisions of politicians. However, a newly elected government is not given a blank sheet of paper on which it can inscribe decisions about what taxing and spending ought to be. Instead, it is parachuted on top of a set of institutions driven by the force of inertia. The political problem is not that of making government move; it is to steer the ship of state in the direction that policy-makers want it to go, and at the speed desired (Rose, 1987a).

A newly elected government is not in a position to decide what to do; it is legally obliged to enforce all the laws that it has inherited from its predecessors. On one side of the budget there are spending commitments that the government is legally bound to carry out, unless and until it can arrest the force of political inertia. On the taxing side, politicians inherit laws that authorize the collection of money to finance spending programmes.

The Thatcher government illustrates the scale of change without decisions. The amount of money that the Conservative administration of Margaret Thatcher has collected in taxation is

93

not what would have been chosen, if it had been free to decide for itself. It was determined by the force of political inertia – and because inertia is a moving force, the amount collected has been continuously increasing. In 1985 the Thatcher administration collected £78b more in tax revenue than did the preceding Labour government in its last full year in office, 1978.

Governing today is not so much about making fresh decisions as it is about living with the consequences of past decisions. The very success of past governments in establishing laws and administrative institutions that can routinely extract tens of billions of pounds from the economy, and increase from year to year, makes it possible to avoid taking unpopular decisions to impose new taxes, as well as greatly limiting the scope for popular decisions to reduce taxes.

To understand how and why changes occur in the amount of tax revenue it is first necessary to distinguish between comprehensive decisions that alter the core of taxation, as against incremental decisions that affect taxation at the margin. Even more, it is important to understand how decisions reflecting the immediate behavioural pressures upon politicians can, in the *longue durée*, compound to have big (and unintended) consequences. Given the importance of non-decision-making in the dynamics of taxation, the final section of this chapter considers the deviant case of conscious decisions about public revenue at the margin.

Comprehensive vs. Incremental Decisions

The capacity to make decisions is both a precondition and prerogative of power. Only if it is possible to decide authoritatively – that is, to make changes in taxation that would not otherwise have occurred – can a government be said to exercise power (Dahl, 1957). If everything is determined by forces external to government, whether economic, social or international, then a government is in fact powerless.

From a revenue-raising perspective, the fundamental question is: what impact do the decisions of politicians in office have upon taxation? Even if the government of the day holds the formal power to alter taxes, the immediate empirical question is: how much tax revenue is redirected, as a consequence of its decisions, from what would be collected by the force of inertia? While some political and economic theories imply that a newly elected government can decide – and implement decisions – to make comprehensive changes in taxation, the theory of political inertia sees the impact of these decisions as marginal. Major changes occur independently of the immediate intentions of decision-makers; they are the unintended consequences of processes that only become manifest long after a government has left office.

How Much Impact Do Decisions Have?

Formal theories of democracy start from the assumption that a legitimately elected government has the power to make whatever substantive impact it wants, subject only to constitutional constraints. Since the size and forms of taxation are normally not written into a constitution, this implies that there is no formal limit to what government can decide about taxation.[1]

In an era of big government, voters cannot be expected to decide matters of taxation. Proposals to alter British taxes are *never* put to the electorate in a referendum, as happens in some American states. The idea is regarded as so inconsistent with Treasury control of taxation that it was immediately abandoned by the Thatcher administration after being mooted in a discussion of local government rates in the early 1980s (Lee, 1986). Nor are voters well informed about the details of tax legislation; the costs of pursuing information are far greater than the likely benefits to be derived from the influence of a single vote (Downs, 1957). Moreover, voters are not simply motivated by their views about issues, let alone the single issue of taxation (Rose and McAllister, 1986: ch. 7).

Theories of representative government assume that elected politicians make decisions that have a big impact upon tax revenue (cf. Rose, 1987a). One set emphasizes that the direction of public policy, including tax policy, is a matter of will: if politicians have a strong enough will, then they can enforce the decisions that follow from their own or their party's ideology, whether it is to cut taxes or raise taxes. Insofar as tax policies do not change with the swing of each electoral pendulum, this may be blamed on weak-willed politicians. A second set of theories postulates that the dominant will within government is that of bureaucrats, who pursue empire-building policies intended to increase the size of their bureau, in the interest of enhancing their own earnings, status, and power (cf. Niskanen, 1971; Breton, 1974; Hood *et al.*, 1984). Both approaches assume that decisions within government, either by politicians or bureaucrats, can account for big changes in taxation.

Many theories of planning assume that government can make a comprehensive range of decisions about everything important in the economy, from taxation and public expenditure to many private-sector activities. Formal models of rational comprehensive decision-making, as propounded by Nobel laureate Jan Tinbergen (1952), start with government identifying a set of goals for the political economy; it is then expected to decide taxing and spending policies that are means to its objectives. The goals can be anything from a general aim of maximizing social welfare to the very specific goal of reducing taxes or winning re-election. Complex mathematical procedures may be employed to produce prescriptions for public policy that are both comprehensive and, given certain assumptions, optimal.

Theories of comprehensive choice are particularly suitable for Britain. The commitment of the Conservatives, especially under Margaret Thatcher, prescribes big reductions in taxation. Labour governments are expected to have a different goal, increasing public expenditure on major social programmes. In turn, this would require a big boost in tax revenue.[2] The centralization of taxing power in Westminster, and more specifically in the Treasury, further enhances the potential impact of decision by the government of the day.

Theories that credit politicians with the power to make comprehensive decisions about public policy can be clear, logical and coherent – but that does not make them true. The approach can be criticized on the grounds that the power of politicians to make big decisions is contingent, not pervasive; some decisions (for example about policing in a rural area) are easier to make effective than others (for example about policing Northern Ireland): cf. Rose, 1987a.

A variety of social scientists have argued that comprehensive decision-making is impossible to achieve in government (for relevant reviews see Mosley, 1984: pt 1; Robinson and Sandford,

1983: ch. 1). Braybrooke and Lindblom (1963; also Lindblom, 1965) raise two fundamental objections. First, politicians do not have goals that can be ordered hierarchically and coherently. Instead their objectives are multiple, contradictory, vague and unstable. A budget cannot be directed at political goals, because these goals are neither consistent nor stable for a year. Secondly, it is impossible to make a comprehensive annual review of alternative possibilities for action, for the problem-solving capacities of individuals and organizations are not adequate to this task. Nor is there sufficient accurate information about the effect that changes in taxing and spending have upon society, the economy or the electorate. At best, politicians are concerned with 'rough tuning' rather than fine tuning, and they have a tendency to switch direction faster than taxing or spending legislation can be altered.

'Satisficing' is the term that Herbert Simon (1952; see also Mosley, 1984), another Nobel Prize winner, developed to describe decision-making by politicians in conditions of un-certainty and inadequate information. In Simon's view, policy-makers need not make big decisions; they need only monitor the status quo to see if it is satisfactory. As long as the status quo appears satisfactory, then nothing need be done. If the operation of routine procedures leads to unsatisfactory results, then small-scale remedial steps should be taken, on a trial-and-error basis, until the dissatisfaction disappears.

Not making decisions is particularly relevant in taxation, for inaction by policy-makers does not prevent taxes from being collected. Instead, past laws and administrative practices con-tinue due to political inertia. If there is a broad consensus about established policies, then non-decision-making is simply maintained by routine. Alternatively, if there is political con-troversy, for example in the American debate about the federal deficit, then President Reagan's refusal to raise taxes to reduce the deficit can be seen as a positive decision to do nothing in the face of demands to act.

Incrementalism

Because taxation is reviewed in the annual budget, a government cannot avoid thinking about tax policy. Given an established set of taxing and spending commitments, the only decisions that politicians need to take involve small increments at the margin of taxing and spending, making alterations in response to circumstances that change a little from year to year. Braybrooke and Lindblom (1963: 48ff.) argue that it is unreasonable to expect politicians to make big decisions, that is, take actions that make a big change, such as restructuring the national tax system, or substantially raising or lowering taxation in total. The incremental model of decision-making is normally applied to the spending side of the budget (see, for example, Wildavsky, 1975; Davis, Dempster and Wildavsky, 1966), but in principle it is equally applicable to the revenue-raising side of the budget (cf. Rose and Page, 1982).

In evaluating a budget incrementally, the first step is to distinguish the base (that is, the revenue that a tax yields in the current year) from incremental changes at the margin (that is, the difference between what a tax yields this year, and what it will yield in the new budget year). At any particular moment in time, policy-makers are expected to concentrate upon incremental changes at the margin, deciding whether next year's taxes should be higher or lower than in this year. The marginal change from year to year is almost always less than the base; only if a tax were more than halved or more than doubled would this condition not hold.

Distinguishing the budget base (not to be confused with the economic activity that constitutes the tax base) from the margin emphasizes the dualistic process of budgeting. One part, the margin, is the object of decision and the other part, the base, is determined by non-decision-making. In France, this procedure has been officially institutionalized. Parliament is only expected to vote additions or subtractions to past budget totals; all past spending is considered a continuing commitment of government (Wildavsky, 1975: 217ff.). In America, non-decision-making is active, when congressional rejection of a presidential proposal to alter a budget results in it remaining unchanged.

Incremental budget-making has three important and linked characteristics: it is piecemeal, it is disjointed and it is serial. It is piecemeal because policy-makers concentrate upon one problem at a time, instead of comprehensively reviewing all taxes. The aggregate consequences of particular choices are not of concern in incremental theories of budgeting. Just as the gross national product is the result of many activities within the economy, so the budget can be seen as the by-product of a number of incremental decisions reached by partisan mutual adjustment (cf. Lindblom, 1965), and the persistence of a base.

Incremental decisions are disjointed, that is, policies tend to be adopted on an *ad hoc* basis, with little regard to previous decisions and no commitment to maintain consistency in subsequent decisions. Furthermore, the criteria for decision can differ from measure to measure. Thus some taxes may weigh specially heavily upon the well-to-do, others upon the poor, and a third set may make proportionately the same claims upon all income groups. In a world of conflicting and unstable goals, it is necessary for policy-makers to act in ways that appear disjointed in order to balance conflicting political pressures.

Because policy-making is a continuing process, decisions are serial. Politicians do not need to make long-term commitments, and would be ill advised to do so. They can proceed experimentally, taking one step at a time. Whereas comprehensive choices are rigid, because all the elements of such a 'mega-policy' are interdependent, incremental policy-making is very flexible. In a system of disjointed decision-making, options are kept open because one step does not predetermine the next. Only after the consequences of one choice are evident is it necessary to decide what to do next. Hood (1985) has gone so far as to argue that decisions about taxation are arrived at through serial experimentation, resulting in some taxes becoming established, and others being abandoned.

Incrementalism is described as a process producing 'decisions effecting small changes' (Braybrooke and Lindblom, 1963: 62ff.). This leaves open the question: how big can a small change be? The point is particularly important in taxation, for an additional claim by the fisc for several billion pounds does not *prima facie* appear small. Braybrooke and Lindblom answer this question by example rather than by statistical procedures. They assert that 'almost everyone would also agree that such factors as rate of progression in income taxation ... belong to a discussion of somewhat less important social change'. Attempts to apply the theory to quantitative analyses of public spending have found that defining the size of an increment is difficult and problematic (Bailey and O'Connor, 1975).

A different approach to the size of a budget increment is taken by Dempster and Wildavsky (1979), who argue: 'There is no magic size for an increment.' They emphasize: 'It is the regularity or irregularity of the changes in size that matter, not the absolute amount of the changes themselves' (Dempster and Wildavsky, 1979: 375). Whether a change in taxes appears large or small in quantitative terms, it can be considered incremental as long as the increase is regular. The predictability of revenue and of spending commitments is a *sine qua non* of making budgets that are consistent with the actual financial practices of government. Unpredictable tax revenue threatens unexpectedly large deficits in some years and surpluses in others, whereas a predictable flow of revenue allows budget-makers to prepare plans that can be met with acceptable margins of estimating error (cf. Table 3.1). Unpredictable and irregular revenue and expenditure are an attribute of poor countries, where national economies are subject to frequent shocks beyond the control of the government (Caiden and Wildavsky, 1980).

To introduce the concept of regularity through the years is to depart from the initial Braybrooke and Lindblom formulation of decision-making as disjointed and serial. From their perspective, regularity is not meaningful, for each decision is taken on a one off basis, without concern for what went before or came after. A politician's attention span is short. The significant time periods are deemed to be: now (today or this week), soon (next week or later in the current budget year), or soon enough (before the next election).

Insofar as incrementalism leads to patterns appearing over a period of years, they occur after the fact. They are not the reflection of a conscious decision by politicians, who have a short time horizon. In the course of time patterns are arrived at as the consequence of the persistence of a revenue base subject to the dynamic pressures of inertia.

Driving Force of Inertia

Government is continuing, whereas the decisions of policy-makers are discrete events. The two statements are not so much

100

contradictory as they are complementary. But just as two lines that intersect at a right angle may be said to join, so from a broader perspective they diverge. Differences in perspective are also crucial in distinguishing the impact of particular decisions upon revenue from the cumulative consequences of political inertia.

An explanation of policy-making by political inertia shares a number of crucial assumptions with the incremental approach. Both reject the idea that policy-makers make a comprehensive review of alternatives. Both emphasize the lack of time, knowledge and political incentives to think very far ahead. The emphasis of incrementalism upon the stability of the base and relatively small, regular rates of change at the margin is complemented by the inertia theory emphasizing that the budget – base and margin – moves slowly, but continuously.

For understanding taxation, political inertia is more appropriate since it also incorporates points that are ignored or rejected by the incremental model. Reviewing differences between the two provides a succinct and explicit way of demonstrating the relative superiority of explaining how the base of tax revenue, amounting to more than 95 per cent of annual tax revenue, increases without politicians bearing the political costs of making any decision.

1) *Long time span*. The incremental model concentrates upon the time span of concern to politicians, the present. In budgeting, the typical issue is a decision about next year's budget. Hence, the annual decision about what to do next year is the limit of concern. A decision about the year after next is a problem of a different kind, and perhaps a different government. Insofar as decision-making is serial and disjointed, a short time horizon is also appropriate. Beyond the horizon there are always more decisions to be made, but they need have no relation to what is done here and now.

By contrast, the inertia theory is concerned with the *longue durée*, a substantial span of time. In the course of decades what was once the present becomes the past, yet remains important today and casts a shadow over the future. Northern Ireland is an extreme example of the way in which past events endure constraining present and future decisions. An incidental feature of viewing time as a lengthy and continuous process, rather than

101

as a series of *ad hoc* choices, is that past decisions are then revealed as having cumulative consequences. A long time horizon is particularly important in understanding taxation, inasmuch as taxation derives from laws, and laws remain in force until such time as they may be repealed. In order to raise this year's tax revenue, a government need not enact any new tax legislation. It can simply continue administering laws enacted in the past.[3] In England the past can go back many centuries.

The oldest taxes in use today in Britain were in effect *before* formal approval by Parliament was required (Dowell, 1888: especially Vol. 1; Anson, 1908, II,ii: ch. 7). The oldest continuous taxes, customs and excise duties, were familiar in the Middle Ages. So too were export duties (on wool in medieval England, as on oil in contemporary OPEC countries). Rates were first levied in the fifteenth century and by 1603 had assumed a form by which they are still recognized. In Tudor and Stuart as in medieval times there were relatively few taxes, because so little economic activity was monetized (Table 5.1).

Table 5.1   Inertia Persistence of Taxation

Tax	Adopted by	Oldest Act
Customs and excise	1347	1706
Wine and spirits	1347	annual
Rates	1427	1845
Tobacco	1604	annual
Beer	1643	annual
Stamp duties	1694	1776
Death duties	1780	1801
Income tax	1799	1931
Corporation tax	1885	1965
Vehicle excise	1910	1969
National insurance	1911	1916
Hydrocarbon oils	1928	annual
Value added tax	1972	1972
Petroleum revenue tax	1975	1975

Source: Principally S. Dowell, *A History of Taxation and Taxes in England* (London: Longman, 1888).

With the coming of the Industrial Revolution a multiplicity of changes occurred in British society. Economic activity diversified, and much more economic activity was monetized, thus making it easier to pay taxes in cash rather than kind, and greatly easing burdens of assessment. The economy grew in aggregate, expanding the tax base and increasing the variety of taxes that could be levied. By the mid-nineteenth century, the administration of government, including taxation, was established on a modern footing. The need to raise money to finance the Napoleonic wars also gave an impetus to revenue collection.

The median taxes in force today were introduced in the late eighteenth century: death duties (1780) and income tax (1799). The income tax was repealed after the Napoleonic wars and reintroduced in 1842. By that time, the Chancellor of the Exchequer was able to collect taxes under a wide variety of familiar headings: income tax; rates; beer, wine and spirits; customs and excise; stamp duties; and death duties. A twentieth-century tax is only relatively modern: national insurance taxes were introduced in 1911, and motor-vehicle licence taxes in 1910. Only two taxes yielding noteworthy amounts of revenue today are innovations of the postwar era, the value added tax, imported from Europe in 1972, and the petroleum revenue tax, enacted following the worldwide boost in oil prices in 1973.

Twelve of the fourteen principal British taxes were enacted before the longest serving member of Parliament arrived at Westminster, and before most MPs were born. As a matter of historical fact, the present House of Commons and Cabinet did not decide the tax system that raises government revenue. It inherited a system that aggregated laws from centuries and generations past. The process for amending and consolidating Acts of Parliament makes it possible to adapt old taxes for use in contemporary circumstances.

Old laws remain potent as sources of money. More than one-sixth of the tax revenue of the fisc today is accounted for by laws enacted before the end of the seventeenth century, and nearly half by taxes first introduced before the end of the Napoleonic wars. Taxes that date from the now distant past – and often from very different eras in that past – today account for more than four-fifths of total tax revenue.

2) *No decisions rather than many decisions.* Inertia does not require

any positive choice by policy-makers; once enacted, an Act of Parliament continues in force until it is acted upon by a stronger force, namely, a parliamentary vote to repeal the Act. As in Simon's satisficing model, there is often a good reason for politicians to do nothing, because of satisfaction with the status quo or because of the negative reaction that changes might produce.

In taxation there is a particular incentive for politicians to do nothing: any action taken to raise taxes is *prima facie* likely to be unpopular. Action is necessary only when the costs of inaction are infinite, and something *must* be done, or the costs of inaction are perceived as greatly outweighing the costs of action (Rose, 1972; Weaver, 1986). For example, if the cost of *not* raising taxes was a major cut in spending on a popular programme, then a decision to raise taxes might be a lesser evil.

Incrementalism, by contrast, assumes that policy-makers are always making decisions, albeit what is at stake is small compared to the base that remains unaltered. A critical feature of incrementalism is that only by making a series of trial and error decisions can policy-makers learn about the consequences of their decisions, and thus determine whether or not they are satisfactory.

3) *Unforeseen consequences.* Both the incremental and the inertia approaches reject the planners' view that actions should be ordered and linked in a comprehensive and coherent plan relating policy means to broad political goals, because it is virtually impossible to foresee all the important consequences of any political choice.

The immediate consequences of a decision are central in the incrementalist model. A policy-maker does not decide the desirability of a measure before action is taken but afterwards, as consequences become evident. If the consequences are popular a decision can be maintained, and if unpopular the course of action can be abandoned and another policy decided upon. The *post hoc* evaluation of consequences is an integral feature of the trial-and-error philosophy of incrementalism. But incrementalism also rejects consideration of long-term consequences. Lindblom (1965: 145f) argues:

As decision-making is in fact practiced, important consequences of policies under analysis are simply disregarded.

104

Forthright neglect of important consequences is a noteworthy problem-solving tactic.

What kind of important consequences are neglected? The answer is: any kind.

The force of inertia makes it unnecessary to anticipate the immediate consequences of actions carried forward by routine. In the *longue durée* the full consequences of a policy are literally incalculable. The story a historian tells after examining the process by which income and national insurance taxes have become the principal sources of revenue is not the story that was (or could have been) foreseen by the participants in initial critical decisions. The process itself was not consciously chosen by any politician or any one Parliament.

4) *Reversibility very difficult.* A necessary condition of serial disjointed incrementalism is that any one decision can easily be reversed. For example, a rise in interest rates may be followed a few months later by a fall in interest rates. In such circumstances, the pattern of change is likely to be cyclical; the long-term consequence will be nil, as movements up and down in a cycle tend to cancel each other out in the process of maintaining an equilibrium. But once a tax proposal becomes the law of the land it cannot be casually abandoned; it remains continuously in force. Tax officials administer the law unless and until it is repealed.

Policies cannot be reversed when a decision is a choice at a crossroads from which there is no going back, for example a decision about war and peace or, less dramatically, about running a highway through the countryside, or razing old houses for a new development (Rose, 1974a). Even if a decision can be reversed, for example interest rates can be returned to the *status quo ante*, the prevailing economic and political environment will not be exactly the same as before, if only because of intervening actions. Policy-makers who assume that history repeats itself may end up drawing the wrong lessons from past experience (Neustadt and May, 1986).

A policy driven by the force of inertia can be redirected with less difficulty than it can be reversed. The most feasible changes involve an alteration of momentum. A slowing down or acceleration can occur by raising or lowering the tax rate, or altering

105

the tax base. It is difficult to overcome the force of inertia by repealing the Act of Parliament that sustains a tax in force, for this also requires politicians to take the blame for introducing new measures to replace the revenue lost.

5) *Linking past and present.* Inertia not only connects what has happened in the past with the present; it implies future actions as well. While a single decision by a policy-maker is an isolated event in time, its significance accumulates – going far beyond the control of the original proposer – when a decision is part of a continuing and cumulative process of government.

Disjointed incrementalism recognizes only one step, the next step. Policy-making is disjointed for no attention need be paid to the rationale for previous decisions; the direction of policy can thus change from day to day. The fact that government adopted a law yesterday creates no presumption in favour of keeping it tomorrow. It does no more than produce consequences for evaluation in the light of today's political priorities, which might lead to the reversal of a measure or its continuance. The time horizon of the incremental model is the present moment, or at most the period until the next election. In boosting public spending without increasing taxes in the run-up to an election, no weight is given to the costs that will subsequently result. For example, Braybrooke and Lindblom (1963: 99f.) describe social security legislation as an example of incrementalism, since it is 'amended every few years to increase incrementally the level of benefits'. The consequences of adding small increments to a growing base are not considered.

Whereas politicians are transitory, government is continuing. The force of inertia moves with glacial speed, but like a glacier it can increase in size as it moves. In an era of big government, no programme will reflect a single decision at a single point in time. Instead, it will be the result of a succession of decisions (Hogwood and Peters, 1983: 101ff.). Understanding the difference between a small change at one point in time and the cumulative effect of many changes is crucial for understanding the dynamics of taxing and spending. Social security legislation, for example, authorized very restricted benefits and required low taxes when introduced before the First World War; today it imposes very substantial taxes, and accounts for nearly one-third of total public expenditure.

Inasmuch as long-term considerations often point in a different direction from short-term political calculations, incrementalists like to quote a hedonistic epigram of Keynes: 'In the long run, we are all dead.' But this epigram prompted the retort from a Cambridge colleague: 'No, Maynard, in the long run, each of us is dead.' Society cannot evade future responsibilities by death, nor can government evade the future cost of commitments already on the statute book.

6) *Compounding change.* The inertia approach emphasizes that a decision taken at one point in time, and subsequently incorporated in the base of a budget, can cumulatively compound. An increase in the tax rate in one year is not forgotten the next; it is incorporated as part of the base to which a further addition may be made in the following year. By contrast, the incrementalist approach tends to regard the base as a constant; change is simply the result of this year's decisions, such as the tax measures announced in the Chancellor's budget speech.

The inertia approach has a very different view of time: it is concerned with the compound consequences of activities begun decades, generations or, in the case of taxation, centuries ago. Compounding seemingly small rates of change through a *longue durée* is the logic applied to such private savings as insurance, or to the purchase of many stocks and bonds; it applies to the public budget as well.

Tax laws are not written to produce a specific sum of revenue for the fisc; they contain formulas that yield a more or less variable amount. Thus, there is no statutory ceiling on the amount of money that a tax can raise in the long run. A small percentage increase in the tax base each year, whether through economic growth, inflation or both, can produce a small increase in revenue each year that can be described as incremental, because it is much less than the base from the previous year.

But compounding each year's change produces a big effect. For example, a 5 per cent annual increase in revenue becomes, by a process of compounding over a decade, a 71 per cent increase, and it will treble in little more than two decades. A compound growth of 8 per cent would double tax revenue in eight years, and more than treble it in fourteen years. A 10 per cent rate of growth doubles tax revenue in seven years and trebles tax revenue in eleven years.

Compounding annual increases in tax revenue does not contradict the logic of incrementalism; it completes it. However, the incrementalist approach does not take compounding into account, because it does not look ahead for many years. This remains true even when attention is given to consistent and regular long-term changes. The concept of regular increments of change focuses upon the consistency of the annual percentage change. Dempster and Wildavsky (1979: table 2) describe the average rate of expenditure change as 'smaller rather than larger' in a twenty-five-year period of federal budgeting. The median programme in the period increased by about 6.5 per cent a year. When the compound effect of this annual change is calculated, expenditure doubles in ten years, trebles in seventeen years, and produces a fivefold increase at the end of the twenty-five-year period of 'smaller rather than larger' annual incremental increases.

Compounding changes for decades is reasonable in Britain, for spending and taxing programmes have histories more appropriately measured in generations than in a 12-month budget. The spending commitments and revenue needs of the budget today are very much influenced by major programmes for health, education and social security launched or expanded in the 1940–5 wartime coalition and the 1945–51 Labour government. Tax laws have had far longer to compound revenue. Whereas an individual politician may measure time in terms of an annual session of Parliament or a two- or three-year period in ministerial office, this is not true of the ministry. It has long had its programmes in place, and they are carried forward by political inertia, independent of the comings and goings of ministers nominally responsible (Rose, 1987).

7) *Large-scale change.* Budgeting is about both macro- and micro-policy. Macro-policy concerns big totals, such as the amount of money raised by taxes in total, including the base, as well as the effects of decisions at the margin. Micro-policy concerns relatively small (or, at least, not so big) numbers, such as the particular amount of money raised by a tax, or a decision that makes a marginal change in one tax.

Decisions about the budget as a whole can start from a top-down or bottom-up perspective. A top-down approach emphasizes aggregate figures, such as the total amount of money raised in taxation, or allotted to public expenditure, and the borrowing needed to finance the deficit. By contrast, a bottom-up approach examines each tax and each spending commitment, carefully considering properties of each, and gradually arriving at a total for both taxing and spending. The top-down approach is preferred by Treasury officials and all who are concerned with the overall position of the public sector in the economy. By contrast, the bottom-up approach tends to be preferred by specialists in particular programmes and particular taxes. Much of budgeting is about reconciling the constraints of top-down decisions with the bottom-up pressures that threaten to burst these constraints.

The bottom-up approach links particular budget lines with aggregate totals. By contrast, incrementalism excludes great sums in order to concentrate upon a particular budget line. By definition, the incremental approach restricts politics to small-scale microscopic changes. The limits imposed by the incremental theory are not so much wrong as they are confining. It can be argued that these limitations are shared by politicians. Even if this be true, the near-sighted concentration upon current marginal changes cannot prevent cumulative changes from having a large-scale impact.

The inertia theory is applicable both to micro-level concerns about particular taxes, and to top-down concerns about long-term changes in the total revenue. From the top-down perspective, the reason to be concerned with particular budget items in a given year need not be that a large amount of money is immediately at stake. Inertia gives special significance to measures that appear small when initially introduced, but, like the camel's nose, appear very large when their full size is evident within the tent.

8) *Variable and potentially destabilizing outcomes.* The incrementalist approach implies that the outcome of any particular political decision can be described by that curious English locution, 'not too disastrous'. The limited scope for alteration at any particular step of an incremental process provides a secure floor, as well as imposing a ceiling upon change. Most writing about incremental budgeting describes a process in which public spending grows slowly, and implies the outcome – more public outputs for popular programmes – is benign.

The inertia approach makes no assumption about whether the consequences of change are benign or dire, but assumes that some are (compounding economic growth can have desirable consequences) just as some are not (compounding debts). The variability of outcomes in the *longue durée* is one of its most significant features. It introduces a high degree of uncertainty about whether a particular measure will turn out as desired, or very different (and perhaps much worse) than intended.

Incremental theories deal with uncertainty by substituting *post hoc* evaluation for prospective calculations of consequences. *Post hoc* evaluation eliminates the need to speculate about events; the consequences of a particular measure can be examined after they are evident and, if benign, sustained; remedial action can be taken if they are unsatisfactory. But ignoring the consequences of actions does not hold them harmless. It only means that long-term consequences of taxing and spending programmes are not considered before they become palpable, when it will often be too late to redress them without pain.

Whereas politicians can live from election to election, government is continuing. Each taxing or spending measure contributes something to the future, for once enacted into law it is carried forward by the force of political inertia. The greater the momentum behind a programme, the harder it is to slow down, redirect or stop. Nearly 2,400 years ago Aristotle spotted the fatal flaw in the politician's sophistical tendency to ignore the long-term consequences of short-term choices:

> The expense is not noticed because it does not come all at once, for the mind is led astray by the repeated small outlays, just like the sophistic puzzle. 'If each is little, then all are little'. This is true in one way, but in another it is not, for the whole total is not little, but made up of little parts. (Aristotle, 1972 edn: 419f)

Because the whole is greater than any one of its parts, the cumulative consequence of seemingly small changes in taxation can result in an outcome that no politican would have consciously chosen, and from which the government of the day cannot extricate itself.

Institutional Behaviour

Anyone with knowledge of government on the inside will recognize much that is familiar in the incrementalist analysis of the behaviour of individual politicians. But strictly speaking, it is impossible to have a behavioural theory of government, for government is not just the sum of the activities of individual personalities; it is an impersonal organization. This point is particularly significant for taxation. The ethos of tax administration and tax law is impersonal, maximizing the certainty and scale of revenue collection by allowing the minimum scope for self-expression. Moreover, politicians welcome the impersonal procedures of taxation, for they do not want to be identified with decisions that enforce the collection of taxes.

Inertia and incremental theories differ in what they define as worth looking at. The incremental theory is a behavioural theory of politicians. The theoretical focus is the same as that of individuals in office; it is short-sighted, and small-scale. The impersonal force of inertia is directed at the base of the budget; the object of explanation is long-term and large, tens of billions of pounds in tax revenue. To explain total tax revenue in terms of decisions by individual officeholders is misdirected. The public-policy model shows that tax revenue is not a question of

Table 5.2 Differences between Incremental and Inertia Models of Policy-making

		Incrementalism	Inertia
1	Time span	Year-to-year	*Longue durée*
2	Government action	Many decisions	No decision
3	Consequences	Immediately unforeseeable	Unforeseeable in long-term
4	Reversibility	Quickly reversible	Very difficult
5	Linkage	Disjointed	Cumulatively linked
6	Compounding	Not considered	Cumulatively important
7	Scale of change	Small, regular	Large, irregular
8	Outcome	Slight changes, short-term equilibrium	Very variable, potentially destabilizing

111

what politicians want; it is a function of laws, administrative procedures and the state of the economy. The inertia theory demonstrates how tax revenue both continues and changes through the *longue durée*.

The significance of the inertia theory for understanding the growth of government is evident in a point-by-point comparison with the incremental approach (Table 5.2). The force of inertia, like government, continues for decades, and routines can continue in motion without any decision by politicians. Cumulative consequences are unforeseeable but, more than that, they are not reversible. Because routine actions can be linked in a process of cumulative compounding, inertia can gradually create change on a large scale, and its consequences can be destabilizing – whether or not they were intended by persons whose actions started a process that can only be manifest in the *longue durée*.

Decisions at the Margins

While inertia is of first importance, it is not all-important. A theory of taxation by inertia must do more than explain the continued flow of revenue to the fisc, and changes in that flow without any conscious decision by politicians. It must also identify the extent to which decisions by politicians can consciously alter tax revenue by fringe tuning at the margin.

In their analysis of regularity in annual budgeting, Dempster and Wildavsky (1979) recognized the possibility of an occasional budget shift occurring, that is, a break in the consistency of annual rates of change due to decisions made by politicians. Such events were regarded as intentional, a singular departure from long-term consistency. When politicial inertia produces discontinuities, they will normally not occur as the intended consequence of political decisions but as the long-term unintended consequences of the compounding of short-term changes.

The public-policy model recognizes four possible ways in which politicians' decisions can shift revenue: new taxes can be introduced or established taxes repealed; a swap of new taxes for old can occur; the rate and base of existing taxes can be altered; or tax administration can be changed. In theory, tax revenue could also be increased by consciously determined economic growth, but the course of the British economy for the past quarter-century emphasizes that the governing party deciding that the economy ought to grow faster does not mean that it does so. As long as the impact of such intentional changes upon revenue is relatively small, they remain minor qualifications to the inertia theory.[4]

Introducing or Repealing Taxes

The repeal of an existing tax or the enactment of a new tax is always possible in theory, but in practice rarely occurs. The great bulk of revenue in Britain today comes from old not new taxes (Tables 5.1 and 6.1).

The logic of maximizing revenue while minimizing political costs explains why the basic tax structure tends to remain unaltered from one Parliament to the next. Although novelty may be immediately appealing to politicians because it attracts publicity, the uncertainty that it induces can also generate forecasts of political disasters. Tax administrators are predisposed to use novelty as an argument against any new tax proposal, emphasizing that neither the administrative nor the revenue effects of a new tax can be known for certain prior to its enactment. Since the revenue effects of a tax repeal can be easily estimated, the Chancellor cannot casually abandon an established source of revenue.

Fringe tuning of taxes is the consequence. Resistance to adopting new taxes or repealing existing taxes can be described by a law (that is, a social science proposition) of inverse reform: *the amount of change that can intentionally be introduced into the tax system varies inversely with its effect on total tax revenue.* The more money that a tax can raise, the greater its inertia force, whether inertia is a force in motion against repeal or inertia is conceived as the force which has to be overcome before a new tax can be adopted. The less money a tax claims in revenue, the less the force of inertia weighing against it.

There is a fundamental disequilibrium in the market for tax reform: supply exceeds demand (Peacock, 1981). The supply of ideas for novel taxes is not constrained by politics; it is a function of the activities of professional tax experts, many of whom work

113

in universities rather than government. There the problems of elected politicians and tax administrators may be ignored, and novelty may be considered desirable in itself providing proof of academic originality. As the supply of reforms is not prompted by demands of politicians in government, it is not surprising, as Peacock notes (1981: 20), that 'tax reform measures are not something bought by government every day'.

A review of two decades of ideas for tax reform in Britain (Robinson and Sandford, 1983) concentrated upon six proposals that were enacted as new taxes: capital gains tax, the classic corporation tax, selective employment tax, corporation tax by imputation, capital transfer tax, and value added tax. Of these, only one, value added tax, has had a significant impact upon revenue. Most new taxes had only a small impact at the margin, and some were repealed as unsatisfactory (Rose and Karran, 1983: Appendix). Dozens more tax proposals never even reached the stage of being put to the House of Commons by government. Robinson and Sandford (1983: 232) conclude: 'We are left with a pretty pitiful result from two decades of enthusiastic tax reform.'

Swapping Taxes

The conditions of the great identity can be maintained if the repeal of an established tax is balanced by the introduction of a new tax or an increase in an existing tax, or a repeal is offset by a compensating increase in revenue. A revenue-neutral tax swap does not reduce the revenue of the fisc.

In the four decades following the end of the Second World War, only one major new source of tax revenue has been introduced in Britain, the value added tax. One reason for its introduction was unique: a value added tax was a condition of Britain entering the European Community. The reason why the introduction of VAT at a relatively high rate of 10 per cent did not cause a political storm was that the revenue raised was 'swapped' for revenue foregone by the repeal of two taxes particularly unpopular among Conservatives. One tax repealed was the selective employment tax (SET) introduced by the 1964 Labour government, and a source of much criticism by business. A variety of purchase taxes levied at different rates, which

114

contained many anomalies that were embarrassing for ministers to defend in the House of Commons, were also repealed. The net effect of the tax swap was to leave total revenue very little altered. In 1970, purchase taxes and SET accounted for 11 per cent of the total tax revenue; in 1974, VAT provided 9 per cent.

Tax swapping is particularly likely to occur within a specific area of taxation. For example, the introduction of a new-style corporation tax by the 1964 Labour government was linked with the repeal of the earlier profits and excess profits tax. The intention was to bring in a better tax on business, rather than to impose an additional tax. Taxes on the transfer of wealth, typically at death, have been subject to three tax laws in the postwar era: estate duty, replaced in 1975 by capital transfer tax, and inheritance tax, which replaced capital transfer tax in 1986. In each case, the swapping of one death duty for another had no substantial implication for total tax revenue.

Altering Tax Rates or the Tax Base

The most common decisions altering tax laws involve alterations to existing statutes, for these have far fewer political and administrative difficulties than the enactment of new laws. The result is not a new law, with all the uncertainties that novelty introduces into revenue forecasts, administration and the economy. The revenue value of a marginal change in an existing tax can be estimated with considerable precision, given the knowledge already at hand (Good, 1980: 11ff.).

Politically, alterations in tax rates and base are relatively attractive *because* they lack the novelty of new taxes. No new principle needs to be debated, nor does a new tax Act need to be steered through Parliament. The only change required is the much less conspicuous alteration in one or two clauses of established legislation. A further advantage of altering established taxes is that changes may be of any size. In order to claim credit for cutting taxes, it is not necessary to make a big cut; a small alteration in the tax rate or base can also be claimed as a cut.

Changes in the *rate* at which a tax is levied are administratively simple, requiring the substitution of one set of percentage figures for another in the tables from which taxes are calculated, or a

115

simple alteration in the money value of a tax with a fixed rate, such as tobacco. The revenue yield from an altered rate is almost as predictable as the yield from the previous rate. For its autumn statement, the Treasury publishes a ready reckoner illustrating the amount by which revenue would change with a variety of hypothetical changes in tax rates (Cm. 14, 1986: 40–44).

The politics of altering tax rates depends upon whether a reduction or an increase is proposed. In a pre-election period, a government reducing a tax rate will feel secure from criticism. However, the great identity makes it difficult to introduce a large cut in the tax rate. For example, to reduce the income tax rate from 27 to 25 per cent would cost the fisc more than £2.9b in a full year. If the change is introduced mid-way through the tax year, the immediate cost is much less – and some of the revenue foregone may be taken back by a post-election tax increase!

A proposal to increase the tax rate invites unpopularity. However, there are times when the government of the day is forced to raise additional revenue, because spending increases faster than tax revenue. In such circumstances, raising the rate of an existing tax is normally preferred to introducing a new tax, for it is a surer source of revenue, and it avoids the political friction of a new tax. It can be justified as a temporary measure; a subsequent reduction that returns the rate to what it had been previously may even be advertised as a tax cut.

The revenue-neutral adjustment of two different sets of tax rates allows a Chancellor to change the tax system for non-revenue reasons. A conspicuous example of such a swap occurred with the newly elected Conservative government of 1979, which believed that tax rates were too high on incomes, especially upper incomes, and was prepared to finance such a reduction by increasing taxes on expenditure. It cut the rate of income tax from 33 to 30 per cent, resulting in a revenue loss of billions. But it compensated for this loss by increasing the rate of VAT from 8 to 15 per cent.

Altering the *base* is another means of modifying a tax. Broadening the base increases revenue: for example, the base for the employer's national insurance contribution can be raised so that the employer is liable to pay a contribution for the whole of a wage, however high it is. Reducing the base of a tax decreases revenue as long as the tax rate remains the same. In an

116

inflationary era, leaving the statutory definition of the tax base unaltered has major revenue consequences. Inflation increases the cash value of every tax base calculated in money terms, such as taxes on income. Moreover, because income tax rates rise with income, not increasing the allowances that single and married people can subtract from gross income causes income tax payments to increase faster than inflation. The higher the level of inflation, the greater the extra revenue generated for the Treasury (and the extra tax imposed upon individuals) due to this fiscal drag.

As long as inflation rates were only a few per cent a year, the Chancellor could claim credit for cutting income tax without reducing revenue by increasing the nominal value of tax allowances against gross income. As long as the resulting reduction in the tax base was compensated for by the increase achieved by inflation, revenue overall remained the same. However, as inflation went into double digits in the 1970s, the credit claimed by this sleight of hand was less than the opprobrium resulting from the increase in the nominal value of taxes paid. The number of pounds collected in income tax increased by 151 per cent from 1970 to 1975, and its contribution to total tax revenue increased by one-quarter.

The Conservative opposition wanted to deprive the Labour government of the opportunity to claim credit for appearing to cut taxes while actually increasing revenue due to fiscal drag. In the circumstances of a Parliament in which the Labour government lacked a working majority, it secured the enactment in 1977 of an amendment requiring the Chancellor to report to Parliament the changes in the income tax base required to adjust fully for inflation. This requirement makes it clear to the Commons whether changes introduced by the Chancellor are correcting exactly for inflation, providing cuts above this correction, or failing to adjust fully for inflation. The change is known as the Rooker–Wise amendment, after the two Labour MPs who broke party ranks to make the law possible.

Indexation is a non-decision-making way of adapting to inflation, and it has been adopted widely in OECD nations, in one or another variant form (Tanzi, 1981; OECD, 1986: ch. 3). The reason why politicians do not want to take credit for apparently cutting taxes is that the explanation – inflation – causes political

117

embarrassment, prompting complaints about inflation. In Britain, the Rooker–Wise amendment has not meant the mechanical determination of changes in the income tax base by legislation; the Chancellor normally makes changes that are either more or less generous than a simple allowance for inflation, depending upon the overall political and economic climate (OECD, 1986: table 3.6). The obligation to publish inflation adjustments has altered political calculations marginally, by revealing to MPs (and to politically attentive taxpayers) the nature of the most important annual adjustment to the tax base.

Changing Administration

Administrative change is a logically possible way of altering tax revenue. Moreover, it is politically appealing to suggest that more tax revenue could be gained by improving the effectiveness of tax administration. A more effective administration would increase revenue by reducing the amount left unpaid because of tax evasion or administrative errors. A more efficient administration would increase the net revenue gain to the fisc by reducing the cost to the fisc of collecting tax revenues. In practice, there is virtually nothing that can be done within an annual budget cycle to alter administration. In the absence of short-term benefits, there is no incentive for a Chancellor of the Exchequer to become involved in improving administration, since potential benefits to the fisc would only occur after he had moved to another office.

The most straightforward way to increase effectiveness, hiring more inspectors to strengthen the enforcement of existing laws, requires several years' authorization, recruitment and training of staff before results can be expected to show results. Introducing new administrative practices to officials accustomed to established routines takes several years of retraining, and the time required can be much longer if there are problems in introducing new routines.

The responsibility for administrative change is not in the hands of the Treasury, but rests with semi-detached Boards of Inland Revenue, and Customs and Excise. In order for politicians to change revenue administration, they would need to engage in inter-organizational bargaining with the heads of the two Boards, who in turn would have to bargain with revenue unions and staff to secure agreement about implementing changes.

The long saga of the Inland Revenue plans to improve efficiency by computerizing the collection of income tax illustrates the constraints upon administrative change. The first attempt to computerize the collection of this major source of revenue occurred in the 1960s. The first (and only) regional computerized centre was opened in East Kilbride in 1968. The Conservative government elected in 1970 suspended further progress pending a major review of taxes and cash transfer payments. Its proposals for new forms of transfer payments were abandoned by the 1974 Labour government, and with it plans to computerize that scheme. Given changes in technology, a new system was developed, with the first pilot scheme launched in 1977. Current plans are for PAYE tax collection to be fully operational by 1989, a quarter-century after this was first mooted (Inland Revenue Report, Cmnd 1985: ch. 4).

Administrative obstacles, combined with political changes of direction and technical developments, have meant that the computerization of tax collection in Britain lags behind that of many other OECD countries. In the absence of the computerized data base of incomes that the system is meant to provide, other possible reforms of taxes and of cash-transfer payments are also stymied. Many tax demands are written out by hand today, as in early Victorian days when Mr Gladstone was Chancellor of the Exchequer.

Non-Decision-Making plus Fringe Tuning

Tax revenue is determined more by what the government of the day does *not* do than by what it decides to do. Political inertia produces more revenue in a given year than decisions taken within any one Parliament. Past laws, established administrative practices and the state of an economy that changes little from year to year are given conditions that the government of the day inherits. While no politician would choose an economy with one of the lowest economic growth rates in the Western world, this is the tax base that a newly elected British government inherits.

The impact of current decisions is best described as fringe tuning, because the effect upon total revenue raised in a year is

119

likely to be very small. The base of revenue that persists from the previous year is far larger than the changes introduced, whether the changes increase or reduce revenue, or leave net tax revenue the same because they are revenue-neutral and cancel each other out. Politicians are constrained to fringe tuning by the terms of the great identity.

The impact of decisions about tax made by the government of the day is primarily in the distant future. The laws and actions of one Parliament become part of the legacy passed to successor governments. To ignore the long-term consequences of short-term incremental choices is to confuse the politician's concern with the present and the government's impact on posterity. To regard this legacy as a conscious calculated choice of the net present value of future consequences is to confuse heuristic models with historical processes.

The inertia theory views taxation over a long time period. It is not so much concerned with how much revenue changes in the short run, but how much change occurs – intended or not – in the long run. This is appropriate, since government is a permanent institution of society, and taxation is a permanent resource of government. If one starts by examining tax revenue shortly after the end of the Second World War, then tax revenue today is the result of the national tax system plus the cumulative effect of all changes in tax laws, in tax administration, and in economic activities in the four decades since. In such a time perspective no one change appears large, but the cumulative effect of political inertia is great.

Notes

1 It also implies that those who wish to limit taxation should write restrictions against high taxes into a constitution (Brennan and Buchanan, 1980; Wildavsky, 1980).
2 For a discussion of the many reasons why these goals are moderated, both prior to entry to office and especially in office, see Rose (1984a).
3 Strictly speaking, the British government must re-enact old tax laws annually, because of the constitutional requirement that Parliament should each year have the right to seek redress of grievances annually before granting supply.
4 It should be noted that the inertia theory does recognize that even

small-scale decisions can, in the fullness of time, have big consequences. But the long-term consequences of a decision are often
not the intent of the decision-maker. It is a fallacy of *post hoc*
reasoning to treat consequences as evidence of intent.

CHAPTER SIX

Increasing Taxes, Stable Taxes or Decreasing Taxes?

When the amount of money collected in taxes in Britain in 1948 is compared with today's sum, a big increase in total tax revenue is evident. But when tax effort is examined, taxation as a percentage of the gross domestic product appears relatively stable over nearly four decades. When particular taxes are compared in terms of their claim on the national product, some taxes are decreasing. Which of these measures offers a true description of the dynamics of taxation in Britain? The short answer is: all three.

To think about tax revenue solely in terms of the total is to confuse the whole and the parts. Whereas the sum can only change in one direction at a time, the terms that go to make up that total need not change at the same rate, or even in the same direction. The increase in total tax revenue since 1948 could result from an infinity of permutations of changes among the taxes that constitute the national tax system.

Theories of the growth of government sometimes imply, if only by treating government as a global entity, that changes in spending and taxation are much the same in every country and, by extension, that all taxes are going up everywhere. There are reasons why homogeneity might be found in Britain, for authority over taxation is very much concentrated in one place, central government, and the Treasury is very much the dominant force at the centre.

There are also good *a priori* reasons for hypothesizing that patterns of change will be tax-specific, with different taxes moving in opposite directions at the same time. One reason is political: insofar as the use of taxes reflects political priorities, then changes in the party in office can lead to changes between taxes in their revenue yields. A second is economic: as sectors of the economy change relative to each other, this will have a differential effect upon revenues from particular taxes, such as those on motor cars and tobacco. A third reason is technical and tax-specific: if the tax rate is an *ad valorem* levy, revenue will rise with inflation, whereas if the rate is specified in fixed money terms, it will not be so buoyant.

The inertia theory of taxation, unlike many theories of the growth of government, does not postulate that government, and with it tax revenue, will invariably grow. The force of inertia guarantees a large and continuing amount of revenue. Nor does it predict that changes will occur uniformly. Differences between annual rates of change sustained by inertia will cumulatively intensify differences between taxes. It leaves open to empirical investigation which particular taxes will grow most, and which will remain stable, or even contract.

Politicians are not in principle worried by differences between taxes, as long as this does not require politically costly decisions on their part. Budget officials are not in principle worried by differential rates of change as long as total revenue continues to match total expenditure. An abnormal increase in one tax will present the opportunity for a reduction in another, or a relative decline in revenue for one tax will force an above-average increase in another if aggregate revenue is to remain constant. Differential rates of change create a situation in which budget-makers can hope to gain on the swings what they lose on the roundabouts.

The dynamics of taxation can only be understood by being explicit and clear about measures of taxation, and the purpose of analysis. Since three different measures are relevant to revenue raising, the answer to a question about changes in taxation must be relative, depending upon the measure used (Rose and Karran, 1983: 12ff.). Taxation must initially be reckoned in absolute terms as the number of pounds collected each year; that is the way in which taxes are collected, and revenue figures reported officially. Since in an inflationary era this measure will invariably show a big increase in taxation, it is also desirable to use a measure that is not so inflation-sensitive. Measuring taxes as a proportion of the national product introduces a control for inflation, for if the national product grows at a faster rate than taxes, tax effort will fall; if it grows slower, tax effort will rise; and if taxes and the national product both grow at the same rate, it will remain stable. Analysing the national tax system by comparing the share that each tax contributes to total revenue is bound to produce movements in opposite directions, for what some taxes gain others must lose. In aggregate there will be the notional appearance of stability, for revenue in the system as a whole must always sum to 100 per cent.

Comparison provides the best means of understanding the dynamics of taxation. The first part of this chapter compares particular taxes according to a number of different measures, in order to show under what circumstances a tax goes up, remains stable or declines. Secondly, a variety of patterns of change are identified in British taxes, and compared with data from other OECD nations to see whether patterns are specific to one country, or cross-nationally characteristic of a particular tax but varying within a nation from tax to tax. Once contrasting patterns are recognized, the relative importance of economic and political influences upon change can be examined by causal models.

Continuity and Discontinuity

Continuity, Innovation and Termination

Whether or not a tax continues from year to year is a basic test of stability. The repeal of a tax or the introduction of a new tax is a discontinuity. Growth in revenue is even more important in financing government. Growth could be a consequence of old taxes continuing in effect and raising more and more money, or newly introduced taxes could account for a substantial amount of additional revenue.

When all taxes contributing at least 1 per cent to the British system since 1948 are reviewed, a substantial amount of discontinuity is evident. Among the nineteen taxes examined, ten

124

have been continuous and nine have not. Most of the taxes that have continued throughout the postwar era originate from Victorian times or earlier (cf. tables 5.1; 6.1). The continuing taxes are familiar taxes: income tax, national insurance, rates, tobacco, hydrocarbon oil, beer, wine and spirits, vehicle licences, customs and stamp duty.

Three different types of discontinuity are evident in the tax system. Six taxes have been introduced in the postwar era, a rate of less than one a Parliament. Three taxes – capital gains tax, corporation tax and the national health service levy – have been in effect for two decades or more. Two other taxes – VAT and petroleum revenue tax – were introduced in the 1970s. Insofar as political inertia carries them forward, then increasingly these postwar innovations will reflect continuity with the past.

Four taxes have been repealed in four decades, including one, Selective Employment Tax (SET), that was introduced and soon repealed. In every case but one, the repeal of a tax was not an attempt to cut taxes; it was part of a swap between one source of revenue and another. Purchase tax and SET were repealed as part of a tax swap in exchange for VAT; profits tax was swapped for corporation tax. Entertainment tax could be repealed without a tax swap, since it was bringing the fisc less than 1 per cent of total revenue when terminated.

When taxes are reviewed in terms of revenue raised, a greater amount of continuity is evident. Of current tax revenue, 79 per cent is raised by measures in continuous operation in the postwar era, or much longer. The taxes most likely to persist are those that raise the most money, such as income tax, national insurance, local authority rates, and a variety of excise taxes (Table 6.1).

The law of inverse reform is evident here: discontinuities in taxation are more likely to involve taxes that make a minor rather than a major contribution to the fisc. In the period under review, the nine taxes introduced raised an average of 4 per cent of total revenue. VAT is the only major new source of revenue introduced to the British tax system in the postwar era. The whole of the revenue required to finance British government in the 1980s could have been obtained by taxes more than half a century old if British government had done absolutely nothing to introduce or repeal taxes in the years since 1948.[1]

125

Table 6.1 Continuity and Discontinuity in Taxes, 1948–85

	Mean % National Tax System[a]	
Continuing taxes (10)		
Income tax	32.7	
National insurance	13.5	
Local authority rates	9.9	
Tobacco	8.0	
Hydrocarbon oil	5.3	
Beer	3.0	
Wine and spirits	2.4	
Vehicle licences	1.8	
Customs duties	1.8	
Stamp duty	0.9	
Total	79.3	
Non-continuous taxes (9)		First/Last full year
(a) Introduced		
National Health Service	1.4	1958
Capital gains tax	1.0	1967
Corporation tax	6.6	1967
Value added tax	11.6	1974
Petroleum revenue tax	3.2	1978
Total	23.8	
(b) Repealed		
Entertainment tax	0.7	1959
Profits and excess profits	4.8	1965
Purchase tax	6.6	1972
Total	12.1	
(c) Introduced and repealed		
Selective employment tax	3.5	1967/72
Total	3.5	

[a] Calculated for last full year in effect.

Under what circumstances do taxes go up? When *current money* is the measure of revenue, then all continuing taxes have gone up in the revenue they contribute to the fisc. In absolute money terms the biggest taxes, such as income tax and national insurance, have gone up most, more than £34b and £21b respectively.

Another way to compare taxes is to calculate increases in percentage terms. Doing so effectively disregards the initial sum of revenue raised; it emphasizes instead the increase relative to the starting point. This measure shows that taxes vary greatly, and differ in their cumulative percentage increase (Table 6.2). Revenue from hydrocarbon oils has increased most sharply, going up by more than 11,000 per cent since 1948. National insurance has increased by more than 6,300 per cent. While income tax has increased its money yield most, its percentage increase in revenue, 2,571 per cent, is actually less than the percentage increase of revenue in aggregate. Tobacco, beer and customs have made cash payments to the fisc that have grown by less than half the average.

Table 6.2   Direction and Scale of Change in Principal Taxes Since 1948

	Change, 1985, from 1948 base		
	Current Money	Share in GDP	Share in National Tax System
Tax (m revenue, 1948)	%	%	%
Income tax £1,327)	2,571	-11	-17
National insurance (£355)	6,308	107	99
Local rates (£317)	4,184	41	33
Hydrocarbon oils (£55)	11,282	260	254
Tobacco (£598)	626	-77	-78
Vehicle licences (£50)	4,678	75	50
Wines and spirits (£121)	1,729	-40	-45
Beer (£305)	534	-81	-81
Customs duties (£114)	1,044	-60	-63
Stamp duty (£59)	1,866	-40	-36
Total tax revenue	3,139	7	n.a.
Number increasing	10	4	4
Number decreasing	0	6	6

When *tax effort* is the measure of change, it is possible for all taxes to increase their share of the national product, if the extra tax effort demanded by government in the postwar years has been spread more or less evenly across all taxes. In practice, the majority of continuing taxes have actually *reduced* their claim on the national product in postwar Britain (Table 6.2). Income tax,

127

tobacco, wines and spirits, beer, customs, and stamp duty claim less effort from citizens today than in 1948. The four taxes that have increased their claims upon the national product, the most stringent expression of demanding greater tax effort, are national insurance, rates, vehicle licence tax and hydrocarbon oils. But the effect of these increases has largely been diminished by the subtraction of taxes claiming less effort.

When the relative contribution of particular taxes to the *national tax system* is examined, inevitably the share of some taxes will contract as a consequence of the share of others increasing. In political terms, it might be hypothesized that smaller (and more numerous) taxes would increase their share most, as politicians would be averse to raising already large taxes higher still. The inertia theory suggests the opposite hypothesis: that the largest taxes would increase by the process that made them big in the first place.

In fact, most taxes decline in their relative importance in the tax system. Of the ten continuing taxes, six have had their contribution to the fisc undergo relative contraction since 1948. But the taxes that have declined are, except for income tax, not specially important to the fisc. Of the four taxes that have increased their share of the national tax system, three – national insurance, local authority rates and hydrocarbon oils – are major revenue sources. In money terms, the change has been greatest for national insurance, which has risen from accounting for 8.0 per cent of tax revenue in 1948 to 15.9 per cent in 1985.

Change through the *longue durée* is much more important than short-term changes. Table 6.2 shows the difference in revenue yields of continuing taxes over a time span of thirty-seven years. In this period all taxes have gone up in current money values, but they have not gone up equally. The increase in claims on the national product has been concentrated too; some taxes, such as tobacco, have declined greatly in relative significance in the tax system, while others, such as national insurance, have grown.

As the inertia theory predicts, there is overall continuity in the principal sources of revenue. But continuity in tax laws is not the same as continuity in absolute or relative amounts of revenue. Propositions about taxation in aggregate will not be true of every tax that contributes to revenue in aggregate. Without differential rates of growth, the tax system would be rigid in its parts. Countervailing movements make the tax system capable of adapting to changes in the economy as a whole.

Patterns of Change

While change can take many forms, the results are not random. We can better understand the dynamics of the tax system as a whole, if we look at the patterns formed by changes in particular taxes.

Annual Inconsistencies

Budget-makers are concerned with short-term predictability, that is, the persistence of a pattern from one year to the next. Incremental theories particularly emphasize consistency, for it is this which makes it easy to predict budget lines, and thus to agree upon regular small increments in taxing and spending. The greater the consistency, the more certain are revenue estimates.

In postwar Britain, budget-makers have not been able to rely upon taxes showing a consistent rate of increase, as the incremental theory postulates. The average annual rate of change has fluctuated greatly up and down, and the range has been great. The average increase in the current money value of a tax was 45 per cent in 1975; in 1952 the average increase was as low as 3 per cent (Rose and Karran, 1983: table 3.5). Each year's revenue forecast must therefore depend upon a detailed assessment of circumstances specific to that year. Changes in tax revenue cannot be estimated by the simple application of an annual average of the rate of change.

There is great variability in the rate at which particular taxes change in a given year. Within a given year, predictability would be simplified if all taxes grew at much the same rate. Statistically, this would result in a low coefficient of variation (that is, the mean of the percentage change of each tax from the previous year, divided by the standard deviation around the mean). In fact, within any given year there is great variation around the mean rate of increase for a tax; the coefficient of variation averages 1.61 (Rose and Karran, 1983: table 3.5).

Nor is there consistent regularity in the rate at which particular taxes annually increase their revenue yield. When the mean rate of annual change in each tax continuing since 1948 is calculated, the coefficients of variation for particular taxes are high, being above 1.00 for five taxes – national insurance, rates, income tax, stamp duty and vehicle licences (Rose and Karran, 1983: table 3.4).

Since there is no homogeneity among taxes in their pattern of change in any one year or across a number of years, budget-makers cannot generalize from an aggregate figure how particular taxes will change. Given the degree of instability across time, the average rate of change for a particular tax cannot be used to forecast its change in a particular year. Changes in taxation are best calculated from assumptions specific to a particular tax, and carefully fitted to the circumstances of a particular year.

Identifying Patterns

A tax's claim on the gross domestic product provides the best measure of revenue through the years, for it is not immediately affected by changes in other taxes. Graphs are particularly suitable to display patterns of change in taxation. Not only can graphic representation show whether the revenue raised by a particular tax is going up, down or remaining steady, but it can also indicate whether changes are occurring in a consistent or unstable manner.

While every tax can claim a historical uniqueness, in the *longue durée* patterns of change common to several taxes can be identified. The grouping of taxes according to different patterns in Figure 6.1 rests upon two distinctions. The first is whether or not the trend is consistent in a tax's share of the gross domestic product. Consistency is measured by calculating goodness of fit to a least-squares regression line; an r^2 value of .50 or better indicates consistency. Secondly, any trend may be up or down, or relatively flat, because of a cyclical pattern. This is indicated by the percentage change in a tax from its trend position in 1948 to 1985; trend changes of less than 50 per cent of the 1948 base are classified as showing no directional movement, and those that are larger as showing a noteworthy movement. (For further details see Rose and Karran, 1983: ch. 4.)

When the movement of taxes is examined through the *longue durée*, the collective result is heterogeneity: taxes differ in their pattern as well as direction of change. Some go up, some down, and others do not consistently move in one direction (Figure 6.1).

Consistently up (3) Only national insurance, local authority rates and vehicle licences conform to the popular stereotype that taxes are always going up. Each of these taxes has substantially increased its trend share of the national product – doubling in the case of national insurance, and going up by more than half in the case of rates and vehicle licences – and the upward trend has tended to be consistent.

Consistently down (4) In an era when total revenue was rising, four taxes nonetheless showed a consistent and substantial downward trend in their claims on the national product. Two of the taxes decreasing in significance – beer and tobacco – have rates fixed in money terms, a feature especially likely to reduce revenue growth in an inflationary era. Customs has declined with the increasing political commitment to international free trade, and stamp duties as traditional taxes on specific transactions have tended to be bypassed by general purpose taxes such as VAT.

Cyclical (2) In the flux of the modern economy no tax will remain absolutely constant in its claim on the national product. As long as fluctuations upwards are offset by movements down, then a tax will show a more or less cyclical movement. In the postwar period, income tax has followed a cyclical trend, sometimes increasing and sometimes decreasing its claim on the national product. The cyclical fluctuations in income tax are of major importance, given the large amount of money that it raises for the fisc. By contrast, the cyclical fluctuations in wines and spirits have involved small ups and downs.

Unstable (1) There is no necessity for revenue to follow a consistent or cyclical pattern. Hydrocarbon oil has had both ups

131

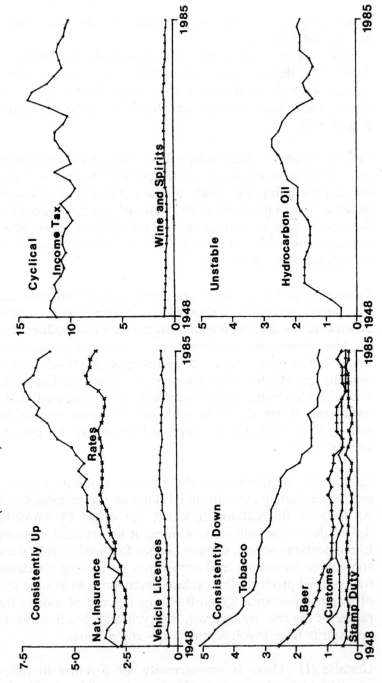

Figure 6.1 Alternative patterns of changes in taxes continuing since 1948 (as % GDP)

and downs, because it is not only sensitive to fluctuations in the national economy, but also to international fluctuations in the price of oil. The changes cannot be described as cyclical, for the underlying trend has been substantially upwards – but not consistently so.

Taxes must be weighed by their contribution to the national tax system, as well as counted. When this is done, the pattern of collective heterogeneity is confirmed. No one type contributes as much as one-third of total tax revenue. The taxes that show a steady trend up in revenue contribute one-quarter of the money claimed by the fisc. The two cyclical taxes also contribute less than one-third of total tax revenue. Taxes that have consistently been falling were significant in 1948, contributing more than one-quarter of the tax system's revenue then. Taxes that have introduced an element of discontinuity since 1948, such as VAT, today account for one-third of total tax revenue.

Tax-Specific or Nation-Specific Trends?

Many contemporary as well as historical accounts of taxation focus exclusively upon activities within Britain. But the fact that particular taxes change in opposite directions raises a fundamental question: in what sense is the British tax system determined by exclusively British influences?

Within-nation differences between taxes are consistent with the hypothesis of between-nation similarities in the movement of particular taxes, especially among nations with similar economies, such as those of the OECD world. An income tax can move in the same direction in Britain, Germany or Japan, and the same could hold for other taxes. Even though the tax rate or base may vary from country to country, the direction of change should remain much the same insofar as it is determined by generic characteristics of a tax, rather than national circumstances.

As far as current revenue is concerned, among OECD nations there is similarity in major taxes in use today. The coefficient of variation for the share of total revenue raised is relatively low for income tax, 0.35; VAT and sales, 0.42; excise, 0.52; and social

133

Table 6.3 Direction of Change in Taxes in OECD Nations since 1955

	% National Tax System (number of countries)		% GDP (number of countries)	
	Up	Down	Up	Down
Income tax	14	3	16	1
Social security	14	2	15	1
VAT and sales	8	8	15	0
Excise	4	13	8	9
Corporation	4	13	6	11
Property	1	11	6	5
Wealth and estate	2	15	4	12
Customs	0	16	2	14

Source: Rose, 1985: table 4, calculated from OECD data.

security 0.60 (Rose, 1985: table 3). Each of these taxes is a major source of revenue in nearly every OECD nation. The fringe tuning hypothesis – taxes contributing a small amount of money to the fisc will vary more – is also substantiated, for the highest coefficients of variation concern relatively small payroll, other, customs and property taxes.

When changes through the decades are examined, only three taxes consistently show movement in the same direction in the great majority of OECD nations. Income tax and social security tend to increase their share of the national tax system and of the national product, and customs to decrease its share. VAT and sales taxes tend to increase their share of the national product, but in about half the countries examined do so at a slower rate than the increase in tax revenue overall (Table 6.3). Taxes declining in their share of a national tax system nonetheless can sometimes show an increase in their share of the national product.

When the consistency of trends is examined, income tax and social security have increased their share of the national product with a high degree of consistency in almost every advanced industrial nation (Rose, 1985: table 5). Customs normally shows a decline in its share of the national product. However, for most taxes the pattern of change tends not to be the same cross-nationally: the taxes consistently going up everywhere are the exception not the rule.

Cross-national attributes of taxes have a limited capacity to explain the dynamics of taxes within Britain. This is most strikingly so in the case of income tax, which has increased its share of the national product in every other OECD nation except Britain. The growing importance of local authority rates also requires a good understanding of British conditions, for such a property tax is unimportant in most OECD nations, and furthermore has tended to decline in significance. The one major increase in British taxes that is consistent with international trends is the growing reliance upon social security taxes. Distinctiveness makes it important to look at the nation-specific influences upon the various ways in which particular British taxes have changed in the postwar era.

Causal Models of Change

The great increase in taxes paid into the fisc is accounted for in general terms as a function of changes in laws, tax administration, and economic activity. We would like to know more than this: why have these changes occurred? and which changes – the decisions of politicians, or inertia – have been most important?

Competing Explanations

Political scientists normally assume that political decisions are important in determining changes in tax revenue. Politicians can alter taxation by changing the rate and base of established laws, as well as by enacting new taxes or repealing established taxes.

Insofar as parties differ, changes in tax revenue could reflect the alternation of Conservative and Labour governments. A Labour government would be expected to favour increasing revenue from income tax, which progressively claims more money from upper-income groups, and reducing revenue from VAT and national insurance, which are not regarded as progressive. The Conservatives would be expected to alter taxes in the opposite direction. Another hypothesis is that, regardless of party, all politicians could react to what is described as the

135

political business cycle (Nordhaus, 1975). A government might schedule its tax increases shortly after it won a general election, and tax cuts shortly before the next general election, in order to minimize the electoral costs and maximize the electoral advantages of introducing tax changes.

The inertia theory emphasizes that non-decision-making is the norm. In the absence of many changes in the tax rate and in the definition of the tax base, political decisions are not a positive cause of changes in tax revenue. The most important characteristic of politicians in the inertia theory is not their willpower but their 'won't power' – that is, firmness in refusing to make changes in tax laws, whether they are recommended by partisan supporters, pressure groups, or experts in theories of taxation.

Insofar as politicians tend not to make decisions about taxation, then, according to the public-policy model, changes in revenue will principally reflect changes in economic activity. The economy is not inert, it is dynamic; it is a force in motion, and gradual changes in the economy can cumulatively have a big impact upon tax revenue, as each year's change is consolidated into the base of economic activity for the following year. Economic growth offers an attractive way to increase tax revenue; increasing income, expenditure and wealth increase the bases of taxation. Inflation offers a less attractive way to alter tax revenue: it increases tax revenues by inflating the value of the tax base, while eroding the relative value of payments made in fixed sums for such goods as tobacco. Changes in consumption can nonetheless affect revenue; a reduction in smoking will reduce tobacco taxes, and an increase in motoring will increase revenue from oil taxes.

Political and economic explanations are statements of relative tendency, not absolutes. To a substantial extent the two theories are complementary, the moving inertia of the economy emphasizing the importance of compounding growth in the base, and political decisions stressing the capacity of politicians to alter revenue from what inertia would otherwise produce.

Specifying the Model

In testing the determinants of change in tax revenues, it is particularly important to distinguish between the influence of intervening variables, such as changes in the rate and base of taxation, and changes in the independent variables that determine revenue through these intervening variables.

Causal modelling is suitable for discriminating between the immediate and the independent causes of changes in tax revenue, since it makes explicit the relationship between them, and measures the influence of each, separately and together (see, for example, Blalock, 1971; Simon, 1957). A causal model emphasizes that tax revenue is immediately a function of the tax base and the tax rate. Any change in either of these figures necessarily produces a change in tax revenue, unless the two alter in ways that exactly cancel each other out. The model can also show influences causing changes in these crucial intervening variables. Economic growth and inflation can increase total tax revenue by changing the tax base, which in turn produces more revenue from a given tax rate. Party government or the electoral cycle can alter tax revenue, insofar as politicians choose to raise or lower tax rates. Standardized beta coefficients measure the degree of direct and indirect influence of intervening and independent variables upon tax revenue in Britain since 1948.

Inflation presents an awkward problem in statistical analysis. Inflation is *prima facie* a major determinant of the big increase in tax revenue in post-war Britain. However, if inflation were all important and affected all taxes identically, then each tax would show much the same rate of increase in revenue as the inflation rate as a whole. This is not the case (cf. Table 6.2). A statistical complication arises because the mean correlation between current money revenue for continuing taxes and the retail price index since 1948 is very high, .88. Moreover, the correlation between the money value of the gross domestic product and the retail price index is virtually total, .998. To use such inter-correlated measures of economic activity would confound the influence of inflation and economic growth (Karran, 1985: 374; 1985a: Table 5).

In order to overcome the statistical problem presented by this multicollinearity, the current money value of revenue has been deflated by the retail price index, and the same has been done for tax rates set in fixed money terms, and the gross domestic product (GDP). Since the principal budget calculations on the spending side were made in terms of 'constant value' currency units for much of the postwar period, deflating revenue is consistent with a form of reasoning applied by policy-makers to the spending side of the budget (cf. Cmnd 1432, 1961; Clarke, 1973; Pliatzky, 1982). Deflating tax revenues reduces but does not eliminate the influence of inflation upon tax revenues. It still allows the indirect effect of inflation to be evidenced, by expanding a tax base subject to progressive taxation (such as income tax or death duties), or by decreasing the relative value of a tax rate fixed in money terms (such as tobacco or beer).

The causal model understates the force of political inertia because it commences analysis in 1948. The accumulated weight of decisions taken by previous centuries of politicians is not allowed for in this statistical analysis. Hence, in interpreting the following statistics, it is important to remember that methodological constraints have lowered the actual effect of inflation and of political inertia, and increased the influence of political decisions and of economic growth.

Applying the Causal Model

Given the markedly different characteristics of taxes in use, a causal model should be tested for a variety of taxes; ten different taxes are examined. Where rates and bases are not consistent for a given tax, adjustments have had to be made to produce an average figure for use in calculations (for details, see Karran, 1985; 1985a). Local rates are not included here, because they are set by hundreds of separately elected local authorities rather than being determined as is central government taxation.

Since *income tax* has been the biggest tax since 1948 and fluctuated up and down in its share of the national product it is particularly suitable for a detailed exposition of causal modelling of taxation (Figure 6.2). The causal model of income tax in Britain has a good fit with the complexities of four decades of history, explaining more than three-quarters of the variance in income tax revenue ($r^2 = .78$).[2] The impact of the influences is not equal, as shown by the very different values of the standardized beta coefficients for each line linking two variables. Following standard statistical practice, only those coefficients significant at the 95 per cent level of confidence, indicated by a * are considered as supporting a hypothesis.

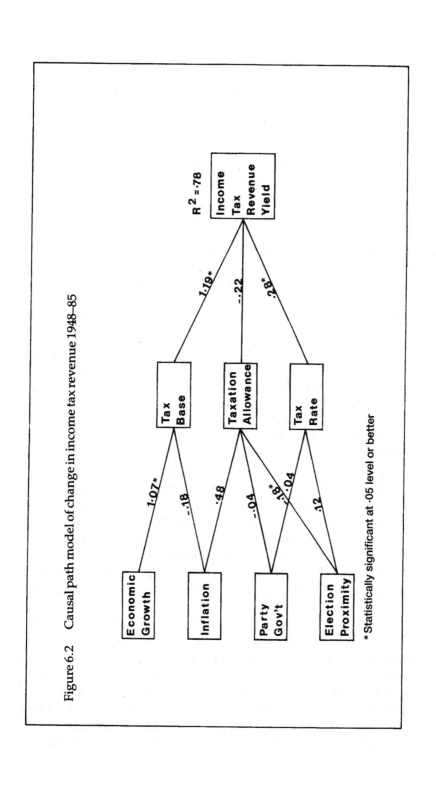

Figure 6.2   Causal path model of change in income tax revenue 1948–85

* Statistically significant at ·05 level or better

The causal model immediately discriminates between intervening influences in the public-policy model. There is a high positive relationship between changes in the tax base and income tax revenue (beta= 1.19). There is also a significant relationship between increases in the tax rate and increases in revenue yield, but the lower value of the beta weight (.28) shows that it is of secondary importance. Changes in tax allowances have tended to reduce the revenue yield (-.22), but the relationship is not statistically significant for the period as a whole.

Inertia changes in the economy influence income tax revenue through intervening variables. In the first instance, economic growth has a very strong impact (beta=1.07) upon the base of income tax. The indirect effect of economic growth upon tax revenue is measured by multiplying the coefficient relating economic growth to the tax base by that for the tax base to revenue. The resulting product (1.07 x 1.19) is very high, 1.30.

After the tax base is deflated by the retail price index, inflation has an insignificant relationship to the tax base (-.18). In the period since 1948 there was a significant relationship with tax allowances (.48). But since tax allowances are not an important determinant of revenue, the influence of inflation through this route (that is .48 x -.22) is low (-.11). The indirect influence of inflation upon revenue through the tax base (-.18 x 1.19) is second in importance in the model overall (-.21).

Neither political hypothesis is supported by the causal model. There is no significant relation between whether the party in government and the tax rate or tax allowances. The electoral cycle also has no significant relationship with tax allowances or tax rates.[3] Changes did occur in income tax rates, albeit not strictly according to the party in government. By comparison with changes in the tax base (1.19), changes in tax rates had much less effect upon tax revenue (.28).

Altogether, the model supports the inertia theory: it explains a high proportion of revenue from income tax, and only one influence – the inertia of economic growth – has a strong effect upon revenue (1.13). If money values had not been deflated by the retail price index, the influence of inflation would be even stronger. As it is, inflation indirectly registers an impact upon tax revenue, whereas political decisions are insignificant.

Applying the causal model to a variety of taxes provides a

robust test of the relative importance of inertia as against political decisions in determining tax revenue. The significant findings can be reviewed by examining taxes in the order of their importance to the fisc. Statistical details are given in Appendix Table 6.1 (see also Karran, 1985).

While *national insurance* is levied upon income, it is not determined in exactly the same way as income tax.[4] There is a good fit between the causal model and revenue raised; 92 per cent of the variance is explained, and changes in the tax rate and base each have a statistically significant effect on revenue.

Changes in revenue from the national insurance tax have principally been determined by inertia. Inflation is the only independent variable that has a statistically significant effect via the tax rate (.44). The greater the increase in the inflation rate, the greater the increase in tax revenue, even after deflating for the retail price index. Economic growth here shows no influence upon revenue, for it has not generated a substantial increase in the number of taxpayers. National insurance revenue is completely independent of the electoral cycle and there is no significant link between the party in government and this tax.

VAT is distinctive in being both a large source of income, and having been in effect for only a short period of time. VAT is also unique in the great change in its rate in a short period of time. When introduced by the Conservative government in 1973 the standard rate was 10 per cent; the incoming Labour government cut the basic rate to 8 per cent in 1974. In 1979 the incoming Conservative government almost doubled the standard rate to 15 per cent. There is a very good fit between the causal model and changes in VAT revenue (r^2: .95).

In the distinctive circumstances of the first years of VAT, changes in party government have been able to explain half (.49) the variance in its revenue yield. Economic growth, by increasing the value of the tax base, has also had a significant effect upon total revenue (.47). The influence of economic growth upon VAT revenue should be continuing, whereas the effect of party is not likely to continue. For this to be the case, the next Labour government would need to make a substantial cut in VAT revenue. But returning VAT to the 8 per cent rate when Labour was last in office would cost the fisc £8b. To replace such a loss would require raising the standard rate of income tax by 6p in the pound.

The taxation of *corporation profits* has involved three different philosophies and sets of tax legislation in the postwar era. Until 1947 profits were taxed in the form of personal income. In 1947 a separate tax was levied upon corporate profits. The Labour government elected in 1964 adopted a new form of corporation tax. Because corporations are inordinately sophisticated taxpayers with resources to reduce tax liabilities, there tends to be a gap between the revenue that the Treasury would like this tax to yield, and what it produces.

A major squeeze on corporate profits in the 1970s and government attempts to counteract the adverse effects of taxation have resulted in this tax being 'in total disarray' (Kay and King, 1983: 162). Therefore it is hardly surprising that the causal model that fits major taxes well explains very little of the change in revenue from profits tax ($r^2 = .13$) or corporation tax ($r^2 = .27$). None of the hypothesized influences had a statistically signifant impact upon either tax.

While a tax has been levied upon *hydrocarbon oils* throughout the postwar era, the significance of oil in the economy has varied greatly in this period. In austerity Britain there was virtually no central heating, and few motor cars. Since then, revenue from this tax has grown more in percentage terms than any other tax, and absolute revenue has also increased by more than £6b. This reflects an increase in the amount of oil being consumed, and an increase in the tax rate. However, international influences upon oil since 1973 have made it difficult to fit a general causal model to revenue from this tax ($r^2 = .23$).

The inertia of the economy affects the growth of hydrocarbon oil revenue, albeit the resulting indirect effect is limited (.11). After deflating for an increase in the retail price index, inflation retains a significant and negative effect on the tax rate, and thus on revenue (-.21). Given the impact of the international political economy upon oil prices, it is hardly surprising that decisions by Conservative and Labour governments have had no significant influence on revenue from this oil tax.

Because the use of *tobacco* is habitual, it is a relatively predictable source of tax revenue, and there is a very good fit between the model and changes in tax revenue ($r^2 = .88$). The inertia of inflation has a significant and negative effect upon tobacco revenue (-.65), because the tax rate is adjusted upwards much more slowly than the rate of inflation. This is a common characteristic of taxes with a rate fixed in money terms. Party politics appear statistically significant (.62) as an influence upon tobacco tax revenue – but contrary to what would be predicted from partisan ideology and interest. The party that tends to raise the tax rate on tobacco is Labour, not the Conservatives. This is surprising, for the tobacco tax falls more heavily upon working-class (and therefore, Labour) voters.

In the postwar era there has been a great expansion in motor car ownership: hence, revenue from *vehicle licences* has risen more than three times as fast as the rate of inflation, and the causal model shows a good fit (r^2= .82). The inertia of economic change has the greatest impact upon revenue from motor vehicles. Economic growth is most important, for it encourages the expansion of car ownership, and thus the tax base, indirectly increasing revenue (.37). Inflation is significantly, albeit negatively, related to changes in the tax rate, which has lagged behind the overall increase in the retail price index. Inflation thus depresses revenue from motor-vehicle licences (-.19).

Taxes on drink are levied according to the amount of alcohol in a product. Since *wines and spirits* vary in their alcoholic strength, only an approximate tax rate and base can be calculated, by averaging tax rates and quantities consumed of different types of alcoholic drinks. In consequence, there is a less good fit between the model and changes in tax revenue (r^2= .27). The inertia forces of the economy are the chief influences. Economic growth is significantly associated with an increase in consumption, and thus revenue (.37). The 'hangover' from inflation reduces revenue, for tax rates are not adjusted upwards as rapidly as prices rise, thus indirectly reducing revenue (-.45). The party in government also has a significant effect upon revenue (.48): Labour governments tend to raise the tax rate on drink more than do Conservative administrations.

Beer is a relatively easy drink to tax, since alcoholic content varies little from beer to beer. There is a better fit between the model and changes in beer revenue (r^2= .55). The inertia of economic growth has a positive and substantial effect upon the amount of beer consumed, but not upon tax revenue, because changes in the volume of beer-drinking are not high in their impact upon revenue, by contrast with the effect on revenue of

143

changes in tax rates. Proximity to an election appears to be the one significant influence upon tax revenue from beer; as expected, the approach of an election decreases the government's willingness to raise the rate of tax on beer.

Table 6.4 **Economic and Political Influences upon Changes in Tax Revenue**

| | R^2 | Statistically Significant Results | |
		Macro-Economic Factors (beta coefficient)	Political Choice
Income tax	.78	Econ. Growth (1.27)	-
National insurance	.92	Inflation (.44)	
VAT	.95	Econ. Growth (.47)	Party Govt (–.49)
Corporation	.27	-	-
Profits	.13	-	-
Hydrocarbon oil	.23	Econ. Growth (.11) Inflation (–.21)	-
Tobacco	.88	Inflation (–.65)	Party Govt (.62)
Vehicle licences	.82	Econ. Growth (.40) Inflation (–.19)	Party Govt (.17)
Wines and spirits	.25	Econ. Growth (.37) Inflation (–.45)	Party Govt (.48)
Beer	.55		Election cycle (.28)

Source: Karran, 1985, updated to include 1985 revenue. (Only statistically significant independent variables that affect statistically significant intervening variables are entered here.)

The Overall Pattern

The large amount of statistical data generated by a multiplicity of causal models can be summarized in a single table that concentrates attention upon the extent to which economic and/or political influences did exercise a statistically significant effect upon tax revenue (Table 6.4).

The force of inertia is the principal determinant of changes in tax revenue. While politicians take few decisions, inflation and economic growth can nonetheless alter revenue. Economic growth appears as a significant influence upon five different taxes, and as particularly important for income and vehicle licences. Even after controlling the overall increase in the retail price index, inflation continues to have a significant influence upon five taxes, and particularly upon national insurance, tobacco and hydrocarbon oil.

Of the two political influences tested, the party in control of government registered a significant influence upon four taxes – but not always in the direction that would be predicted from conventional assumptions about partisan values and the incidence of taxation. Labour governments have been more inclined than Conservative governments to put up taxes on such consumption goods as tobacco, wines and spirits. The proximity of an election appears to have very little influence upon particular taxes once account is taken of other influences. Nor is this surprising, for the great identity implies that even in a pre-election year a government will need to raise big sums in taxation to finance big budgets (see Chapter 4).

The forces of inertia provide the only significant influences accounting for changes in income tax, national insurance, and hydrocarbon oil, and the single most important influence upon changes in tobacco and vehicle licences. The party in government has been of first importance for revenue from wine and spirits and VAT, and election proximity is important for beer.

The impact of inertia upon revenue-raising is even greater than indicated by Table 6.4, which reflects influences *after* controlling for inflation and discounting the effects of legislation prior to 1948. When the budget is viewed in the *longue durée*, the inertia of laws and administration is of primary importance, ensuring that a tax remains in force. While much political attention is focused upon what the Chancellor of the Exchequer may (or may not) do in his annual budget, the great bulk of the revenue secured by that budget is not determined by decisions of the Chancellor of the moment. In forecasting next year's revenue, tax officials do not wait for the budget speech to see what is new. Instead, they look to old laws to calculate how much money established taxes will raise.

145

Appendix Table 6.1 Significant and Not Significant Influences Upon Changes in Tax Revenue

Tax (Years Covered)	R²	Intervening Variables Base/Volume	Rate	Independent Variables Economic Growth	Inflation	Party Government	Election Year
Income tax (1948–84)	.78	1.19*	.28*	-1.07*	-.18	.04	-.18*
National insurance (1950–74)	.92	.49*	.66*	.03	.67*	.19	.00
VAT (1973–85)	.95	-.52*	.50*	.91*	-.03	-.98*	-.00
Corporation tax (1966–82)	.27	.48	-.06	-.05	-.72*	.17	-.19
Profits tax (1948–65)	.13	-.14	-.34	-.06	-.45	-.34	.25
Hydrocarbon oil (1948–85)	.23	.24*	.48*	.46*	-.45*	.10	.23
Tobacco tax (1948–76)	.88	.48*	1.01*	-.03	-.64*	.61*	-.05
Vehicle licences (1948–85)	.82	.82*	.59*	.48*	-.33*	.29	.22
Wines and spirits (1948–84)	.25	.43*	1.10*	.86*	.41*	.44*	.19
Beer duties (1948–85)	.55	.08*	.78*	.84*	-.04	.26	.36*

* : Beta coefficient significant at 5 per cent level.

1   This assumes that at least 79 per cent of revenue would have come from continuing taxes, and 12 per cent from taxes that had not been repealed. Adjustments in tax rates and bases could have provided the additional 9 per cent of revenue to make up the total actually raised, e.g. the increase of purchase taxes, a tax amendment, rather than the introduction of a generalized value added tax.

2   Because the analysis concerns a series of years, autocorrelation could severely distort the results (Johnston, 1974). The Cochrane and Orcutt (1949) iteration method was used to transform the dependent and independent variables to remove autocorrelation (Karran, 1985: 376).

3   The party in office is scored as a dichotomous dummy variable, with a value of 1 for a Labour government and 0 for a Conservative government. To test for the effect of the electoral cycle, each election year was scored as zero, on the assumption this is the year when taxes would be lowest. The year immediately after an election, the most likely for a tax increase, was scored as 5, with subsequent years having values of 4, 3, and 2; the immediate pre-election year, the point in the cycle when a tax cut would be most likely, was coded -1.

4   Because of changes in national insurance contributions in 1974, subsequent figures are not comparable with those for the earlier period. Hence the analysis here covers the longer period, from 1950 to 1974.

CHAPTER SEVEN

Fringe Tuning:
The Chancellor's Decisions

To speak of a politician making decisions about taxes leaves much unclear. It does not say whether decisions are about the revenue base, or only represent modifications at the margin. Nor does it indicate whether decisions are revenue-neutral, changing the way in which a given amount of money is raised, or alter how much money is raised in total. It is possible for a Chancellor to make marginal adjustments up and down in taxes, yet leave the total revenue the same.

The ceaseless stream of proposals for new taxes or altering existing taxes implies great scope for decisions that change taxation. The Chancellor of the Exchequer, by virtue of his position as the Cabinet minister responsible for introducing tax legislation into the House of Commons, appears to make sweeping decisions about taxation. By contrast, political inertia hypothesizes that whatever decisions the Chancellor makes they will have little effect upon total revenue: he inherits a commitment to raise nearly 150 billion pounds in total revenue, and it would be political suicide to repudiate the spending programmes that mandate this commitment. The most that a Chancellor can do is engage in fringe tuning.

The decisions of the Chancellor can be viewed in two very different time perspectives. Immediately, the most important decisions concern the next budget. A Chancellor has a unique degree of personal responsibility for what the budget contains; therefore, a host of pressures are directed at him from the Cabinet, Parliament, and by organized interest groups. A

Chancellor's political status will rise or fall according to the way his annual budget is viewed. Given the frequent reshuffling of officeholders in Britain, a Chancellor lives with the prospect that the current budget may be his last.

While Chancellors come and go, government remains. In this book, the most important questions concern the *cumulative* effect of the decisions of successive Chancellors. Do changes in taxation tend to be in the same direction, thus reinforcing each other, or do the actions of successive Chancellors move in opposite directions, thus cancelling out? To taxpayers and to the fisc, it is important whether the actions of one Chancellor accentuate what has gone before or, alternatively, whether the money that a Chancellor gives away by tax cuts in one budget is taken back in the next.

The politician's desire to cut taxes and the government's need to raise revenue can both be met. This will occur if the forces of inertia increase the base of the revenue by so much that this offsets the revenue lost by the Chancellor trimming taxes at the margin. The Chancellor can then get the political credit for making reductions in the rate or base of some taxes, while the fisc, due to the effects of inflation and economic growth, gets the money it needs to satisfy the great identity of the budget.

The political institutions of Britain permit very precise answers to questions about the importance or unimportance of annual budget decisions, for the Chancellor is centrally responsible for decisions about changing taxes, and the Treasury publishes detailed figures of the impact upon revenue of each decision. The first section of this chapter describes the institutional setting within which the Chancellor makes decisions. The second section analyses the annual impact of these decisions upon public revenue. Since the budget is an expression of political strategy, its impact upon political popularity must be examined too. The concluding section reports the cumulative impact upon revenue of all the decisions that a party makes during its term of office; this impact is compared in size against sums raised by the force of political inertia.

The View from 11 Downing Street

The formal answer to the question – who decides about taxes? – is simple but opaque: the government. But what, or who, is the government? In Britain, this question permits a much clearer answer than in the United States, where authority is very fragmented. The government is effectively the Prime Minister and Cabinet, acting as the executive committee of the party with a majority of seats in the House of Commons.

Immediately, the decisions of the Chancellor are about tax legislation rather than tax revenue. If he decides to do nothing, then officials will calculate how much will be raised by the inertia of established legislation. If he makes decisions about raising revenue, a Chancellor must introduce legislation to modify the inertia of established laws.

The Chancellor of the Exchequer is *ex officio* an important member of the Cabinet, and normally a politician of very high status in the governing party. No other minister can put tax legislation before the House of Commons, and only the government can propose an increase in taxes to Parliament. Such is the political weight of the Chancellor – and such is the secrecy that is still meant to surround tax changes – that it is virtually unknown for a Chancellor to be forced to adopt a tax measure against his will.

The Chancellor is central but not sole in the decision-making process: he is at the centre of a network in which the inner circle consists of other Treasury ministers, Treasury civil servants, Inland Revenue and Customs and Excise advisers, and any special adviser that he may choose to appoint. The outer circle includes those ministries indirectly affected by tax policy, such as social security, energy or transport, and which may be consulted on an *ad hoc* basis (Robinson and Sandford, 1983: 87ff.).

Chancellor and Prime Minister

The Chancellor of the Exchequer normally resides at Number 11 Downing Street; the location is of practical and symbolic significance. Occupying the residence next to the Prime Minister signifies that the Chancellor is very close to the head of government in authority as well as in status. Residence in

Downing Street also allows the Chancellor to discuss problems of the economy privately with the Prime Minister on a day-to-day basis.

The closeness of the Chancellor to the Prime Minister means that major decisions of the Chancellor must also be endorsed by the Prime Minister, if they are to become government decisions. Once the two have agreed, it is virtually impossible for any other member of the Cabinet to change the policy to which they are together committed (for an example, see Donoughue, 1986).

In considering taxation, the Prime Minister and Chancellor have different interests. The Prime Minister must think in terms of political imperatives: she or he is responsible for the governing party winning or losing popular support. Proposals about taxes are not only part of the Chancellor's economic policy; they are also part of the Prime Minister's political strategy. The Chancellor is more concerned with fiscal imperatives. Whether or not the Prime Minister likes it, the great identity of the budget makes it difficult to dispense with politically unpopular taxes, if they account for a significant amount of revenue. The Chancellor's political strategy is not identical to that of the party leader, for the Chancellor, as an ambitious politician, may think about becoming Prime Minister in the future.

Dialogues between 10 and 11 Downing Street involve a process of mutual education. A Prime Minister's job is to demonstrate 'won't power', that is, to remind the Chancellor about political constraints, vetoing proposals that risk losing political popularity, whatever their technical merits. For example, Mrs Thatcher has vetoed the idea of making changes in tax relief for mortgage payments, changes that would invite criticism from electorally strategic home-owners. A Chancellor's job is to educate the Prime Minister about fiscal realities. Since the Prime Minister's political strategy normally is designed to have the economy booming in the months prior to a general election, the views of the Chancellor, as the minister immediately responsible for managing the economy, cannot be ignored – nor can Treasury judgements about the economic consequences of politically motivated actions.

Notwithstanding the importance of the economy, first-hand experience of the Chancellor's job is not necessary in a Prime Minister. Of nine postwar Prime Ministers, only two had

151

previously been a Chancellor of the Exchequer, Harold Macmillan briefly, and James Callaghan, unhappily responsible for devaluation in 1967. By contrast, four of the nine postwar Prime Ministers have previously been Foreign Secretary.[1] Moreover, the ambitions of a Chancellor to move from 11 to 10 Downing Street are usually frustrated; only two of sixteen postwar Chancellors have moved that distance.

Within the Treasury

Because the Chancellor's position is central, he is constantly bombarded with demands to act on many different fronts. The Chancellor is concerned with the whole of the British economy, for what happens in the private sector affects the budget, and decisions about the budget affect the private sector. As Britain's position in an open international economy is a continuing source of vulnerability, the Chancellor is also much concerned with international economic trends, where Britain is more often a taker than a maker of events. The Chancellor spends a substantial portion of each year at meetings abroad, or dealing with foreign officials who come to London. Overload is part of the Chancellor's job description.

In order to deal with this multitude of responsibilities, a Chancellor has a large team of ministers. Currently, these include a chief secretary, who is also a Cabinet minister, a financial secretary, an economic secretary, and a minister of state. The Treasury also has a disproportionate number of the ablest recruits to the civil service. The complexity of the Treasury's work is indicated by the number and importance of the divisions into which it is divided: economic assessments and forecasting; macro-economic policy; overseas finance; public expenditure; civil service pay; financial management in the public services; and public finance. Fiscal policy is but one of three units within the public-finance division of the Treasury, alongside home finance, and an international-finance unit. The Under-Secretary in charge of the Fiscal Policy Group is one of dozens of Under-Secretaries seeking the attention of the Chancellor.

In considering tax measures, the Chancellor is both helped and constrained by the fact that the principal revenue-collecting institutions of government are detached or semi-detached from the Treasury. Separate Boards of Inland Revenue and of Customs and Excise and the local administration of rates relieve the Treasury of the very great administrative burden of collecting taxation. Separation of revenue collection from daily supervision by politicians also reduces allegations of political interference or corruption in tax administration. A Chancellor benefits politically by being able to avoid blame for collecting taxes, or making rulings in difficult individual cases.

However, the bifurcation distances the Chancellor from officials whose knowledge of the tax system is based upon first-hand experience of tax administration. While Treasury officials tend to view taxation in terms of its theoretical implications for the economy as a whole, the revenue boards have the expertise for evaluating taxes in practice. Because the Inland Revenue and the Customs and Excise are deeply involved in the day-to-day task of tax collection, these officials may be insensitive to the broader political and economic priorities of concern in Downing Street. The difference in perspective between the two institutions – differences exacerbated in local government by independently elected councils – can place the Treasury at loggerheads with those who collect revenue.

While tax decisions of the Chancellor are significant, they must be taken within the context of the Chancellor's overall economic responsibilities. The Chancellor's decisions about taxation must be made within a short- and longer-term financial strategy. The budget represents the inertia force of taxing and spending commitments as well as involving marginal decisions. If total spending and revenue are not equal, as the great identity requires, a judgement is required about the best way to cover the resulting gap. Raising taxes or cutting expenditure are but two options. On macro-economic policy grounds a higher level of borrowing may be recommended. A variety of creative accounting practices are also possible.

The budget cycle starts after Easter in one year and concludes before Easter in the next (see Lipsey, 1983; Harris, 1985). In the first stage, the Treasury is responsible for preparing the autumn forecast about the likely state of the economy in the financial year starting in the following spring (cf. Cm. 14, 1986). The forecast of the overall state of the economy is central. From this can be calculated the effect of political inertia – that is, what tax revenue

153

and public expenditure would be if no change is made in existing laws and spending commitments. From these figures the Chancellor can get a sense of the problems to be addressed in the budget. Macro-economic concerns with economic growth, inflation, unemployment or public-sector borrowing are usually central issues of the budget. Changes in taxation, and especially the total amount of tax revenue, are usually regarded as means to the end of realizing a larger economic and political strategy (cf. Harris, 1985).

Concurrently, the Prime Minister is getting signals from autumn party conferences and monthly opinion polls. If the trends are against the government, then the Prime Minister will want the Chancellor to bring in a 'happy' budget. But insofar as economic difficulties are the cause of the government's unpopularity, then the Treasury's economic forecasts are likely to emphasize unpopular measures, including tax increases. In such circumstances, the Chancellor is likely to emphasize the need to get the economy right as a precondition to a political recovery. If the Prime Minister is secure, then an unpopular budget can be introduced in one year in order to provide a popular budget before the next election. But if a Prime Minister is nervous about maintaining office and an election is imminent, then 10 Downing Street will put pressure on 11 Downing Street to make political rather than economic calculations central to the budget.

In a good year, the initial budget forecast will allow some scope for increasing public expenditure, reducing taxes, or both. In a bad year, the economic prospects will point to cuts in public spending and to tax increases. Whatever the economic forecast, a dozen Cabinet ministers will put forward proposals to increase spending above the forecast total. The Chief Secretary of the Treasury acts as the Chancellor's deputy in dealing with negotiations with spending ministers (Barnett, 1982; Pliatzky, 1982). Since spending ministers have no responsibility for taxation, it is in their interest to avoid saying how their proposals are to be financed.

The Chancellor is most of all concerned with the total increase in spending, for this affects the need to raise taxes, or the scope for tax cuts. The Chancellor is only concerned with details of battles about particular budget items insofar as they relate to winning his war to prevent total expenditure from forcing tax increases deemed harmful to the economy and disastrous to his own political career. As part of the battle to contain public expenditure, the Chancellor emphasizes a general need to prevent a politically unacceptable increase in taxation. The definition of what is unacceptable is a matter of art, not science. It can be argued that any increase in taxation will stimulate political criticism. But it can also be argued that a failure to increase spending on desirable programmes will attract criticism.

From January until the budget, the Chancellor is continuously subject to lobbying about the budget from many quarters. A Schedule of Representations is drawn up to enumerate the 400 or more proposals requiring decisions (Lipsey, 1983). The vast number of representations emphasizes the variety of pressures upon the budget, as well as the small size of many concerns. Pressure groups may defer to the Chancellor's authority to determine principles of taxation, and seek to advise on matters of implementation and administration, where employers and other organizations collecting large sums on behalf of the fisc will have both knowledge and interest. The Chancellor may use consultations or public speeches to float trial balloons about taxation, in order to gauge the extent of support and opposition to ideas. Consultations also allow the Chancellor to lobby pressure groups to support government proposals (Robinson and Sandford, 1983: ch. 7).

Attempts made by a host of pressure groups to influence the Chancellor's decisions often cancel each other out, for the Confederation of British Industries and the Trades Union Congress have different interests to protect when the question at issue is: who pays? Economists' comments sometime concentrate upon the macro-economic impact of taxes: will they make the economy work better or not? This question is immediately relevant to the Chancellor's concern with growth in the base for future tax revenue, as well as relevant to the Prime Minister's overall electoral strategy. Questions about the notional fairness of the distribution of the tax burden are not relevant to the Chancellor's revenue concerns. Insofar as such points are politically relevant, they are matters to be resolved by political evaluations.

The submissions of the Inland Revenue and the Customs and Excise are privileged. They calculate the likely revenue to be derived by inertia, and the revenue gained or lost by changing taxes at the margin. These institutions are the chief source of expert advice on tax matters. The responsibility of the Boards for collecting taxes gives their views particular weight, especially on such matters as the ease of administration of a tax, or whether a proposal to change the tax law will make administration and compliance worse.

Some spending departments have an interest in particular aspects of taxation. For example, the Department of Transport administers the motor vehicle excise duty, and is concerned with its relation to transport policy. Because of the interaction between taxes and social security benefits, there are discussions between the Treasury, the Inland Revenue and the Department of Health and Social Security about tax decisions that affect social security beneficiaries, such as the point at which persons become subject to income tax while also in receipt of cash-transfer income supplements.

On the spending side the Chancellor is bound by agreements reached in bilateral negotiations with other ministers collectively endorsed by the Cabinet. But on matters of taxation, the continued insistence upon secrecy concerning tax changes (and the fear of a political reaction against budget leaks) excludes Cabinet colleagues as well as the public from the making of tax changes that appear in the budget. The words of an economic journalist about budget-making are particularly apt as a description of decisions about taxation:

> Senior Treasury people spend their weeks in purdah, working long hours and passing their lunchtimes together to provide each other with alibis in case of leaks. Those out of the know operate less efficiently, out of ignorance. The Treasury's relationship with other departments, never warm, cools to sub-zero temperatures as the budget approaches. (Hogg, 1985)

Given a majority in Parliament for the governing party, whatever decisions the Chancellor announces in his budget speech are almost certain of adoption. Many tax increases take effect immediately, such as changes in excise duties on petrol, tobacco and drink. More complex changes, for example in corporation tax or capital transfer tax, may not take effect at once, or may be deliberated upon at length in Parliament before the new Act or clauses can be in effect. The Chancellor's power to make *effective* decisions contrasts with that of the American President, whose tax proposals to Congress are only the start of a lengthy negotiating process from which the President never gets all that he asks.

Immediate Impact on Tax Revenue

The Chancellor must always be concerned with the annual impact of his budget, because it could be his last. The average postwar Chancellor is in office for about two-and-a-half years. Given the frequency of reshuffles in Britain, the prospect of changing jobs (or losing his seat in Cabinet) is ever-present.

In his first year in office, a Chancellor spends a large amount of time learning about the complexities of working in an open international economy, the institutions and personalities involved in his work and the attempts made to influence his actions, the vulnerability of plans to unexpected events, and the alternatives about which he can decide, each with some advantages and disadvantages. The overriding issues of concern are likely to be a few central and often volatile things, such as the economic growth rate, interest rates, inflation, balance of payments problems and unemployment. Because taxation is largely determined by the force of inertia, it does not produce the same urgent pressure for decisions. Nor is taxation a major issue for discussion in the many meetings that the Chancellor will have with foreign governments jointly concerned with the state of the international economy.

In his second year, a Chancellor will have more time to come to grips with tax problems, because many features of the budget process will now be familiar. If the opportunity of the first budget is used to introduce a dramatic political initiative, the second budget may then be left to consolidate matters by fringe tuning. At this time a Chancellor will be thinking more about his political future, which depends upon the proximity of a general election, and upon the chances of moving from the Treasury to the Foreign Office, to 10 Downing Street, or to be sacked by the electorate

157

or the Prime Minister (cf. Rose, 1987: ch. 4). Insecurity remains even if a Chancellor has four years in office.

While political constraints and incentives are constant, economic conditions are variable, and political perceptions of what is economically practicable further increase variability. A Chancellor who takes office when the economy is booming faces the politically desirable prospect of being able to approve increased public expenditure *and* cuts in tax rates, for in a booming economy lower tax rates can produce more revenue. But a Chancellor who takes office in a recession faces demands for increased public expenditure when tax revenue is not rising at so fast a rate.

The number of tax changes can be greatly increased insofar as a revenue-neutral approach is employed, offsetting increases by decreases. But insofar as political objections are greater to decisions that increase taxes than is approval for the benefits of reducing established taxes, such decisions will *not* be politically neutral. The concept of fringe tuning postulates an inverse law of tax reform: the less the impact of a change upon total revenue, the easier it is for a Chancellor to make a decision.

In examining the impact of the Chancellor's decisions, the starting point is the Treasury's estimate of the effect upon revenue of a particular change in the tax law. These figures are initially prepared for internal use when budget proposals are under consideration; they are a necessary part of the budget calculus. They are published among the documents issued by the Treasury on the day of the Chancellor's budget speech.

Fringe Tuning or Decisions with a Big Impact?

The fringe tuning hypothesis is that the decisions of a Chancellor have little impact upon the amount of tax revenue that government raises in a year. The proportion of total revenue affected by changes in tax legislation should therefore be far less than the proportion that is raised by laws continuing by the force of inertia. Alternatively, if a Chancellor makes a big impact upon taxation through his budget decisions, then a large portion of annual revenue should be determined by these changes. This view is consistent with much journalistic writing about the budget, and with the image that a Chancellor often projects about

158

his responsibility. These competing hypotheses can be tested by examining the value in the next full tax year of the changes announced in each budget since 1953.

1) *The Chancellor's decisions have a very limited impact upon gross tax revenue.* When the Chancellor announces a billion pounds or more of changes in his annual budget speech, this may seem like a large amount of money to an individual, but it is only a very small percentage of the total budget. When total spending is over £140b, changes can only impact the central structure of taxation if they involve more than 10 per cent of revenue. But decisions are not made on so big a scale.

When the impacts on revenue of all the Chancellor's annual budget decisions are added together, the gross total is marginal. The sum of annual changes averages 4.5 per cent of total tax revenue (Table 7.1). Only once, in the 1979 budget that swapped a big cut in income tax for a big boost in VAT, did changes exceed 10 per cent. If the effect of the Chancellor claiming credit for tax cuts by adjusting allowances to take account of inflation is allowed for, the impact of his decisions upon the budget is even less.[2]

In the postwar era policy-makers have been much readier to view changes in taxation not only as an end in themselves, but also as a means to the end of overall economic policy goals. This implies that the scale of tax change should be increasing as governments have been under increasing pressure to improve Britain's generally disappointing economic performance. But this has done little to increase marginal changes in the budget. When figures for the percentage of taxation subject to gross change are plotted, there is only a slight upward trend; it averages little more than 0.5 per cent in the life of an average Parliament. Moreover, there are substantial fluctuations down as well as up in the gross marginal changes that the Chancellor decides.[3]

2) *The Chancellor's choices have an even more limited impact upon net tax revenue.* In a budget speech, a Chancellor announces many decisions; hence, he can both raise *and* lower revenue from particular taxes. There are good political reasons for giving away some money in tax reductions to court popularity, and imposing some tax increases to replace revenue lost through tax reductions. If Peter is robbed to pay Paul, then at least Paul may be pleased. The recirculation of tax liabilities through increasing and

Table 7.1 Revenue Impact of the Chancellor's Decisions

Year[a]	Increase £m	Decrease £m	Gross £m	%	Net £m	%
1953	-	288	288	5.6	-288	-5.6
1954	14	2	16	0.3	12	0.2
1955	123	156	279	4.9	-33	-0.6
1956	58	50	108	1.8	8	0.1
1957	25	121	147	2.3	-87	-1.4
1958	4	112	116	1.7	-108	-1.6
1959	-	359	359	5.1	-359	-5.1
1960	105	33	138	1.9	72	1.0
1961	157	100	257	3.2	58	0.7
1962	227	217	444	5.0	9	0.1
1963	15	572	587	6.5	-557	-6.2
1964	126	10	137	1.4	116	1.2
1964	415	75	490	5.0	340	3.5
1965	373	150	523	4.8	223	2.0
1966	361	3	364	3.0	358	3.0
1967	8	20	28	0.2	-12	-0.1
1968	926	3	930	6.1	923	6.1
1969	414	69	345	2.0	345	2.0
1970	11	228	239	1.3	-213	-1.1
1970	-	440	440	2.3	-440	-2.3
1971	8	684	693	3.4	-676	-3.3
1972	-	1,814	1,814	8.4	-1,814	-8.4
1973	120	190	310	1.3	-70	-0.3
1974	2,081	684	2,765	9.2	1,397	4.7
1974	243	1,109	1,352	4.5	-866	-2.9
1975	2,023	554	2,577	6.7	1,469	3.8
1976	793	1,765	2,560	5.7	-970	-2.2
1977	811	2,375	3,183	6.3	-1,564	-3.1
1978	25	2,610	2,635	4.7	-2,585	-4.6
1979	5,050	4,624	9,674	14.4	406	0.6
1980	2,338	3,105	5,443	6.6	-767	-0.9
1981	3,310	649	3,959	4.1	2,661	2.7
1982	1,192	4,675	5,867	5.5	-3,483	-3.3
1983	662	3,465	4,127	3.6	-2,803	-2.4
1984	3,441	5,717	9,158	7.4	-2,276	-1.8
1985	1,321	2,897	4,318	3.2	-1,476	-1.2
1986	1,280	3,160	4,440	n.a.	-1,880	n.a.
1987	340	3,230	3,570	n.a.	-2,890	n.a.
Mean				4.5		-2.4

a. In three years a general election resulted in two budgets being introduced, each by a different party.

decreasing taxes is a form of churning, that is, stirring up the tax system by movements in opposite directions. In only four years since 1953 have budgets failed to include both increases and decreases in taxation; the last time a budget contained no increases to offset cuts was 1972.

Because the budget normally includes both tax reductions and tax increases, the net revenue impact of a Chancellor's decisions will necessarily be less than the gross impact. On average, the net impact of the Chancellor's decisions is 2.4 per cent, and it has not exceeded 5 per cent since 1972. The impact is relatively low whether the net effect in a year is to raise taxes (average, 1.8 per cent) or to reduce taxes (average, 2.8 per cent). Notwithstanding the Treasury's increasing need for revenue to finance the growth of government, there is *no* upward trend in the net revenue impact of the Chancellor's decisions. The changes that a Chancellor introduces in the 1980s affect much the same proportion of revenue as changes introduced two or three decades ago.[4] Short-term economic influences rather than long-term trends in government appear to influence the size of the marginal changes that a Chancellor can introduce in a given year.

3) *The inertia of established tax laws accounts for 97.9 per cent of revenue in the average year.* The Chancellor's budget speech and the publicity that surrounds it focuses on what is new. This is politically understandable, for change is likely to generate controversy. But in the course of a year, old taxes account for the overwhelming proportion of annual revenue. In any given year, the actual amount of money raised by taxation is the sum of the revenue impact of the year's changes in the rates and bases of existing taxes and of new taxes, plus the revenue raised by established taxes that have continued in effect by the force of inertia.

The inertia of established tax laws is consistently important. In every year examined, inertia accounted for more than 90 per cent of all revenue, and in five-sixths of budgets inertia accounts for more than 95 per cent of revenue. In three years – 1953, 1959 and 1970 – established laws accounted for 100 per cent of tax revenue, for no tax increases were introduced. Whatever the political intentions, the personality or the economic circumstances of the Chancellor of the day, the decisions he makes about taxation only affect revenue at the margin. In a

161

Table 7.2 Inertia of Established Laws the Principal Source of Revenue

Year	Total Revenue £m	Revenue from Tax Increases £m	Inertia of Established Taxes £m	%
1953	5,174	-	5,174	100.0
1954	5,357	14	5,343	99.7
1955	5,746	123	5,623	97.9
1956	5,995	58	5,937	99.0
1957	6,406	25	6,380	99.6
1958	6,801	4	6,797	99.9
1959	7,062	-	7,062	100.0
1960	7,260	105	7,155	98.6
1961	8,080	157	7,922	98.1
1962	8,796	227	8,569	97.4
1963	9,022	15	9,007	99.8
1964	9,715	541	9,174	94.4
1965	11,007	373	10,634	96.6
1966	12,131	361	11,770	97.0
1967	13,509	8	13,501	99.9
1968	15,140	926	14,213	93.9
1969	16,960	414	16,546	97.6
1970	19,104	11	19,093	99.9
1971	20,256	8	20,248	99.9
1972	21,476	-	21,476	100.0
1973	24,085	120	23,965	99.5
1974	30,027	2,324	27,703	92.3
1975	38,506	2,023	36,483	94.7
1976	44,628	795	43,833	98.2
1977	50,761	811	49,950	98.4
1978	56,376	25	56,351	99.9
1979	67,392	5,050	62,342	92.5
1980	82,157	2,338	79,819	97.2
1981	96,910	3,310	93,600	96.6
1982	106,619	1,192	105,427	98.9
1983	114,530	662	113,868	99.4
1984	123,358	3,441	119,917	97.2
1985	134,970	1,421	135,549	98.9

given year, the additional revenue resulting from all the Chancellor's decisions accounts for only 2.1 per cent of total tax revenue.

It would be entirely possible for the government of the day to finance the next year's budget even if the Chancellor decided to make absolutely no alterations in tax legislation. If the political calculation was that no change was the most satisfactory or the least unsatisfactory alternative, then the government would continue to collect tax revenue under established laws. At the end of the year, it would have more money than otherwise, given the tendency for decisions by the Chancellor to favour a net tax reduction.

Changes Within the Fringe

While the revenue impact of a Chancellor's decisions is small, the political significance remains important – not least to the Chancellor – for it is his annual opportunity to be identified with popular or unpopular tax measures.

For any given amount of fringe tuning, a Chancellor must strike a balance on two counts. First of all there is a question about whether to use the money at hand to make a few larger changes, or many smaller changes. The greater the number of changes, the smaller the size of any one change, everything else being equal. Politically, a Chancellor may think it a good idea to spread tax cuts widely in order to gain favour from many different groups. Alternatively, a Chancellor may prefer to concentrate upon one or two measures, in order to make tax cuts more visible. For example, to deliver a 1p reduction in the rate of income tax will cost the fisc £1,450m in a full year.

Secondly, the number of changes involving tax increases or tax cuts reflects the Chancellor's calculation about whether the political impact of a tax increase is different from that of a tax cut. If all cuts are popular, then there is an incentive to make the average value of a cut less, in order to introduce more cuts. If all tax increases are unpopular, there is an incentive to introduce fewer increases, albeit each having a higher value on average.

4) *Fringe tuning has many threads.* While a fringe is a singular term, it is made up of many threads. So too, the net figure by which a Chancellor alters total taxation is made up of many small changes in taxation. An average postwar budget speech contains a number of small changes in taxes. In the decades since 1953, there have been an average of eighteen tax changes in each budget. The number of changes has been growing steadily throughout the postwar era. From 1953 to 1964, the average

budget speech contained twelve changes. From 1964 to 1973, the average budget speech contained thirteen changes, from 1974 to 1978 nineteen, and from 1979 to 1987 an average of thirty-six changes (Table 7.3).

The average value of a tax change has always been low; it is measured in tenths of 1 per cent of total tax revenue. In the three decades examined in Table 7.3 the mean tax change has been equal to 0.40 per cent of total tax revenue. The individual threads (that is, particular changes in taxes) that constitute the fringe are exceedingly thin, for the bulk of tax changes have a value less than the mean.

Moreover, the size of the average budget change has been falling. In the period when changes were fewest, 1953–63, the average tax change affected about 0.75 per cent of tax revenue. In the 1964–70 Labour government the mean value of a tax change averaged 0.56 per cent. In the Heath administration, the value fell to 0.29 per cent of revenue. As the number of tax changes has increased since 1974, so the value of the typical change has fallen further. In the 1974–9 Labour government it averaged 0.38 per cent. After 1979, when a few big changes were made in taxation, the Thatcher administration has introduced numerous tax changes of very little value, averaging 0.25 per cent of total revenue. Given the impact of a change in a major tax, such as income tax, upon the calculation of these averages, it follows that the revenue value of more than half the tax changes is smaller than the average.

In nearly every budget, some decisions of a Chancellor are about increasing revenue, while others decrease revenue. In this way both political and economic constraints can be satisfied. A Chancellor can both cut and increase a given tax simultaneously, by reducing one term and raising another. To take a simple example, in 1986 the Chancellor wanted to make changes in the stamp duty on share transactions, in order to prevent the City of London from losing business abroad. The rate of stamp duty was cut from 1 per cent to 0.5 per cent, at an estimated cost of £70m a year to the fisc. To replace this revenue, the base of the tax was broadened, so that stamp duties would be charged on transactions previously exempt, such as takeover and mergers. The broadening of the base was estimated to yield an additional £70m a year to the fisc. The pair of changes thus cancelled each other out.

Table 7.3 Number of Decisions by Chancellor and Average Value

Year	Chancellor	Number of Changes		Mean Value of Change as %Total Revenue	
		Decrease	Increase	Decrease %	Increase %
1953	Butler	7	-	0.79	-
1954	Butler	2	3	0.02	0.09
1955	Butler	8	3	3.57	7.51
1956	Macmillan	6	3	0.14	0.33
1957	Thorneycroft	8	2	0.24	0.20
1958	Amory	11	2	0.15	0.03
1959	Amory	7	-	0.73	-
1960	Amory	8	2	0.06	0.72
1961	Lloyd	6	4	0.21	0.48
1962	Lloyd	7	9	0.35	0.29
1963	Maudling	19	1	0.33	0.17
1964	Maudling	2	7	0.05	0.19
1964	Callaghan	1	3	0.77	1.42
1965	Callaghan	3	11	0.46	0.31
1966	Callaghan	2	7	0.01	0.43
1967	Callaghan	6	3	0.02	0.02
1968	Jenkins	2	16	0.01	0.38
1969	Jenkins	11	11	0.04	0.22
1970	Jenkins	8	3	0.15	0.22
1970	Barber	2	-	1.15	-
1971	Barber	16	1	0.21	0.04
1972	Barber	13	-	0.65	-
1973	Barber	6	4	0.13	0.12
1974	Healey	3	14	0.76	0.49
1974	Healey	8	3	0.46	0.27
1975	Healey	2	13	0.72	0.40
1976	Healey	15	7	0.26	0.25
1977	Healey	12	5	0.39	0.32
1978	Healey	22	2	0.21	0.02
1979	Howe	14	5	0.49	1.50
1980	Howe	24	14	0.16	0.20
1981	Howe	16	15	0.04	0.23
1982	Howe	32	10	0.14	0.11
1983	Howe	32	10	0.09	0.06
1984	Lawson	30	19	0.15	0.15
1985	Lawson	27	15	0.08	0.07
1986	Lawson	24	17	n.a.	n.a.
1987	Lawson	16	5	n.a.	n.a.

165

5) *The Chancellor usually introduces more tax cuts than tax increases*. In nine out of ten budgets, the Chancellor introduces both tax cuts and tax increases. The politically significant point is that tax cuts are usually more numerous than tax increases. Taking one year with another, the average budget contains eleven tax cuts and seven tax increases. While on balance the net effect is a reduction, most of the changes do no more than cancel each other out. The gross impact of the budget is distributed in the proportion of 59 per cent for tax cuts and 41 per cent for tax increases. In effect, the net cut in taxation is worth only one pound in six of the gross changes in the budget.

Notwithstanding arguments that can be advanced as to why tax cuts and tax increases should differ in size, the practice of Chancellors is that marginal increases and decreases are usually much the same in value. The one exception is the Thatcher government, which has consistently produced a greater number of tax cuts than increases. This preference for making tax cuts more numerous has been registered even when, as in 1979 and 1981, the overall impact of all changes was to increase taxation.

6) *Patching taxes rather than innovation or repeal*. When the Chancellor chooses to make a change in taxation, he has two choices: to introduce or repeal a tax, or to patch the existing system by changing the rate or base of an established tax. Even though the revenue impact of a new tax or a tax repeal is small, its political significance may be large. By contrast, amending a law that is already there is more likely to minimize political reaction, for no principle is challenged, as is the case with tax innovations or repeal.

In practice, Chancellors almost invariably resort to tax patching. In an average budget, 92 per cent of revenue change involves alterations in the base or rate of existing taxes. Even more striking, in more than half of all budgets, 100 per cent of the revenue changes are the result of tax patching. This is as likely to occur in the post-1974 period as in the seemingly quieter days of the 1950s. Patches are as likely to be applied to the clauses defining the tax base as to the tax rate.

The chances of radical cuts in taxes, in the sense of a tax being repealed, are slight. *In three out of four budgets a Chancellor does not repeal any tax*. Revenue reductions are normally made by changes in the rate and base of taxes. Implicit in such a strategy is the possibility of subsequently recovering revenue by putting the rate up again, or returning to a broader base. In five-sixths of all budgets, tax increases are introduced by raising the rate or base of an existing tax. It is unusual for an increase in tax revenue to be the result of the introduction of a new tax.

Immediate Impact on Political Popularity

The fact that the Chancellor's annual budget decisions have little impact upon tax revenue suggests that perhaps these decisions are not so much about fiscal matters as about politics, that is, the electoral popularity of the government of the day, and the Chancellor of the moment.

There are good theoretical and practical reasons why the Chancellor and Prime Minister should think about the views of the electorate when making decisions about budgets. Normative theories of democratic government postulate that the party winning an election ought to do what the majority of voters want; and positive theories of government may present politicians as vote-maximizing politicians, for whom taxation is electorally important.[5] The practical incentive for politicians to think about taxation is that they hold office on the basis of election victory – and will lose office if the vote at the next election goes against their party. Taxation directly or indirectly affects every citizen, and it does so visibly. Insofar as taxation is important in determining voting behaviour, then decisions about the taxing side of the budget can immediately affect the governing party, and the Chancellor's own political career.

But do decisions about taxation make a big difference to how people vote? Taxation is, after all, only one of many issues that can concern voters. Studies of voting behaviour in Britain consistently find that taxation does *not* have a significant in-fluence upon voting behaviour. One reason is that the decisions of voters are influenced by their social background, broad political principles, and judgements of the general competence of parties (Butler and Stokes, 1974: 297; Alt, 1979: 53ff., 196, 222; Rose and McAllister, 1986: ch. 7). Even when attention is concentrated upon economic issues, the things that count are unemployment, inflation and strikes, rather than promises of tax cuts (Sarlvik and Crewe, 1983: 272ff.; see also Chapter 8).

The absence of a major impact of taxation upon voters is consistent with the theory of political inertia, which posits that whatever the party in office there will be few changes in total taxation, or in the taxes levied. Doing nothing is politically safer than introducing radical changes in taxation, and this guideline is recognized by both Conservative and Labour governments. However, since electoral pressures are continuous and politicians concentrate upon gaining immediate advantage from handling issues before them, each spring the Prime Minister and Chancellor can ask themselves: how much short-term popularity can the government get from a tax-cutting budget?

Popular Perceptions of the Budget

The budget is the primary occasion each year when political attention focuses on taxation. Spending decisions have already been publicized earlier in the year, and the macro-economic features of the budget are far more difficult to communicate through the media than actions about taxation that relate to everyday circumstances, such as putting income tax up or down 1p, or adding something to the price of beer or cigarettes. On budget day, if at no other time, both the government and the electorate are encouraged to give political attention to decisions the government makes to lower or raise taxation.

Popular perceptions of the budget are documented by an unusually long series of Gallup Poll questions asked immediately after the budget since the early 1950s (*Gallup Political Index*, No. 307, 1986: 40). The Gallup Poll has produced two measures of popular assessment, one about the fairness of the budget, and the other an evaluation of the performance of the Chancellor.

While popular perceptions of the budget are likely to be influenced by whether taxes are put up or down (which itself is an indication of the overall state of the economy), they are not simply determined by the size of tax cuts or increases. The art of politics is to make small tax cuts appear prominent, for example by making easily publicized changes, and to keep increases in taxation in the shadows. Insofar as the Chancellor is successful in doing this, then the image will differ somewhat from the reality.

168

Asking voters about the fairness of the budget allows individuals to make an on balance judgement about everything in the budget. This is realistic, for most voters do not learn about the budget by studying the pages of details published in the *Financial Times*. They learn about it from the evening television news, or by seeing headlines in the *Sun* or the *Mirror*. When the Gallup Poll asks voters immediately after the budget whether it is considered fair, on most occasions most voters say they think the budget is fair.[6] But the response can vary greatly, according to the terms of a particular budget (Table 7.4). The most popular budget was in 1978: 68 per cent considered it fair. This budget, which was viewed by the Chancellor as a prelude to an autumn 1978 election, cut taxation by 4.6 per cent. The budget regarded as least fair was that of the Conservatives in 1981, which put up taxes by 2.7 per cent; only 22 per cent thought it fair.

Judgements of whether the Chancellor is doing a good or bad job are strongly correlated (0.83) with judgements about the fairness of the budget. Nine out of ten times the Gallup Poll reports that most voters think the Chancellor is doing a good job. The only budgets that have produced a negative majority were Nigel Lawson's 1985 proposals, the 1981 budget of Sir Geoffrey Howe, and Denis Healey's 1977 budget. On average, 49 per cent voice approval of how the Chancellor is doing his job, as against 29 per cent saying he is doing a bad job. Since the overall rating of a Chancellor can be influenced by personality and other economic matters,[7] this analysis will concentrate upon the relation between the budget's fairness and electoral popularity, the measures that affect everyone in office, starting with the Prime Minister.

The simple materialist hypothesis is that if the government cuts taxes its popular support will rise, and if it raises taxes its support will fall. Data is readily available on both counts. The net impact of the budget upon taxation is given in Table 7.1. The change in support for the governing party in the Gallup Poll shortly before and after the budget indicates its impact upon the popularity of the government.

A 'good' budget – that is, a tax-cutting budget – helps the popularity of the governing party – but not by much. While there is a correlation between tax cuts and a rise in popular support (r= 0.28), it is not statistically significant. Only 8 per cent of the

169

Table 7.4   Popular Evaluation of the Budget

Year Chancellor (Net %Tax Change)	Rating Chancellor as Good %	Rating Fair %	Budget: Not Fair %	Change in Party Support %
1953 Butler (-5.6)	63	50	37	2.8
1954 Butler (0.2)	53	n.a.	n.a.	-0.2
1955 Butler (-0.6)	57	50	32	3.0
1956 Macmillan (0.1)	42	43	43	-1.7
1957 Thorneycroft (-1.4)	50	42	40	-0.6
1958 Amory (-1.6)	n.a.	62	23	-0.8
1959 Amory (-5.1)	58	59	34	0.2
1960 Amory (1.0)	43	41	47	-1.7
1961 Lloyd (0.7)	36	33	51	-0.5
1962 Lloyd (0.1)	42	48	34	-6.2
1963 Maudling (-6.2)	59	59	24	0.0
1964 Maudling (1.2)	47	41	48	0.5
1964 Callaghan (3.5)	48	56	33	1.4
1965 Callaghan (2.0)	48	51	34	-1.5
1966 Callaghan (3.0)	61	60	24	0.8
1967 Callaghan (-0.1)	51	56	23	-4.7
1968 Jenkins (6.1)	41	43	47	-4.2
1969 Jenkins (2.0)	49	59	32	-0.3
1970 Jenkins (-1.1)	61	66	24	6.0
1971 Barber (-3.3)	56	61	29	-1.3
1972 Barber (-8.4)	57	64	27	1.5
1973 Barber (-0.3)	57	55	34	0.2
1974 Healey (4.7)	43	56	32	7.0
1974 Healey (-2.9)	53	59	27	6.8
1975 Healey (3.8)	44	51	37	-2.8
1976 Healey (-2.2)	60	63	23	1.3
1977 Healey (-3.1)	38	36	54	1.0
1978 Healey (-4.6)	57	68	24	3.0
1979 Howe (0.6)	38	44	49	-6.7
1980 Howe (-0.9)	51	57	36	1.8
1981 Howe (2.7)	24	22	73	-4.0
1982 Howe (-3.3)	49	56	38	8.8
1983 Howe (-2.4)	51	33	39	0.2
1984 Lawson (-1.8)	57	60	36	-2.2
1985 Lawson (-1.2)	33	41	51	-5.3
1986 Lawson (n.a.)	43	49	44	-1.0
1987 Lawson (n.a.)	50	49	37	n.a.

Source: Gallup Political Index and Table 7.1.

variance in party support before and after the budget is explained by the direction and size of tax changes.[8]

Calculating regression coefficients shows that for every 1 per cent net cut or increase in taxation, the popularity of the governing party goes up or down by only 0.26 per cent. In other words, a tax cut of £1.3b would not visibly alter a party's support in the opinion polls. On the basis of these statistics, the governing party would need to cut taxes by more than £5b in order to achieve a 1 per cent boost in the immediate post-budget opinion polls. Equally important, a budget that increases taxes does not cause the government to lose much support. A 2 per cent increase in taxes would be likely to reduce further the government's popular support by only 0.5 per cent.

The governing party does not see its vote go up or down according to budget-day tax decisions because they reflect economic conditions that have *already* made an impact upon public opinion. A government is only in a good position to introduce tax cuts when economic conditions look favourable. The evidence of this will not only affect the Chancellor's outlook but also the governing party's standing in the opinion polls in the months *before* the budget. A Chancellor forced to introduce tax increases will be in charge of an economy that has already eroded popular support for the government. For example, the Conservatives had already dropped 10 points in the Gallup Poll in the six months before Sir Geoffrey Howe introduced his unpopular 1981 budget increasing taxes, and had begun to see their support rise prior to the 1982 tax-cutting budget. Similarly, Labour had begun falling in the Gallup Poll before Denis Healey introduced a big net tax increase in his 1975 budget, and Labour had recovered 10 points in the Gallup Poll before Healey introduced big tax cuts in his 1978 budget.

The interconnection between attitudes toward the budget and other opinions is also shown by the correlation between party support and views about the fairness of the budget. The relationship is positive (0.42) and statistically significant. But the direction of causation is moot. The most realistic interpretation is that Conservatives are predisposed to regard the budget of a Conservative Chancellor as fair, and Labour voters to regard a Labour Chancellor's budget as fair. Yet even here there are severe limits in gaining political advantage. Prior to the 1987

171

budget, the Gallup Poll asked voters whether tax cuts would make them more likely to vote Conservative. Among those expecting taxes to be cut, 83 per cent said this would make no difference to their vote, and the few who claimed it would were but a minority of Conservative supporters (*Gallup Political Index* No. 317, 1987).

While the Chancellor's budget decisions determine changes in taxation in the year ahead, they do not determine the popularity of the governing party. The Chancellor's responsibility for managing the economy does give him an indirect influence upon the popularity of the government, but only so far as he can succeed in promoting favourable economic conditions on a year-round basis. But this goal is not unique to the Chancellor, nor are the Chancellor's fiscal decisions of sole importance.

Cumulative Impact

Annual budgets have a cumulative impact. A Chancellor who decided to change taxes in the same direction for several years running, and even more a governing party that did the same throughout a Parliament, could cumulatively make a substantial impact upon the national tax system, multiplying by four or five the effect of a single year's change. What seems small in a single year could cumulatively become large – insofar as there is consistency from year to year in the decisions of a particular Chancellor or governing party.

Insofar as the force of inertia and fluctuating economic events dictate the terms of the budget, the Chancellor of the moment and the government of the day will find that the decisions they make tend to be cumulatively inconsistent. As the world economy changes, or simply as domestic political priorities change, a Chancellor might accept there was justification for *ad hoc* decisions without regard to previous actions. The theory of disjointed incrementalism emphasizes that this is likely. The cumulative consequence of frequent reversals would be little change in tax revenue in the longer run. Instead of a steady trend, the net effect would be churning, that is, a great deal of motion created by Chancellors going around in circles of tax increases and cuts, in *ad hoc* response to changing circumstances.

How Much Difference Do Parties Make?

Although the Chancellor of the day has the immediate responsibility for making choices about taxation, he does so as an agent of the government. The appointment of the Chancellor rests with the Prime Minister, and a Chancellor is sustained in office by maintaining the confidence of the Prime Minister, and of the governing party. The crucial distinction between budgets is not the name of the Chancellor, but of the party in power. Insofar as parties make a difference, then it would be expected that a Conservative government would change taxation in one direction, and a Labour government in the opposite. But insofar as there is 'something stronger than parties', there should be little difference in the direction of tax changes in a Conservative or Labour government (cf. Rose, 1984a; Castles, 1982).

The evidence shows, however, that 97.9 per cent of tax revenue is determined by something stronger than parties, the force of political inertia (Table 7.2). The inheritance of past legislation, the constraints of the great identity, and the desire to maximize political benefits while minimizing costs lead Labour and Conservative politicians to continue acting in much the same manner as their predecessors. Activities at the margin of government revenue-raising can nonetheless be significant to political parties, for reasons of internal party politics (evidence of Socialist or Conservative principles), or as a means of cultivating a distinctive electoral appeal. The need for a party to appear marginally different, if only to avoid a continuous circulation of floating voters between all parties, supports the idea that insofar as tax changes are concerned, the party in office should make a big difference to such decisions as are actually made.

Notwithstanding areas of agreement, the Conservative and Labour parties through the years have differed in their attitudes toward taxing and spending. The Conservatives have tended to favour lower taxes, even if this requires spending less on popular programmes, whereas Labour has tended to favour spending more on popular programmes, even if this means higher taxes. The implications for the annual budget are clear. Conservative Chancellors should be more likely to cut taxes, and Labour Chancellors to increase taxes.

But party ideology is not the only influence upon party

politicians, or necessarily the most important influence. Everything else being equal, political leaders favour cutting taxes rather than raising them. Insofar as conditions are not equal, this could be the result of changes in the economic climate rather than in the party in office. When the economy was booming then the government of the day, whatever its party, would cut taxes, and when there were economic difficulties, particularly the inflation that marked the post-1973 recession, then taxes would not be cut, or might even be increased.

The potential for partisan differences in taxation can here be tested in five different terms of office, each long enough to show internal consistency in a party's record, as well as differences between parties:[9]

1957–64: Conservative government. Macmillan and Douglas-Home, Prime Ministers; Thorneycroft, Amory, Lloyd and Maudling, Chancellors.

1964–70: Labour government. Wilson, Prime Minister; Callaghan and Jenkins, Chancellors.

1970–3: Conservative government. Heath, Prime Minister. Anthony Barber, Chancellor.

1974–9: Labour government. Wilson and Callaghan, Prime Ministers. Healey, Chancellor.

1979–84: Conservative government. Thatcher, Prime Minister. Howe and Lawson, Chancellors.

When the budgets of Conservative and Labour governments are compared in the direction and cumulative effect upon revenue, there are both similarities and differences – albeit the differences are not always along party lines. Four out of five governments have more often introduced a budget that cut taxes than one that increased taxes (Table 7.5). This is consistent with the hypothesis that politicians, regardless of party, prefer to be identified with decreasing rather than increasing taxation. The exception was the Labour government of 1964–70. In introducing measures that resulted in a net tax increase, the first Wilson government not only differed from its Conservative predecessor and successors, but also from the 1974–9 Labour government. Since 1974, the Labour and Conservative governments have each had a similar record, in some

174

Table 7.5 Impact of Budget Decisions on Taxes by Party

Party in Office	Total Tax Changes		Cumulative Change as % Total Revenue (per budget)		Churning as % Gross Change[a]
	Up	Down			
Conservative, 1957–64	4	4	-11.3	(-1.4)	57
Labour, 1964–70	5	2	15.4	(2.2)	44
Conservative, 1970–4	0	4	-14.3	(-3.6)	7
Labour, 1974–9	2	4	-4.3	(-0.7)	88
Conservative, 1979–85	2	5	-6.3	(-0.9)	86

a. Churning: % of gross revenue change not included in cumulative revenue change.
Source: Derived from Table 7.1.

years being forced to defend net tax increases, but in most years claiming credit for tax cuts.

When the overall direction of a party's budget decisions is analysed for the whole of its period in office, four out of five governments showed a pattern of cumulative tax cuts. The 1964 Labour government again is egregious, having a cumulative pattern of tax increases. The capacity of a governing party to introduce tax cuts has, however, been substantially diminished by the downturn in the economy since 1974. In the Macmillan government, net tax cuts could be introduced at the rate of 1.4 per cent a year. In the Heath government the absence of indexation and inflation made claims to cut easier; they were announced at the rate of 3.6 per cent a year. But after the economic troubles of the mid-1970s, the 1974 Labour government could only claim credit for cuts at the rate of 0.7 per cent a year, and the Thatcher government has done little better (Table 7.5).

The irony of the Chancellor's decisions is that while budgets since 1974 announce more and more tax cuts, the net effect of this has become less and less. Most of the changes announced since then have been part of a process of churning, in which tax increases cancel out tax cuts, and vice versa, within a party's term of office. From 1957 to 1970 only half of decisions altering revenue were part of a churning process, and in the Heath government, only 7 per cent. Since 1974, five-sixths of all the revenue changes

175

announced in budget speeches have had the effect of cancelling each other out.

The great increase in churning since 1974 is consistent with the greater volatility in the international economy, and greater difficulties in managing the British economy, as growth has been less (and sometimes negative), inflation has accelerated and decelerated rapidly, and the exchange value of the pound has fluctuated greatly too. The greater the scale of volatile changes in other parts of the economy, the greater the pressures for the Chancellor to make tax changes that appear inconsistent, if only because they are responding to changing circumstances.

The significance of churning can be illustrated by comparing the total gross changes introduced with net change in revenue during a party's term of office (Table 7.4). In the Macmillan government, the gross changes totalled 26.1 per cent, and net changes just under half that, 11.3 per cent. In the first Wilson government, the gross change was 27.4 per cent, and the net change slightly more than half that. In the Heath government, the total gross change introduced, 15.4 per cent, was only 1.1 per cent more than the net change, emphasizing that nearly all changes involved tax reductions.

The 1974 Labour government was more inclined to introduce tax cuts than tax increases, but the size of the increases tended to cancel out cuts. While the gross impact of changes introduced by Denis Healey was equivalent to 37.1 per cent of revenue, the net impact was equal to a 4.3 per cent reduction in revenue. The experience of the Thatcher government is even more striking, for the Prime Minister and Chancellor would ideally like to do nothing but cut taxes. In fact, the great bulk of their tax cuts have been offset by tax increases; the gross impact of 44.8 per cent is thus reduced to a net revenue reduction of 6.2 per cent.

Choosing Cuts But Collecting More Money Due to Inertia

The paradox of the Chancellor's choice is that while there is a cumulative tendency for each party to introduce more cuts than increases in its term of office, simultaneously tax revenue increases. The gap between what the Chancellor proposes and how the fisc imposes taxation is shown in Figure 7.1. The dotted lower line indicates the cumulative effect of the Chancellor's decisions each year about decreasing and increasing particular taxes in the budget. If the only changes in tax revenue were those announced in the annual budget, then by the end of the 1957–64 Conservative government, total tax revenue would have fallen by 11 per cent; by the end of the Heath government by 14 per cent; by the end of the 1974 Labour government by 5 per cent, and by 1985, after six years of Thatcher in office, by 6 per cent. Only under the 1964 Labour government did the sum of decisions to increase taxes exceed tax cuts.

However, while Chancellors are claiming credit for cutting taxes, the force of inertia is pushing up tax revenue. Without any action by the Chancellor, established laws and administrative agencies will collect tens of billions in revenue. More than that, tax revenue will rise with inflation and economic growth. The increase in revenue generated by the forces of inertia is much greater than the decrease announced in the budget by the Chancellor.

The solid top line in Figure 7.1 shows how political inertia has consistently been pushing tax revenue up in each period of party government. In the 1957–64 Conservative government, the force of inertia resulted in taxes actually increasing by 50 per cent in the seven-year period. This came about because, even though tax cuts implied an 11 per cent reduction in total revenue, the gross effect of inertia was more than five times as great in the opposite direction. When decreases in the budget are subtracted from increases due to inertia, the net effect is that tax revenue rose by 50 per cent in seven years.

Atypically, the 1964–70 Labour government could actually receive credit for a portion of the total increase in tax revenue then, for Labour's budget decisions assumed that they would add 15 per cent to total revenue. But this was less than one-sixth of the total increase in revenue of 80 per cent. For every extra pound raised in consequence of announced budget decisions, the forces of inertia accounted for more than four pounds.

The Heath government was unusual in consistently introducing tax reductions in its budgets from 1970 to 1973. Notwithstanding this, total tax revenue rose by 37 per cent during the short life of the Heath administration. The force of inertia accounted for more than three times the change of revenue by conscious decisions of the Chancellor, thus arriving at a net increase of 37 per cent.

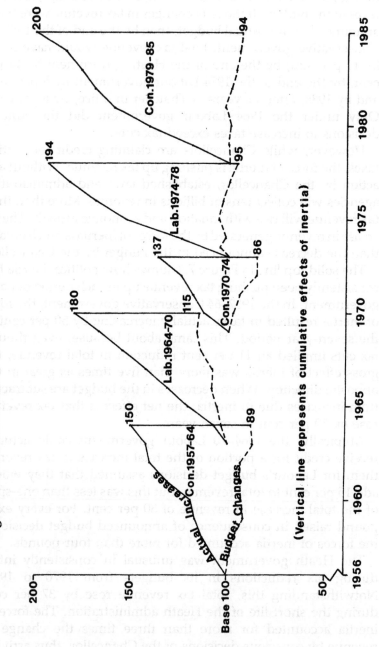

Figure 7.1 Paradox of Chancellor's cuts and cumulative tax increases

(Vertical line represents cumulative effects of inertia)

Since 1974, the world economic recession and prolonged difficulties with the British economy have increased the impact of political inertia, particularly through inflation, and further decreased the limited significance of tax cuts. Hence, the net increase in taxation under the 1974 Labour government was 94 per cent; the tax cuts of Denis Healey had very little effect against the force of inertia.

The strength of political inertia is even more evident when juxtaposed against the will of Margaret Thatcher and her Chancellors to reduce taxation. Adding together the annual impact on revenue of each budget since 1979 implies a cumulative 6 per cent reduction in taxation. By contrast, the force of political inertia has pushed up tax revenue by more than 100 per cent. As a result, the money paid by British taxpayers since Mrs Thatcher took office has more than doubled.

The *dissociation* between the Chancellor's choice and what government does is measured by the distance between the lines in Figure 7.1. Not only is political inertia far stronger than the Chancellor's decisions to cut taxes, it is growing in force, while the net impact of budget decisions during a party's term of office is becoming smaller still. As the amount of money collected in taxes goes up, the proportion of money that can be devoted to tax cuts goes down.

The public-policy model can easily explain the unimportance of the Chancellor's decisions. Tax revenue reflects the interaction of tax laws, administration and economic activity. When established laws and administration are left unchanged and the current money value of economic activity rises steadily due to the combined effects of inflation and economic growth, then tax revenue is bound to rise as well. The cuts that the Chancellor introduces in each annual budget are real, in the sense that there is a reduction in the tax rate, or a narrowing of the tax base that would, *if all other conditions remained the same*, result in a reduction in money paid in taxes. But the buoyancy of the economy means that all other conditions do *not* remain the same. Political inertia is a moving force, and it pushes tax revenue up far more than the Chancellor reduces it.

The paradoxical relationship between the Chancellor's choice and tax revenue is politically convenient . Politicians can usually be identified with doing what they like to take credit for, spending money and cutting taxes. Without any active intervention by the Chancellor, tax revenue can concurrently rise to finance the continuously rising cost of government.

Notes

1 Winston Churchill's tenure at the Treasury, 1924-9, is excluded from these calculations, as it was outside the period examined here and, as Keynes's pamphlet on *The Economic Consequences of Mr Churchill* showed, it was an obstacle to his becoming Prime Minister.
2 Double-digit inflation first became significant in the early 1970s. It was not until 1977 that there was some statutory provision for indexation of income tax allowances to prevent fiscal drag, the Rooker–Wise amendment. For all figures since 1978, the value of the tax cut by the Chancellor are *inclusive* of changes necessary to maintain inflation indexing of tax allowances.
3 When a least-squares regression line is fitted to the annual figure for gross percentage change in revenue for each budget (Table 7.1) the goodness of fit is low $r^2= .19$, as is the b value of the annual rate of change 0.14.
4 Fitting a least-squares regression line to the annual percentage net change in tax revenue (Table 7.1) shows no consistent pattern (r: .00) or direction of movement (b: .00).
5 However, the bulk of the public-choice literature concentrates upon the popular side of the budget, public expenditure. For example, only one four-page reference to taxation is indexed in Mueller's (1979: 167–70) 297-page survey. Whiteley's (1985) study of the politics of economic management in Britain contains no index references to taxation. For an exception, see Brennan and Buchanan, 1980.
6 The mean for descriptions of the budget as fair is 52 per cent; the standard deviation, 10 per cent.
7 In particular, the overall economic climate is likely to affect judgements of the Chancellor before the budget, and also his prospects for making tax cuts or being compelled to introduce increases.
8 Government support is reckoned as a three-month average of the per cent saying they would vote for the governing party. It is not a single monthly figure in order to reduce the effect of random fluctuations in survey results. The change in government support is the difference between the average for the three months before the budget and the three months after. If a monthly figure is used to test the impact of budget changes in taxation, the correlation is less, 0.13.
9 The period 1953–6 is omitted as a time of transition from Sir Winston Churchill's last years through a brief period of Sir Anthony Eden in office. Neither was interested in economic policy. Iain Macleod's name is omitted as a Conservative Chancellor in 1970 as he did not live long enough to present a budget.

CHAPTER EIGHT

The Decisions of Citizens

Taxes demonstrate the government's powers of compulsion; they are not voluntarily contributions. Laws lay down the sums that citizens *must* pay, and the procedures that *must* be followed in order for civic obligations to be met. If government depended solely upon voluntary contributions from altruistic citizens, it would not have enough money to maintain the contemporary welfare state; it could not even provide the minimal services of a nineteenth-century nightwatchman state.[1]

At the extreme, a citizen who dislikes British taxes could 'vote with his feet', emigrating to a country with lower taxes. This would rule out most European countries, where taxes are higher than in the United Kingdom, albeit post-tax income is usually higher too (cf. Table 2.2). British emigrants tend to head for old Commonwealth countries, such as Australia and Canada, or the United States. In each of these countries taxes are marginally lower than in Britain, but this is usually not the principal motive for emigrating there.

For people going into tax exile from Britain, the Channel Islands and the Isle of Man are the usual destinations. Their rates of taxation are much lower than Britain, the distance from Britain is slight, the customs are similar, and often the weather is drier and sunnier. However, the number of Britons emigrating to these tax havens is very few. The total number of British-born persons domiciled in the Channel Isles and the Isle of Man is only 44,500, equivalent to 0.08 per cent of the British population.

For reasons of birth and culture, the overwhelming majority of British people are locked in to living in Britain. By remaining

181

subject to Acts of Parliament, people are obliged to pay British taxes. Even if taxation is not popular, there is widespread recognition of the need to collect some taxes to finance the costs of government, and of a citizen's duty, for prudential as well as moral reasons, to obey laws (Rose, 1985c: 129ff.).

Whilst laws heavily constrain what must be paid as taxes, they do not determine the way in which people arrange their affairs to take account of tax laws. The collection of taxes is a process in which individuals as taxpayers interact with officials acting as tax collectors. If we follow Barnard's (1938) idea of 'the customer as a part of the organization', then the taxpayer is as much involved in the administration of taxation as is the government. The two depend upon each other, albeit they are not equal in their authority. The taxpayer is a peculiar kind of customer, a person who wants to receive *less* of the service that tax collectors offer.

The acceptance of taxation is so widespread that government can routinely collect billions of pounds each week in taxes. Nor is this achievement exceptional; most OECD nations collect as much or more tax revenue as Britain. Moreover, the taxing capacity of authoritarian regimes is not so much constrained by their lack of legitimacy as it is by the poverty widespread in many authoritarian countries. After surveying many countries and cultures distant in time and space, Webber and Wildavsky (1986: 33) conclude:

> Tax revolts are rare. Either the alternative, if one exists, is regarded as worse, or members of polities do accept the right of others to rule over them. How can this be?

This chapter considers four reasons why Britons accept a level of taxation that, in money terms, is higher than ever before in British history, and in tax effort has been high for decades. The first reason is that popular attitudes towards taxation are less unfavourable than is often assumed. Familiarity with high and rising taxes can encourage resigned acceptance, even if not active approval. Secondly, compliance with taxation is secured by giving citizens little choice. Effective tax handles secure compliance without requiring each individual to decide whether to pay taxes, or how much to pay. A third possibility is that citizens do not accept taxation and illegally evade paying large sums. This is often alleged, but the evidence tends to be anecdotal rather than systematic. The concluding section considers that acceptance of tax laws is widespread because the laws offer loopholes as well as compulsions, thus making it possible for many people liable to pay high taxes to avoid doing so through legal methods of tax avoidance.

Public Opinion About Taxation

Laws work best when they are accepted by the general public; the higher the level of popular approval, the greater the degree of voluntary compliance. Laws authorizing popular benefits such as pensions are very easy to implement, for people will want to collect the benefits to which they are legally entitled. By contrast, laws regulating motoring speeds will not be so effective because of a lower level of popular acceptance by motorists of speed limits.

Public opinion about taxation is not so much about the desirability or popularity of taxes as it is about the tolerability of taxation. While in theory it would be desirable to know what the majority of the public consider the right amount of taxation, asking such questions presents difficulties, for there is a limited connection between figures for tax revenue in aggregate, as recorded in the national budget, and perceptions of taxation in the minds of ordinary people.

'The general public is fiscally ignorant', concludes Alan Lewis (1982: 49) in a major survey of *The Psychology of Taxation*. This does not mean that citizens are unaware of having to pay taxes, but that most people lack specific knowledge about how much they pay in taxes each year, both directly and indirectly. Even more, they are without knowledge of the tax price of the programmes that their money funds. To judge ordinary citizens by the standards of fiscal experts is to employ a standard that is unrealistic and even unfair. Ordinary people do not need to have detailed knowledge of taxation in order to react in ways that concern politicians.

The answers in opinion surveys about taxation are sensitive to the phrasing of questions. A question about the desirability

183

of tax cuts will produce more anti-tax replies than a question that asks whether tax cuts are favoured if this means reducing spending on public programmes, a necessary consequence of the great identity. The term tax increase is profoundly ambiguous. Experts may use this term to describe any of the following phenomena: an increase in current money tax revenue; an increase in tax effort (that is, total taxation as a proportion of the national product); an increase in the rate or base in one or more tax laws; or an increase in the taxes paid by a particular category of taxpayer.

Popular Expectations

The expectations that citizens have about taxation are important, since popular expectations condition politicians' views about what must be done to maintain electoral popularity. If there is a widespread expectation of tax cuts, politicians will be more anxious than usual to avoid blame for raising taxes, whereas a widespread expectation of a tax increase makes it easier to announce such a decision. Failure to produce expected tax cuts could be a source of popular frustration, leading voters to turn the governing party out of office. Frustration may lead to aggressive attitudes generating a tax revolt at the ballot box or in the streets (cf. Gurr, 1970; Wilensky, 1976; Sears and Citrin, 1982; Peretz, 1982).

The Gallup Poll asks Britons each December what they expect will happen to taxes in the year ahead: will taxes rise, fall, or stay much the same? Since the question has been asked annually since 1957, there is evidence of popular expectations across many decades. If voters were naively optimistic, then they would consistently expect taxes to fall. If they were resigned or pessimistic, public opinion would consistently expect taxes to rise (Figure 8.1).

Voters are realistic in their expectations about taxation. Most voters usually expect taxes to rise. An average of 52 per cent of voters expect higher taxes in the year ahead. A substantial fraction of the electorate expects the status quo to continue; an average of 30 per cent report that they believe taxes will stay the same in the year ahead, or have no opinion. In thirteen years those expecting no change have been the largest single group in

Figure 8.1 Popular expectations of taxation in the year ahead: Gallup Poll

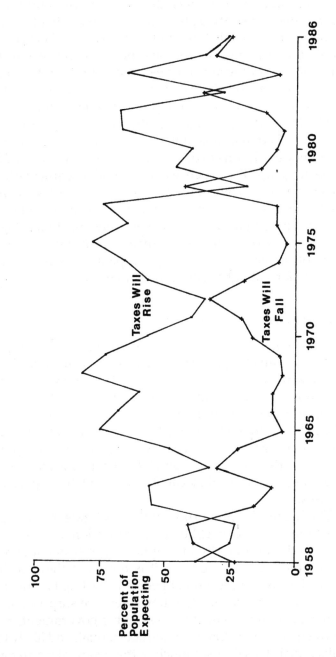

the electorate, or have included the median voter (Figure 8.1). At no time in twenty-eight years has a majority of the electorate expected taxes to fall. Since the money collected in taxes has been consistently rising, voters have been correct in not expecting taxes to fall. In the average year, only 18 per cent of voters have expected taxes to fall. Since Mrs Thatcher's entry to office, there has been no trend up in the proportion expecting tax cuts.

Contrary to expectations of the invariant growth of government or of popular resentment of increased taxation, there is no tendency for Britons to become more and more inclined to expect taxes to go up. The absence of any trend[2] is particularly striking, given that the current value of tax revenues has risen consistently in the postwar era. One reason why expectations of tax increases are steady is that tax effort is relatively steady (cf. Figure 2.2). Another reason is that immediate circumstances, such as the state of the economy or party competition, may cause popular expectations about taxation to change.

Implications for Government

Because voters are not all of one mind about taxation, politicians can play conflicting pressures off against each other; they are not faced with massive electoral pressure to move in a particular direction. Politicians can decide whether or not to cultivate that portion of the electorate expecting tax cuts, or to say nothing about taxes. In such circumstances, the fact that voters divide into three significant groups, with the largest group expecting taxes to rise, makes it possible for politicians to promote spending increases that can be financed by expected tax increases.

The higher the proportion of the electorate expecting taxes to rise, the less the likelihood of frustration resulting from an increase in taxation. By raising taxes, government is doing just what voters expect – even if it is not what they ideally might want. The low proportion of people expecting tax cuts is equally significant, for it means that few voters are surprised by the fact that they do not occur. In an era of big government, four-fifths of voters recognize that taxes are substantial, and likely to remain substantial. This defuses much of the potential for an aggressive tax revolt.

Popular expectations of taxation change through time, and can be shaped by the party in office. Under a Conservative government, voters may expect taxes to decrease, thus generating disappointment if this does not happen. Equally important, if most voters expect taxation to rise under a Labour government, then Labour would not lose support if it met these expectations.

In fact, voters expect taxes to rise whether there is a Conservative or Labour government. The percentage expecting a tax increase fluctuates, but this appears to have more to do with the state of the economy than the colour of the party in office. The proportion expecting a tax increase averaged 43 per cent for the Conservative government of 1957–64, 59 per cent for the 1970–4 Heath government, and 47 per cent under Mrs Thatcher. The expectation of a tax increase under the 1964–70 Labour government was only 4 per cent higher than that for the Heath government, and only 2 per cent higher than that for the Thatcher government.

Fairness in Taxation

Popular attitudes toward the fairness of taxation are particularly important, for the greater the proportion of people who think taxes are unfair, the less government can rely upon popular co-operation in collecting taxes. The higher the proportion who think taxation is fair, the greater the likelihood of people co-operating in the payment of taxes.

There is not a substantial amount of evidence about popular attitudes toward the fairness of taxation. Gallup Poll surveys often find voters critical of the distribution of tax benefits and burdens in a particular budget (Table 7.4), but assessments of particular tax measures (see, for example, *Gallup Political Index*, No. 307, 1986: 12) appear to reflect partisan values as much as, or more than, attitudes toward taxation generally. The available evidence suggests the absence of a widespread positive belief in the fairness of the tax system. When the Gallup Poll asked a national sample of voters (*Index* No. 302, 1985: 13) what they thought of the taxes they pay, only 15 per cent said they were fair, and another 22 per cent said that they were about right, compared to 41 per cent saying that they thought their taxes unfair.

Compliance Without Decision

The most effective taxes are those that leave citizens with no choice but to pay. Offering a citizen the opportunity to decide about a tax is to offer an opportunity for tax evasion. The art of designing taxes is to secure compliance more or less automatically, as a byproduct of normal economic activities, or even unwittingly by having taxes deducted before an individual receives money nominally due him, for example through the PAYE system of collecting income tax from employers on behalf of employees.

Compliance with tax laws is most readily secured when those liable to pay taxes have little or no opportunity to hide the resources that constitute the tax base, or to escape the attention of tax inspectors. The propensity to pay taxes is not meant to be a matter of decision, but a recognition of inevitability. As long as laws give weight to these administrative concerns, the extent of tax evasion will be limited, for bureaucratic organizations could not carry out evasion without abandoning the commercial and accounting practices on which many of their daily activities depend.

Making Taxes Effective

In drafting tax legislation certainty is always a major concern, for tax officials do not want to be ordered to enforce an act that, in their professional judgement, cannot be carried out with a very high degree of certainty. A tax that is relatively ineffective not only reduces the revenue flowing to the fisc; it also increases the criticism directed at tax officials. Nor do politicians want to defend in Parliament a tax that is widely known to be ineffectual.

In defining the base for a tax, administrators prefer taxing economic activities for which a money value can readily be calculated. With income tax it is easy to ascertain the weekly wage of an employee, for it is recorded in the books of the employer, and its value is printed on a wages slip. By contrast, with income in kind it is more difficult to impute a cash value. The Inland Revenue can identify employees who have the use of a company car, but assessing the value of a company car to the recipient can only be done in a rough-and-ready way.

188

Assessing the value of an expense-account lunch is even more difficult. An employee might argue that big expense-account meals are a liability rather than an asset, inducing overeating and ill-health damaging to long-term earning capacity!

The advantage of taxing income rather than wealth is that income is denominated in current money terms, whereas wealth consists of a schedule of assets accumulated through the years. While each asset – a house, car, furniture, jewellery, shares, etc. – will have had a money value when purchased, the historic purchase price will not be the same as its current value. Some assets appreciate in value in an inflationary era, such as a house; other assets depreciate with use, such as a motor car; and the value of a number of assets, such as jewellery, can only be estimated through an item-by-item valuation.

Tax officials can more readily secure compliance if responsibility for paying the tax to a revenue agency is placed upon large, bureaucratic and easily accessible organizations, rather than upon individuals whose records will be inferior, who have smaller resources, and who may be difficult to track down. The ideal tax-paying organization is a large firm, particularly a public-sector organization with a direct interest in public revenue. The self-employed are the most difficult to collect taxes from. It is easier for a taxi driver to evade payment on a 50p tip than for a company director to evade payment on a £5,000 bonus, for the former is a cash transaction without any written record, whereas the latter is well documented by the firm paying the bonus, and by the bank records of the recipient.

Income tax is usually collected from organizations employing wage-earners, and not from the employees whose income is liable to the tax. It is far easier to collect taxes 'wholesale' – that is, from employers or from sellers of goods – than to collect taxes 'retail' from millions of individuals. Equally, it is far easier to collect tax at the point of production than at the point of consumption. For example, the liability to duty on whisky is that of the distiller rather than the retailer, or the individual drinker. By monitoring the inventory of distilleries, the Excise can effectively determine the tax base, leaving to the distiller the task of passing on the cost of the tax to those who buy his product to bottle for retail sale as whisky.

A final and increasingly important concern is to minimize the amount of skilled manpower needed for making assessments, and collecting taxes. The revenue boards, especially the Inland Revenue, are short of the trained technical personnel required for the expeditious despatch of tax matters. The main reason is that tax authorities tend to suffer a loss of trained personnel to the private sector; a gamekeeper turned poacher (that is, a tax inspector turned tax consultant) can enjoy a big increase in salary and fringe benefits by changing sides in the contest between tax collectors and taxpayers. Even though every trained tax official can bring in far more money than he or she is paid by improving tax collection, the government remains chronically short of skilled tax officials. In consequence routine tasks such as answering mail fall behind, and controls and checks are not carried out as fully as is suitable (Public Accounts Committee, 1986).

Compliance Costs

Whatever the method used to collect revenue, the individual taxpayer or the organization acting as agent must inevitably spend time and effort, in addition to the money actually paid to the fisc. From the perspective of tax officials, the more work that the taxpayer can be compelled to do, the easier is their job. But from the perspective of those who must pay taxes, the addition of a substantial administrative burden is a further aggravation.

Compliance costs – financial burdens incurred by the taxpayer or by a third party such as an employer, over and above the tax paid and any indirect effects upon economic behaviour – have been described as the 'hidden costs' of taxation (Sandford, 1973). In reckoning the total cost of operating the tax system, taxpayers' compliance costs must be added to the administrative costs of public agencies. Compliance costs are not tabulated in the accounts of the Inland Revenue or the Customs and Excise. They show up in the accounts of those who pay taxes, and in the unremunerated labour that individual taxpayers have to spend in correspondence with the Inland Revenue, or with their accountant. As taxation increases in money value and as organizations and individuals become more self-conscious about the cost of their activities, compliance costs have become increasingly a matter of concern.

The cost of complying with income and national insurance taxes does not fall upon individual wage-earners but upon their employers. It is the employer who must collect and report the information from which the Inland Revenue determines how much tax is to be deducted. The employer also withholds the tax, and makes regular payments to the Inland Revenue. The employer is thus involved in a continuous process of correspondence with the Inland Revenue about the payment of more than £52b due each year in taxes from employees.[3]

The gross compliance costs to employers of administering income tax and national insurance deductions is more than half a billion pounds, approximately 1 per cent of the tax money paid. This is a substantial sum of money, albeit a small percentage. It is similar to the administrative cost to the Inland Revenue (cf. Cmnd 9831, 1986: 39; Godwin et al., 1983). The net cost to employers of complying with PAYE and national insurance is less, and a very efficient large employer may even be able to make a profit as a middle-man between employees and the Inland Revenue. A firm with computerized payroll and personnel records can administer taxation at a cost below the 1 per cent average. Furthermore, it can improve its cash flow by not immediately paying the fisc the money it deducts from wages; deductions are held for an average of a month before payment to the Inland Revenue. The sum held can augment a firm's working capital, reducing the overdraft it runs with a bank or providing a positive return by being deposited at interest.

The compliance costs to businesses of value added tax are much heavier, for a firm must calculate and record VAT every time it buys or sells goods and services. Since a firm is likely to have hundreds or thousands of transactions subject to VAT each week, a very substantial amount of book-keeping is required. Most of the operating costs of VAT fall upon firms collecting VAT. The administrative cost to the Customs and Excise for VAT is virtually the same, as a proportion of revenue, as that for income tax. Whereas the Inland Revenue pays more than half the gross cost of administering income taxes, trading firms bear more than five-sixths of the gross cost of administering VAT (Sandford, 1986).

A detailed study of VAT compliance costs shortly after its introduction, carried out by the Centre for Fiscal Studies of the

University of Bath, estimated that the administration of VAT added 9 per cent in compliance costs to the payments due the government as tax in 1977/8 (Sandford *et al.*, 1981: 45). Subsequently, VAT regulations have been simplified and traders have become more familiar with procedures, thus reducing the compliance cost. An incidental effect of raising VAT to 15 per cent has been to reduce further the compliance cost as a percentage of total VAT payments. In the 1984/5 fiscal year, the gross compliance cost of VAT to traders was £940m. This was 5 per cent of the total value of taxes paid in VAT, a decline from the figure for 1977, but still five times the relative compliance cost to employers of the payment of income taxes. Concurrently, the administrative costs of Customs and Excise have fallen to 1 per cent of VAT revenue (Cm. 5, 1986: 8; cf. Sandford, 1986).

Calculating the net cost of VAT is more complex. A trading firm may derive two types of measurable cash benefits from VAT, the cash flow benefit of VAT payments made to it by other traders, and the addition to working capital arising from the delay in paying taxes to Customs and Excise. Sandford (1986: 110) estimates that these benefits can reduce net compliance costs by more than half; the extent of the benefit depends upon interest rates. In addition many firms, particularly smaller firms, have received management benefits because of improving their accounting practices to cope with VAT.

The total gross compliance costs for taxpayers are more than £2.5b a year for income taxes and VAT together (Sandford, 1986: 110). When administrative costs are added – for the Inland Revenue £834m in 1985, and for the Customs and Excise, £411m – the total cost of operating the tax system rises to more than £4b. Total compliance costs are more than the sum raised by the tax on motor vehicles, wines and spirits or beer, and equal to the revenue on tobacco. But because total tax revenue is more than £134b taxation remains a low cost government activity, for operating costs are a very small percentage of total revenue raised.

There remain intangible psychic costs for taxpayers who believe 'it is bad enough to have to pay taxes; to have to incur costs for the privilege of doing so is to add insult to injury' (Sandford, 1986: 111). These costs fall disproportionately upon the self-employed and individuals whose tax payments are so large that they seek professional advice and actively monitor tax payments. An individual who is subject to an Inland Revenue investigation will have substantial costs, in time and in professional fees. The Inland Revenue's view is that this is appropriate; a citizen should meet the costs of complying with the law (Cmnd 8822, 1983: 332; cf. Sandford, 1973).

Pursuing Non-Payers of Taxes

The responsibility of collecting taxes includes a duty to investigate whether taxes due are actually paid. Both the Inland Revenue and the Customs and Excise devote a significant portion of staff to inspecting tax returns, and monitoring activities where evasion may be taking place.

The immediate task facing the Inland Revenue is to collect tax known to be due. For income tax, 98 per cent of tax assessed is paid promptly. Of the other 2 per cent, the Inland Revenue eventually collects 1.7 per cent, through negotiation, legal action, or by invoking legal procedures to secure payment. In 1985, the solicitors of the Inland Revenue acted in 96,500 cases to recover tax due. Only 0.36 per cent of income tax due (£195m in 1984) is written off as irrecoverable. The most common reason for writing off income tax is that the payer is insolvent, for example a firm goes bankrupt before it has made all its PAYE payments to the Inland Revenue. Taxpayers going abroad or otherwise untraceable account for only £51m a year in lost revenue, and £15m is written off because it is not worth the cost of recovering it (Cmnd 9831, 1986: 54).

The Customs and Excise administers a wide variety of taxes; VAT accounts for more than half its £35.5b revenue. In 1984 it wrote off £227m in taxes as irrecoverable, a higher proportion and amount of money than written off by the Inland Revenue. However, the amount was only 0.6 per cent of total revenue collected (Cmnd 9655, 1985: 35). Of this figure, nearly all was written off as non-payment of VAT or car tax. In five-sixths of the cases insolvency was the reason.

In addition to pursuing those who do not pay taxes when they are due, tax officials also investigate firms, individuals and trading records in search of evidence for tax liabilities that have not been properly reported. The complexities of the tax code are such that misreporting is not proof of fraud. The Inland Revenue does not seek prosecution when it finds that a taxpayer has not paid the full sum due. It regards its primary role as that of collecting money. Hence, unless an important point of principle is at stake or a violation is flagrant, it normally prefers to settle matters without reference to the courts. It can collect interest on sums that are paid after the date initially due, and penalty payments for errors by the taxpayer, actions that avoid charges of criminal negligence or fraud.

Only a few hundred people a year face criminal proceedings instigated by the Inland Revenue; 338 cases were tried in 1984. Fraud is the usual charge, and convictions are secured in 98 per cent of cases (Cmnd 9831, 1986: 53). The Customs and Excise in 1985 instituted proceedings against 4,527 business entities for failure to furnish returns, and against 444 for failure to pay taxes. In most cases it collected what was due (Cm. 5, 1986: 23). The Customs and Excise was involved in 431 proceedings for fraudulent evasion, resulting in 167 convictions and imprisonment.

The Inland Revenue makes tens of thousands of investigations in each year. Attention is particularly concentrated upon unincorporated businesses, in which there can be substantial opportunity for the owner–operator to take benefits in forms not readily identifiable as taxable income. Given the tens of billions of pounds flowing through the PAYE system annually, the Inland Revenue audits about 63,000 employers a year; in 33 per cent of these cases, irregularities are discovered resulting in further tax payments. Specialist investigations are also made into complex schemes where tax avoidance may be outside the law. A total of £549m was collected through investigation and audit work in 1985, increasing the Inland Revenue's take by 1.1 per cent.

The actual amount of money collected per investigation is more than the cost of the average investigation, but not large in an absolute sense. It averaged £7,700 per income-tax investigation, and £1,000 per PAYE audit in 1985. The sum collected per VAT audit averaged £1,250. Investigations confirm the effectiveness of existing tax handles in squeezing revenue from law-abiding taxpayers. Tax inspectors with a vested interest in increasing tax payments conclude that, in the accounts they inspect, 99 per cent or more of money due is actually paid.[4]

But investigations also show that there is a consistent record of taxpayers being more likely to make underpayments than overpayments. In 1985 nearly half of all VAT-registered traders visited in 370,000 routine inspections were found to have made underpayments, resulting in further payment of £451m. The inspections found only a very small proportion of traders making VAT overpayments with a total value of £6m. In sum, 98.7 per cent of the value of the errors found were in favour of taxpayers (Cmnd 9655, 1985: 22; see also Cmnd 8822, 1983: 74).

Limits of Evasion

Everybody talks about tax evasion, but only a minority are actually in a position to evade taxes. That some people escape payment of taxes legally due is undoubted. But as Dilnot and Morris (1981) comment: 'The black economy can be large enough to yield a rich vein of anecdotes without necessarily being a phenomenon of quantitative significance.' The history of taxation is a story of the development of more effective tax handles, in order to minimize the opportunity for evasion. For example, rates on houses were imposed many centuries ago, when the capacities of government were weaker, because the impossibility of concealing a house provided an effective tax handle.

Conceptualizing Tax Evasion

Different forms of illegal activity, not all of which are tax evasion, are often confused in anecdotal discussions. Hence, it is important to understand exactly what is and is not included in the concept of tax evasion.

Tax evasion must first be distinguished from criminal activities, that is, activities that are illegal whether or not taxes are paid. The sale of hard drugs remains a crime, even if VAT were paid on the proceeds, and robbery is a crime, even if a self-employed thief declared his receipts for income tax. A person who draws social security benefit as unemployed while simultaneously earning money on which no tax is paid is not only evading tax, but also defrauding the social security office.[5]

Tax evasion must also be distinguished from tax avoidance, the

195

arrangement of activities so that an individual is liable for less tax than would otherwise be the case. It is of the essence of tax avoidance that the arrangements are within the law, and known to appropriate revenue authorities. If the taxpayer's definition is disputed, it is adjudicated, and if a claim for tax avoidance is wrongly founded, then payment can be collected.

Tax evasion is the non-reporting of a tax liability for activities in which money or taxable benefits change hands. If a person pays a gardening firm to work around his house and the firm pays tax on the money received and wages paid to workmen, no evasion occurs. If a jobbing gardener is paid in cash and does not file a tax return, this is evasion. If an individual decides to do gardening himself or herself, with the assistance of family, this is not tax evasion, for no money changes hands in the domestic household.

The goods and services produced in society are the sum of three separate sets of activities (Rose, 1985d), those of the Official Economy (recorded in the official national accounts and subject to taxation); the Unofficial (often called the black or shadow) Economy (bought and sold for cash but unrecorded in the national accounts and not declared for purposes of taxation); and the Domestic Economy (produced and consumed in the household without any money changing hands).

Working in the Official Economy is the norm – both statistically and in terms of social values – in every industrial society. Industrialization increases the number of taxpayers by creating factory and office jobs, and urbanization has greatly decreased unpaid or unofficial work in a farm household. A majority of women, who formerly worked without a wage or a tax liability at home, are now wage-earners and taxpayers in the Official Economy. Today government provides positive incentives to work in the Official Economy: social security benefits and eligibility for unemployment compensation supplement fringe benefits from employers.

Employment in the tax-free Unofficial Economy is constrained on both the supply and the demand sides. Such transactions will occur only if both buyers and sellers will be better off. For tax evasion to pay, two conditions must be met: i) the Unofficial Price to the purchaser must be less than the Official Price; and ii) the Unofficial Wage of the worker must be higher than the Official Wage.

Take-home pay and taxes on earnings are only one part of the cost of any product: the materials used and capital equipment are also costs. Goods cannot be produced in the Unofficial Economy if capital costs are high, as is the case with steel, for example. Nor can goods be produced at great saving if the cost of materials is a large proportion of total cost. Workers in the Unofficial Economy may reduce capital costs by borrowing equipment from their principal employer in the Official Economy, or pilfering materials from work. Borrowing or pilfering does not, however, eliminate the need for the consumer to pay a wage that is an inducement to a supplier to work without tax.

Only when wage costs are the bulk of the cost of a product is there a potential for selling it 'tax free' at a price that will satisfy both potential buyer and seller. For example, a person will find it cheaper to purchase a machine-produced carpet from a store than to commission a carpet which would have to be made by hand in the Unofficial Economy. But it could be cheaper to have the carpet laid in the Unofficial Economy, for labour is the primary requirement for carpet fitting.

The paradigm cases for the Unofficial Economy are services that can be produced with virtually no investment in materials or capital goods, such as baby-sitting or window-cleaning. The Unofficial Economy is ill-suited to the production of manufactured goods. Whereas a motor mechanic may borrow equipment to do repair work on the side, an employee of a motor-car manufacturer cannot borrow a production line to build cars to sell to friends on a cash-only basis. If industrial workers pilfer goods after they have been manufactured and recorded in the Official Economy, this does not increase the total product of a nation, it redistributes it.

The incentive for workers to enter the Unofficial Economy is very sensitive to marginal tax rates. A worker will only pay income and social security tax after earning money in excess of the allowance against gross wages appropriate to family circumstances. There is thus no incentive to draw all of one's income from the Unofficial Economy. The incentive to work for cash only is strongest as a *supplement* to a job in the Official Economy. At that point an individual is likely to have a marginal tax rate of more than 35 per cent in income tax and national insurance contributions. Hence, he can offer a 20 per cent discount off the gross cost of his wage and still be earning significantly more than by working in the Official Economy. If VAT is charged on services, the incentive is increased to work for cash in hand.

However, an income in the Official Economy limits the time available to work in the Unofficial Economy and the marginal attractiveness of additional work. If a worker views such an activity as the equivalent of overtime, then he or she will want virtually the same amount of money as a worker in the Official Economy. If the work is paid at straight time-rates, then there is limited incentive to devote a lot of time to such activities after working an official 40-hour week. Studies intended to highlight moonlighting (that is, a second job on top of regular employment) conclude that less than 10 per cent of the labour force in the Official Economy also has a second job, in which tax evasion might possibly operate (de Grazia, 1980; Smith, 1986: 45ff.).

The constraints on would-be purchasers are also substantial. This is most obvious for public employees, nearly one-third of the labour force in Britain today (Parry, 1985). It is also true for employees of large private-sector organizations, which must have stable work forces, and keep accurate records of their personnel and of their purchases, conditions that make it very easy for tax officials to assess the taxes due, not only on the firm's account, but also as PAYE and national insurance contributions on behalf of their employees.

Estimating the Size of the Unofficial Economy

By definition, tax evasion – the illegal non-payment of taxes due – is a subject for which official records are inadequate. If tax authorities could identify the exact sources and amounts of evasion, they could better act to collect sums due. The trivial number of criminal proceedings launched by government confirms the *a priori* assumption that official records are inadequate indicators of illegal tax evasion. But anecdotes about cash only plumbers and waiters pocketing tips give no idea of the actual scale of tax evasion.

The extent of activity in the Unofficial Economy can never be known for certain, but it can be estimated on the basis of the above parameters. Since most people working in the Unofficial Economy are also in the Official Economy, the starting point is to analyse the Official Economy according to the capacity of different sectors of the work force to participate in the Unofficial Economy.

There is a relatively high opportunity for tax evasion in services requiring a moderate amount of capital and materials, and produced by small-scale enterprises or by the self-employed. Construction trades are the best example in a modern society, and agriculture or peasant farming in the pre-industrial economy. Most anecdotes about the Unofficial Economy usually feature payments to plumbers, painters or related tradesmen. A striking feature of the sectors where off the books work is most likely – construction and agriculture – is that they are small, accounting for less than 9 per cent of the total British labour force (Table 8.1).

There is virtually nil opportunity to engage in the Unofficial Economy for workers in capital-intensive industries, such as heavy engineering, chemicals, metals, and so forth. There is also virtually no possibility to work in the Unofficial Economy for persons in highly bureaucratized employment, whether in public-sector areas such as central government, local government or national health service hospitals, or in such private-sector fields as banking and insurance. Altogether, these sectors employ nearly half the total labour force in Britain.

A third category of the labour force contains persons who have some – even if relatively low – opportunity to work in the Unofficial Economy: professional people, those in shops or distributive trades, and what the census classifies as providers of miscellaneous services. This category accounts for 44 per cent of the labour force.

Given the far greater opportunities for tax evasion by the self-employed as against employees, the distribution of the labour force should also be sub-divided by this criterion as well. The proportion of those with greater opportunity to avoid taxation is low, 9 per cent of the total labour force. Employees constitute 91 per cent of the labour force. The unemployed are a larger proportion of the labour force than the self-employed. But empirical studies emphasize that while the unemployed may have more time to work off the books, they tend to lack the

Table 8.1 Employment According to Opportunity to Work in the Unofficial Economy

	Total (000)	Self-Employed (000)	Of Labour Force %
Relatively high			
Construction	1,438	389	6.2
Agriculture, forestry and fishing	599	245	2.6
Total	2,037	634	8.8
Limited but possible			
Distributive trades	3,173	467	13.7
Professional and scientific services	3,981	213	17.2
Miscellaneous services	2,994	390	12.7
Total	10,148	1,070	43.8
Virtually nil			
Engineering and allied industries	2,697	51	8.6
Other manufacturing (food, chemicals, metal, clothing, etc.)	3,198	92	13.8
Transport and communication	1,508	125	6.5
Public administration	1,549	0	6.7
Insurance, banking, finance	1,405	84	6.0
Gas, electricity, water	340	0	1.5
Mining and quarrying	326	1	1.4
Total	10,933	353	47.3
Overall total	23,110	2,057	100.0

Source: Calculated from *Social Trends* 14 (London: HMSO, 1984), tables 4.7, 4.8.

equipment and materials, the contacts with customers, and often the skills to do so.

The skills and opportunities to work in the Unofficial Economy are not strictly aligned with sectors of the labour force, but since exceptions are likely to operate in both directions, they will not greatly distort estimates. To test the robustness of conclusions, a high and a low estimate can be made of the propensity to work in the Unofficial Economy.

Opportunities to work in the Unofficial Economy would be heavily utilized if three-quarters of those with a high opportunity increased their working time by half; if one-third of those with limited opportunity worked an additional one day a week in the Unofficial Economy; and if one-tenth of those with virtually nil opportunity managed to work one-half day a week. Altogether, these estimates assume that almost 6 million Britons do at least a little work in the Unofficial Economy. Since such work is a supplement to normal employment, it would add only 6.8 per cent to labour in the Official Economy. On a lower and more realistic estimate, it could be calculated that three-quarters of those with a high opportunity to do Unofficial work increased their labour by one-third; that one-quarter of those with a low opportunity increased their effort by one-half day a week; and one-tenth of those with nil opportunity increased their labour by 5 per cent. If millions of Britons acted thus, it would add only 4.6 per cent to labour in the Official Economy.

Since most of the output of the Unofficial Economy consists of services, the productivity of such work is relatively low. For example, the labour of an electrician wiring a house will produce less output than an engineer tending an electricity generating station, for the latter is working in a capital-intensive field. Hence, the Unofficial Economy adds less in proportion to the official national product than might be implied by the additional labour it mobilizes.

The foregoing is not the only way to estimate the product of the Unofficial Economy. The importance of the subject has generated a large number of attempts to do so in Britain and other countries (Tanzi, 1982; Smith, 1986). Estimates may be derived from: the discrepancy between income and expenditure in national income accounts or sample surveys of family expenditure; statistics about holders of second jobs (moonlighters); Inland Revenue sources; public opinion surveys about the popular predisposition to avoid taxes; or records of financial transactions and currency in circulation.

The striking feature of the great variety of estimates is agreement that the Unofficial Economy is small in proportion to the Official Economy (see Rose, 1985d: table 4, for a summary). The median estimate is that it adds about 4 per cent. The above labour force estimate is thus consistent with most other estimates, including the Inland Revenue view that the Unofficial Economy could be equivalent to 7.5 per cent of GDP (Cmnd 8160, 1981: 27).

To speak of the Unofficial Economy as small is to use relative terms; the median figure suggests that the Unofficial Economy adds £18b a year to the national product, and it could be as much as £28b. While such sums are large in absolute terms, they remain relatively small in an economy that has a national product of more than £400b a year. The tax revenue lost through the Unofficial Economy is smaller still, since it is only a proportion of earnings in the Unofficial Economy, and if tax laws were 100 per cent effective, this would discourage a portion of such earnings.

The limited importance of the Unofficial Economy is further underscored by comparing it with the Domestic Economy, that is, the non-monetized labour of women and men in the home, making meals, cleaning house and clothes, repairing or renovating furnishings, gardening and so forth. An estimate based upon time-budget studies shows that labour in the Domestic Economy is equal in quantity to that in the Official Economy (Rose, 1985d: table 6; Rose, 1986b).

From the viewpoint of the family and the fisc, the Domestic Economy is the more important source of untaxed labour. Government cannot tax it because no money changes hands. In order to levy a tax, it would first of all have to force households to complete a time-budget each month, and then impute a money value to work done in the home.[6] No popularly elected government would consider imposing such a draconian obligation. Today, people find that the most economical and efficient way to work outside the tax system is to engage in unpaid self-employment in their own home. Because do-it-yourself labour is free of charge or a labour of love and affection, the family does not need to pay for household services of the Domestic Economy from its post-tax income. No issue of tax evasion arises, because no money changes hands.

Opportunities for Tax Avoidance

Taxation is contingent. Whether or not an economic activity is subject to tax depends upon laws that define whether and in what ways it may be the base of a tax, and circumstances in which different rates apply. The money due to the fisc is the outcome of a process in which clauses in tax acts are applied to specific economic activities.

Economic activity is contingent too. Given a choice between receiving money in a form that involves higher or lower taxes, most people would prefer to arrange their affairs in ways that attract less tax. For example, a specialist consultant would rather be paid as self-employed, without tax being deducted, so that a variety of personal expenses could be deducted and tax paid a year later under Schedule D. Tax avoidance occurs when individuals or organizations so arrange their economic activities so that tax liabilities are reduced, or do not occur.

Legality of Avoiding Tax

By definition, tax avoidance is within the law. Tax authorities can challenge the particular interpretation of the law invoked to justify tax avoidance, but they cannot collect a higher tax simply because a transaction could have been conducted differently. The initial guideline was laid down by the courts in the case of the Inland Revenue Commissioners vs. the Duke of Westminster (1936):

> Every man is entitled if he can to arrange his affairs so that the tax attaching under the appropriate Acts is less than it otherwise would be. If he succeeds in ordering them so as to secure that result, then, however unappreciative the Commissioners of Inland Revenue or his fellow taxpayers may be of his ingenuity, he cannot be compelled to pay an increased tax.

The Inland Revenue has since succeeded in having the courts narrow the scope for tax avoidance. But given the incentives for pursuing tax avoidance and the variety and complexity of tax legislation, often 'the Revenue put themselves in the position of men who go to shut the stable door every time they see a horse has bolted' (Kay and King, 1983: 39; cf. *Butterworths*, 1984: 3ff.).

Tax avoidance can take two forms: it may eliminate any liability to tax, or it may reduce the amount of tax paid. For example, an individual may invest in national savings certificates rather than deposit money in a building society in order to avoid paying tax on interest received, since national savings certificates (which are issued by the government) often pay interest free of tax, whereas building societies deduct interest at source. A person whose marginal rate of taxation is 50 per cent may choose to receive part of his corporate remuneration in the form of an expensive company car, since the tax claimed for the use of the car for private purposes will be much less than the pre-tax earnings required to purchase an expensive car from post-tax income.

While tax avoidance can be done legally, it cannot be done casually. Planning is required *before* money changes hands, in order that the form of a transaction is such as to reduce tax liabilities. Planning is most evident in reducing liability to death duties. After a wealthy person has died, it is too late to take steps to reduce the liability to an inheritance tax. An elderly person may greatly reduce or completely avoid tax on his or her estate by a variety of carefully planned steps, including making gifts to relatives, establishing trusts, or even by investment in forms of property, such as timber, which is specially treated for tax purposes (*Butterworths* 1984: part 8). Given the capacity to reduce so greatly the liability for estate tax this is often described as a voluntary tax paid only by those who are unwilling to take decisions necessary to leave a tax efficient inheritance.

Conditions of Tax Avoidance

The capacity of an individual to practise tax avoidance is contingent upon circumstances. First and most importantly, an individual must have an income sufficient to justify the additional effort required to reduce or avoid taxation. Most employed people in Britain are subject to income tax at the standard rate of 27 per cent; national insurance contributions claim up to 9 per cent more each week. If through tax avoidance a person can gain the use of £100 rather than £64 of earnings, then this is a 56 per cent increase. For a person paying the highest rate of tax, 60 per cent of income, complete avoidance of tax increases the value of a pound earned by 150 per cent.

The basic rule is: the higher the income, the greater the incentive to practise tax avoidance. Today, 95 per cent of British income-tax payers are subject to tax only at the standard rate; those paying at higher marginal rates are substantial in number, 980,000, but still a small proportion of total taxpayers. The number subject to capital gains tax on the ownership of stocks and shares or other assets sold during a year has been equal to only 0.6 per cent of persons paying income tax.

Secondly, a taxpayer must be organized to manage money in ways suited to minimize taxation. A company, and especially a large corporation, is well organized to make use of professional advice, and often has staff concerned with tax and accounting matters. The sums of money involved in corporate cash flows are large enough to make small percentage savings worthwhile in absolute money terms. Moreover, a large firm will attract attention from tax authorities, which can see significant gains in finding even relatively small sums due from big taxpayers. There are 560,000 firms paying corporation tax, and thus having the potential capacity to practise tax avoidance. A multi-national company has a particular advantage, the capacity to organize the flow of transactions within the company in such a way as to minimize liability to tax in countries where rates are highest.

Thirdly, tax avoidance often requires co-operation between two parties, a payer of money and the recipient. In the case of small businesses, this may be the same person, when the owner pays himself salary and also expenses. But most people work for large organizations which have bureaucratic systems of payment that inhibit or prevent tax avoidance schemes. This is most notably the case for employees in the public sector, which is concerned with maximizing tax revenue, including revenue from their own employees. Large firms typically design tax avoidance schemes only for a very small fraction of their employees, the company directors and senior executives.

Fourthly, given the technicalities of the system, a taxpayer requires professional advice in order to be informed about the means of arranging activities to reduce tax liabilities. This may be the motive for seeking professional advice, or advice may be sought simply to complete standard tax transactions. Kay and

King (1983: 32) note that for the average British taxpayer 'filling in a tax return is not a purposive activity. It does not enable the recipient to check how much tax he owes or is owed, or indeed to do anything except post the form back to the tax inspector'.

Professional advice on tax matters can be given by a variety of people: accountants; ex-tax inspectors who use the knowledge gained working for the Inland Revenue or Customs and Excise to advise clients about how to get around their former employer; and lawyers. Advice given by Citizens' Advice Bureaux or newspaper columnists usually involves the resolution of disputes about small sums, rather than advice about avoiding tax on larger sums (Sandford, 1973).

The growth in the number of persons qualified as accountants is one indicator of the growing importance of tax planning, and tax avoidance. The number of accountants in Britain has increased by six times in the past half century, and two-and-a-half times since 1951. The number of chartered accountants has grown very substantially as a proportion of the work force too. In 1931 accountants constituted less than one in a thousand of the labour force. By 1951 they were 1.6 per thousand, and in the 1980s they are 3.6 per thousand (Table 8.2).

Table 8.2   Growth in Number of Accountants, 1931–81

Year	Number	Per 1000 in work
1931	15,592	0.7
1951	36,773	1.6
1971	76,610	3.1
1981	91,290	3.6

Source: Census Occupation Tables for England and Wales, and for Scotland (London and Edinburgh: HMSO).

Most people do not consciously and consistently practise tax avoidance, for they lack the income, the organization and the professional advice to do so. In order to practise tax avoidance, an individual will need, in addition to a substantial income, professional advice from an accountant, and sufficient influence or authority over payments received so that they arrive in a form that is tax efficient for the recipient.

Forms of Tax Avoidance

Anyone with sufficient income and wealth to make tax avoidance financially worthwhile is confronted with a great variety of means of reducing tax payments. Actions that can be taken include:

Earning less money Living without money is hardly practicable in a money economy, and when money is spent, it is subject to VAT and other taxes. But it is possible to decline the opportunity of earning more money. As taxation at the margin is higher than the average tax rate, marginal earnings will always be more highly taxed. This is true, for example, of overtime payments to factory workers, and bonuses or salary increases for well-paid businessmen and professional people.

Dozens of studies by economists have found no conclusive evidence of tax rates acting as a systematic disincentive to work or to seek additional earnings (see, for example, Brown, 1983; Atkinson and Stern, 1980; Huhne, 1986). Even when tax rates are above average, an increase in marginal earnings will always generate an increase in total earnings. Moreover, higher marginal rates may sometimes encourage persons who have the ability to increase their labour input, working more hours to increase their after-tax income substantially, notwithstanding high marginal rates. If tax rates are cut, a person can then receive the same income for slightly less work, or have an increased income without doing more or better paid work. In any event, most employed persons cannot control the number of hours they work and are paid for.

Becoming self-employed Whereas employees pay income tax weekly or monthly on a Pay As You Earn basis, self-employed persons pay income tax when it is assessed in the year following receipt. For example, self-employed income received in the tax year from April 1986 to April 1987 is taxed in two instalments due in January and July 1988. Thus, a self-employed person can borrow from the Inland Revenue up to two years of taxes, a substantial addition to working capital, or investments paying interest. Furthermore, self-employed persons usually have more latitude in deducting expenses than is allowed employees.

Transmuting income into payments in kind An employer can provide employees with a variety of goods and services of material advantage, but not attracting any tax. These benefits include meals at work, special-purpose clothing, some low-interest loans, removal expenses if transferring jobs, and, for persons on above average incomes, a host of other perks. A variety of benefits in kind may be taxed at their secondhand value, which is much less than their cost to the employer or their value to the employee. For example, an individual given exclusive use of a company car, including private motoring, may receive a benefit worth £3,000 a year in pre-tax income, but attract a tax bill of only a few hundred pounds.

Transmuting income into capital gains A well-to-do person who pays income tax at a marginal rate of 60 per cent will increase the cash value of a transaction by three-quarters if the money is received as a capital gain rather than income, for capital gains are normally taxed at half that rate. Moreover, if capital gains in a year do not exceed £6,600, the sum received is free of all tax, adding 150 per cent to the cash value of what is gained. To achieve this benefit, a person may buy securities or bonds that pay very little or no interest but are redeemed at a price that is substantially above their purchase cost, thus generating a capital gain, or invest in shares or property that may appreciate in capital value.

Transmuting income into pension While a pension is not current income, it can be financed by contributions from current income. Any money deducted from an individual's gross salary as a contractual pension contribution is not counted as part of taxable income. Nor is the sum contributed by an employer to a pension counted as part of an individual's taxable income. Since the total can be equivalent to 10 or 15 per cent of total gross earnings, this allowance effectively increases by 41 per cent the value of the pension contribution above what would have been paid on a post-tax basis. For persons paying tax at a higher rate, the value of pensions payments is greater.

The money in pension funds may be invested without the income earned attracting tax. The ability to reinvest at a gross rate of, say, 10 per cent rather than a post-tax rate of between 4.0 and

7.3 per cent greatly enhances the cumulative value of a pension upon retirement. In a period of 20 years, £1,000 would compound to £4,092 if tax at 27p were paid before the interest was reinvested, but to £6,725 if interest is reinvested gross. Only after a person retires need tax be paid on a pension.

Transforming the payment of rent into interest A tenant who pays rent does so from post-tax earnings; no tax allowance is given for the sum paid as rent. By contrast, the monthly interest payment for buying a house on a mortgage is deductible from gross income on payments of interest up to £30,000 of the purchase price. For a standard rate taxpayer, the net cost of every £100 paid in interest thus becomes £73, and the savings are higher for persons on higher tax rates. In an era of rising house values, buying a house with a small down payment and a mortgage financed in part by tax rebates will normally generate a substantial capital gain in the course of time. The capital gain will be untaxed, as long as it is an individual's residence.

Reducing or writing off profits Companies are in business to make money, but since government levies a tax on the profits, it is rational for businesses to arrange their accounts in such a way that the value of the company grows more than does the profit subject to tax. One way to reduce gross profit is to invest money in the corporation's activities, for investment is not only meant to produce future profits, but also can provide an immediate reduction in current tax liabilities, as up to 100 per cent depreciation of the cost of the investment has been allowed for deduction from the base for corporation tax. In the case of North Sea oil, which has involved huge sums in investments and profits, more than £3b in allowances were deducted in 1982/3 (cf. *Inland Revenue Statistics*, 1983: table 1.5). Reinvestment also has important implications for shareholders, as it affects the relation between dividends taxed as a form of income, and capital gains taxed at a much lower rate (Kay and King, 1983: chs 11–12).

A tax system that generates a large amount of tax avoidance is likely to be unpopular among those who do not enjoy the opportunity to reduce their tax liabilities. Those who do enjoy the advantages may nonetheless still feel annoyed at having to arrange their financial affairs in ways that they would deem unreasonable, but for the fact that doing so produces a reduction in tax. The government too may feel dissatisfied, because the erosion of the tax base by tax avoidance forces it to levy higher rates of tax than would otherwise be needed to raise a given amount of revenue.

From a revenue-raising perspective, tax avoidance, tax evasion and public opinion towards taxation are of secondary concern. They are but intervening variables, influencing the decisions that citizens make as participants in the process of financing big government. They do not reduce government's need to find tax handles sufficient to collect nearly two-fifths of the national product for the fisc.

Notes

1 Even the literature on the relationship of voluntary services to publicly provided services consistently emphasizes the necessity of public effort to complement volunteer effort (Willmott, 1986; Bulmer, 1986). For example, blood freely given from altruistic motives is transferred by paid and unionized employees of the state-funded national health service. Notwithstanding the moral significance of altruism in Titmuss's (1970) work, altruism cannot finance the welfare state that he favoured.

2 The variability of opinion is shown not only by the movements recorded in Figure 8.1 but also by the absence of any fit between a least squares regression line and public opinion; the r^2 value for expectations of higher taxes is .00; for lower taxes, .00, and for taxes staying the same, .01.

3 In addition, the employer bears the cost of workers pressing for wage increases treating their 'real' wage as take-home pay net of tax and national insurance deductions. To add an additional £1 to a worker's take-home pay requires the employer to lay out an additional £1.87. These indirect costs are real, but are not defined as compliance costs.

4 There is also a very small amount of money collected by the wrongful application of the law by public officials, for example payments made through an accounting error, or because a tax official's ruling was incorrect but not challenged. Of 275 appeals against Customs and Excise assessments decided by VAT tribunals in 1984, 45 were allowed in full and 20 allowed in part (Cmnd 9655, 1985: 90).

5 Hence, even if a person on the dole were to pay tax on earnings, he or she would still be defrauding the social security system.

6   Imputing value to services that are not marketed is not unknown in
    the British tax system. Flor more than a century this was done to
    calculate the old Schedule A levy on the imputed value of an
    owner-occupier renting (*sic*) his house from himself.

CHAPTER NINE

What Scope for Future Change?

The future of taxation is already here; it has been delivered by the inertia of the past. Most taxes that will be in force in the year 2001 are already on the statute books. Most tax laws of future importance were decided generations or centuries ago. Political inertia ensures that the bulk of public revenue at the start of the next millennium will depend much more on old laws than upon new ones.

While the inertia of the past is very important in raising revenue, it is not all-important. Each year the Chancellor has scope for fringe tuning, and some citizens have opportunities to alter their taxes a little through tax avoidance measures. In the course of a decade or a quarter century, changes in economic activity can cumulatively cause substantial change in the relative importance of particular taxes in the system.

The scope for change appears greater the further ahead we look. The logic of compounding emphasizes that the longer any seemingly small change is in effect, the greater its cumulative impact can be. The current levels of revenue from income tax and national insurance were not achieved overnight; they reflect the accumulation through the generations of decisions and non-decisions. In the case of national insurance, there have been positive decisions to raise tax rates. Doing nothing about income tax rates has generated even more revenue, as inflation and economic growth have greatly increased the tax base.

However, the longer the *durée* in which change occurs, the more difficult it is to identify its cause as a single decision by a politician or party in office. Politicial inertia leads to changes occurring slowly, almost imperceptibly. Each party avoids introducing big changes in taxation, because of the criticism this would attract. It is not in a politician's interest to be identified as responsible for the taxes that claim most revenue today. He would prefer to avoid blame, or plead diminished responsibility because of laws enacted by predecessors at an earlier point in the *longue durée*.

As the future becomes the present, it is manifestly evident that taxes are changing. But future changes need not follow from the intentions and actions of present-day policy-makers. Within the life of a Parliament in which it is introduced, a novel tax is likely to generate little revenue, because politicians are averse to being blamed for big new taxes, and tax administrators are risk-averse. If the tax does subsequently become a major source of revenue, such a consequence is not proof of initial intent. Certainly, the level of income tax today was not intended by Pitt or Gladstone, nor were high rates of tax used to finance the Second World War intended to be maintained for decades after the war.

Even if politicians do introduce a major change in the tax system with a clear long-term intent, it does not follow that a new tax will have the consequences intended. For example, the Selective Employment Tax of the first Wilson government, was a much-heralded innovation of Nicholas Kaldor of Cambridge, an internationally known economist. It was intended to raise more revenue and to give a competitive advantage to manufacturing industries exempt from it. It was repealed by the Heath government, and not reintroduced by Labour subsequently.

In the pages that follow, attention is first directed to the limits imposed by decisions in the historic past. These limits are real but not rigid; the moving force of inertia means that a national tax system cannot be static. The second section emphasizes that current political and budget realities also limit the scope for decisions about revenue; proposals for major changes in tax must be sub-divided into those that are currently outside the bounds of political acceptability, and those that are inside the bounds. Pressures to increase expenditure create pressures to increase revenue. The third section examines the extent to which politicians can avoid raising taxes by increasing revenue through other means. The final section of this book poses the fundamental question: given that the great identity compels revenue and expenditure to go up or down together, do citizens actually want

213

a big change in the costs and benefits currently received from government?

Inertia of the Historic Past

While economic theories of taxation tend to be stated in universal terms, the collection of taxes is cast in the mould of national history. The taxes that a national government collects each year are those that were enacted by the nation's Parliament at some time in the more or less distant past. Even in societies where war and revolution have created political discontinuities, there is a surprising degree of persistence in tax practices from one constitutional regime to the next.

National History Persists

Economic texts, academic tax journals, and meetings in inter-governmental bodies such as OECD and the International Monetary Fund promote the international dissemination of current ideas of tax experts. An innovation in one country is watched by experts in other countries, partly from professional interest and partly with the idea that tax innovations may be transferable across national borders. Implicit in many evaluations of tax concepts is the idea that there is a standard that identifies best practice in taxation, and that sooner or later all advanced nations ought to adopt it. The increasing openness of the international economy is a further inducement to tax harmonization.

In the contemporary world, in which economic discourse, including ideas about taxation, is transnational, the significance of national history tends to be overlooked. But trade in taxes is far more like autarky (that is, national self-sufficiency) than is trading in conventional manufactured goods. Whatever the prominence of expert opinion in public discussions, it is of no importance unless, and until, ideas are translated into national Acts of Parliament. The existence of an international market for the exchange of ideas is neither a necessary nor a sufficient step for such thinking to replace national history in determining national tax systems.

214

Theories of political culture suggest that a government ought to reject the importation of alien ideas about taxation. Each nation's culture represents a distinctive or unique mix of values, beliefs and symbols, distilled from centuries of experience, and transmitted from generation to generation through political institutions and Acts of Parliament as well as through political socialization, which encourages practices from a nation's past to persist (Rose, 1985c: chs 4–5; cf. Webber and Wildavsky, 1986).

Political cultures incorporate the values by which citizens judge taxing and spending. In Scandinavian political cultures and in Britain, people have learned to expect a higher level of taxing and spending than in American or Japanese society. Furthermore, cultures reflect attitudes toward tax morality. In Southern Europe and in France, the cultural tolerance for the evasion of income tax is so high that the tax system is designed to rely upon other measures with strong enough tax handles to prevent evasion. In Britain and most Northern European countries, there is sufficient trust between citizen and state to support the expectation that people ought to and will pay taxes due.

Insofar as differences in national history do persist, then we would expect major differences to exist between national tax systems. Since there are virtually no new taxes under the sun, this means that even when the same taxes are in use there would remain substantial differences between nations in the proportion of revenue collected by particular taxes, and thus in the structure of national tax systems. The persistence of diversity among national tax systems is the cross-national complement of the persistence of political inertia within a nation.

Insofar as generic ideas about taxation are valid and powerful across national boundaries, we would expect to find national tax systems virtually identical in countries of a similarly high level of national wealth and freedom of inquiry and travel, that is, among the advanced industrial nations belonging to OECD. Even if different national histories cause marginal differences to continue, at a minimum the international circulation of ideas about best practice should lead to increasing convergence among national tax systems. In the postwar era, initial differences should be less significant than convergence toward a single standard (cf. Kerr 1983).

215

The extent of commonality in the tax systems of OECD nations can be measured statistically by comparing the tax system of each nation with a *Standard Tax System*, constituting the unweighted average of the percentage of revenue that each tax contributes to its national tax system. For example, income tax contributes an average of 33 per cent of total tax revenue in OECD nations, social security 24 per cent, and so forth, down to 1 per cent from payroll taxes and otherwise unclassifiable taxes (Rose, 1985: table 1).

The extent to which a given national tax system is identical with the Standard Tax System can be measured by a *distance index*, the arithmetic sum of the differences between the percentage of total revenue raised by a tax in the standard system, and that raised in a particular country. For example, if the contribution of social security to the Standard Tax System is 24 per cent and in Britain it is 19 per cent, this adds 5 per cent to the distance index. The sum of these differences measures a nation's distance from the Standard Tax System. The greater the similarity between a country's national tax system and the Standard Tax System, the closer the distance index is to 0; the greater the difference, the higher the index number. Insofar as most advanced industrial nations have much the same tax system, then the average distance for OECD countries should be close to 0.

In fact, advanced industrial countries differ from each other in taxes used to raise national revenue (Table 9.1). The Standard Tax System is an analytic abstraction rather than a description of common tax practices. The average OECD nation deviates by 42 per cent from the Standard Tax System. Britain is less distant than most nations; its distance index is 31 per cent. One major cause of British distinctiveness is the rating of housing and other buildings, a tax little used in countries not having historic ties with Britain. The countries that deviate most from the Standard are New Zealand, Australia and Denmark, all countries in which little use is made of social security taxes; and France, where income tax is of slight importance.

The convergence hypothesis is consistent with substantial differences among national tax systems today, for it postulates that the differences today are less than in the past – and that they will be further reduced in future. Given a distance in the 1980s

Table 9.1 How Nations Differ from the Standard Tax System

	Distance Index, 1955[a]	Distance Index, 1965[a]	Distance Index, 1982[a]	Convergence(-) Divergence(+) 1955–82	1965–82
New Zealand	30	55	65	+35	+10
Australia	36	50	64	+28	+14
Denmark	56	54	61	+5	+7
France	n.a.	65	60	n.a.	-5
Spain	n.a.	44	50	n.a.	+6
Finland	29	34	49	+20	+15
Japan	36	44	48	+12	+4
Italy	57	52	46	-11	-6
Luxembourg	n.a.	40	40	n.a.	0
Austria	59	40	39	-20	-1
Netherlands	27	31	39	+12	+8
Ireland	72	64	38	-34	-26
Canada	34	40	37	+3	-3
Norway	35	43	35	0	-8
Switzerland	28	41	33	+5	-8
United Kingdom	24	35	31	+7	-4
Germany	45	26	29	-16	+3
USA	44	37	28	-16	-9
Sweden	61	44	25	-36	-19
Belgium	48	37	23	-25	-14
Average	42	44	42	-1.6	-2

a The distance index measures the difference between a particular country's national tax system and the Standard Tax System. The index is calculated by subtracting the share of revenue yielded by a given tax in a given country from the average OECD share of revenue raised by the tax, and summing the results without regard to the sign. The taxes used in compiling the standard system are income tax, social security, VAT and sales, excise, corporation, property, wealth and estate, customs, payroll and otherwise unclassifiable taxes. In 1955 excise and customs must be collapsed into a single category, and data for three countries is missing. Cf. Rose 1985: tables 1, 2.

of 42 per cent, it might be as high as 84 per cent in the 1950s, when economic and social structures were more varied among OECD nations. The country closest to the standard then was Britain, an old industrial nation, and the country furthest was agrarian Ireland.

In fact, there is no tendency for tax systems to converge in response to transnational influences; national differences in taxation have persisted through the postwar era. The average distance from the standard in 1982, 42 per cent, was exactly the same as the distance in 1955 (Table 9.1). The inertia persistence of historic British taxes has, in the course of three decades, caused the United Kingdom to diverge from the Standard. Whereas in 1955 Britain was closest to the Standard (distance index: 24 per cent), by 1982 it was fifth (31 per cent).

Through the years nations are as likely to move away from the standard system as move towards it. The changes in taxes occurring between and within nations tend to cancel each other out. In this period, seven of the seventeen nations for which comparable data is available have moved towards the Standard Tax System. Concurrently, nine have moved away, and one did not change. Each country seems to follow a course directed more by the political inertia of national history than by current international ideas of best practice in the operation of tax systems.

Change Within Britain

The persistence of national distinctiveness is consistent with gradual change within a nation. Moreover, the theory of political inertia predicts that in the *longue durée* significant changes are likely. Changes will not reflect conscious decisions of the Chancellor of the day, for this typical decision scarcely affects the amount of money that each tax contributes to the fisc. Changes occur through the cumulative and unintended compounding of unintended changes in economic activity, augmented by changes in tax administration, and such consistency as successive governments bring to amendments in tax rates and tax bases.

The extent of change in the British tax system since 1948 can be measured by a national distance index, calculated by the same logic as above. The standard or base for this index is the percentage that each tax contributed to the British tax system in 1948. The value of the distance index in a given year represents the sum of the differences between the percentage that each tax contributed to the system in 1948, and its share in a given year.

If the decisions of politicians were the sole cause of change in

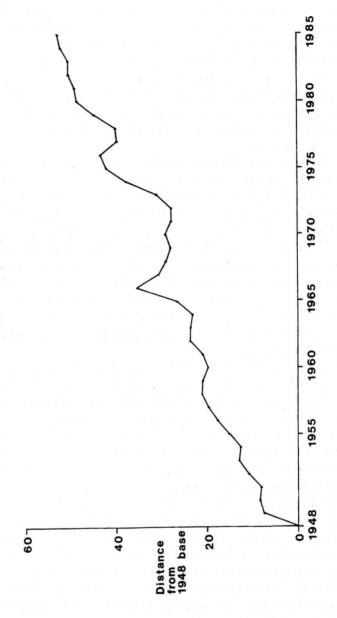

Figure 9.1   Inertia changes in the tax system from the base in 1948

the national tax system, then the tendency of British chancellors to avoid making decisions with a large and immediate impact on revenue should result in the distance index remaining low from decade to decade, as each year's revenue is derived by virtually the same tax legislation as the year before (cf. Table 7.2). However, insofar as inertia is a dynamic force, because of the interaction of persisting laws and a changing economy, then unintended changes would alter the tax system substantially. The gradual increase in the distance index would reflect the absence of active decisions necessary to maintain the tax system in a steady state.

The course of the British tax system since 1948 has been directed by political inertia (Figure 9.1; cf. Figure 7.1). There has been a slow but steady trend away from the 1948 structure. A decade later the distance index had risen to 21 per cent. By 1968 the distance from the base two decades earlier was 29 per cent; in 1978, 40 per cent, and by 1985, 53 per cent. In short, the difference between Britain today and in 1948 is even greater than that between the average OECD nation and the Standard Tax System.[1] Changes within Britain due to the inertia of national history are just as great as cross-national differences caused by historical variations in the direction in which inertia moves particular countries.

In total tax effort, the British tax system today differs very little from 1948; in the former year 35.5 per cent of the national product was levied in taxation, and today 38 per cent. But the sources of tax revenue are substantially different. Tobacco is no longer a significant tax, and national insurance taxes have greatly increased in importance. In place of a variety of *ad hoc* purchase taxes there is now a value added tax that applies more widely, and raises much more money.

Even though no Chancellor has chosen to make a radical break with the past in taxation, the unintended nth-order consequences of big changes in the economy and small-scale decisions about tax rates and bases have cumulatively produced a big change in the British tax system. But the slow pace at which it has altered demonstrates that the change has not been the result of a single decision, or even the decisions of a single Parliament. The changes have been as gradual and persisting as the force of inertia.

Constraints Upon 'Reform'

Many kinds of tax reform are conceivable, but that does not make them equally possible. The imagination of theorists can in the abstract create tax systems of great clarity and logic, by comparison with the hotch-potch system that is the result of political inertia. The aspirations of politicians in opposition can lead to proposals for tax changes that are meant to be as attractive as they are vague. But that is not an indication of the adoption of these proposals in the years ahead, for they are usually outside the bounds of realization.

The rhetoric of tax reform is not to be confused with the realities. The phrase tax reform is appealing to many audiences because it is ambiguous. The phrase symbolizes dissatisfaction with the status quo; it leaves open the direction and consequences of change. On the radical right, it may refer to proposals to abolish taxes. To the left-of-centre, it promises more revenue to spend on programmes for the masses by increasing taxes on the few.

The inertia theory emphasizes continuity, not decisive reform. While change is possible, it is confined. The great identity constrains how much money can be devoted to tax cuts without also imposing expenditure cuts, and it similarly constrains expenditure increases to what beneficiaries, in their role as taxpayers, are deemed ready to bear. Limits are also imposed by history, politics and administration.

Constraints upon Change

History limits reformers, because it imposes an inheritance of established tax laws and institutions, and an immediate need for revenue to meet historically determined spending commitments. Reformers cannot decide what situation they will inherit; it is imposed upon them. In the words of a politically sophisticated Harvard economist:

> Discussions of optimal taxation implicitly assume that the tax laws are being written *de novo* on a clean sheet of paper. Such tax design is a guide for tax policy in the Garden of Eden. The optimal tax laws for the next year are not the same as they

221

would be if taxes were being introduced for the first time. Optimal taxation depends on the historical context. (Feldstein, 1976: 77)

As Feldstein learned as Chairman of President Reagan's Council of Economic Advisers, an optimist can be confronted with a sub-optimal context.

Electoral politics too impose vetoes. Whereas an academic or a journalist may recommend an increase in taxation with no harm to his future career, it could prove suicidal for a politician or a political party to be identified with a proposal to double VAT or increase income tax by half. Even if a tax change is revenue-neutral, those aggrieved by tax increases are likely to protest more loudly and effectively than those benefited. An American tax expert, Richard Goode, has reckoned as a rule of thumb that the beneficiaries must outnumber the losers by a ratio of about 4 to 1 for a tax reform to be politically acceptable. The major 1986 American federal tax act divided individual winners and losers in about this ratio.[2]

The economy also confines change, for it is far easier to make alterations in the tax system when the Chancellor has money to give away than when there is not the extra revenue to finance big tax cuts. The ideal for a tax reform is that no one should be worse off because of a change in the law. Since some people are bound to be better off (otherwise there is no material advantage in change), the fisc loses money. The money surrendered to finance reforms can be recovered if a booming economy increases the tax base. If income is generally rising, the Treasury can remove anomalies in income tax at a cost to the fisc that can be offset by more revenue from continuing taxes. A hold harmless approach to tax reform that is, no one is worse off and some people are better off, is politically attractive, but it is limited by the amount of money that the fisc can afford to give in tax reductions. Britain's low postwar rate of economic growth has not made it easy to finance reforms painlessly by economic growth.

Administrative politics present additional obstacles to tax reform, for tax officials are well informed, and have a special interest in avoiding difficulties in the implementation and administration of novel taxes. Any proposal to swap a new tax for an old tax invites the administrative rejoinder in defence of the status quo: it works, and we can prove it, because the tax is already there. A novel tax proposal will by definition be untested, and its administrative practicality unknown. Tax administrators are not interested in debating the theoretical advantages of new taxes as 'their prime task is to keep the system going and the revenue flowing in' (Robinson and Sandford, 1983: 227).

Persons campaigning for tax reform often castigate the Inland Revenue for failing to do what reformers think is easy to achieve. So great is the gap between what reformers and the Inland Revenue want that John Kay, director of the Institute of Fiscal Studies, has concluded that the primary lesson he has learned from a decade of work is: 'We shall not reform the British tax system unless we reform the Inland Revenue first' (Kay, 1986: 2). Whereas critics may damn the status quo as intolerable, opponents of reform can damn proposals for change as impossible. Each term is used rhetorically in an attempt to influence judgements about what is to be done. The very fact that a tax has been in effect for years is evidence that it has been tolerated, if only as a lesser evil. However, criticism is evidence that a tax is not entirely acceptable, and may sooner or later be classified as intolerable. Labelling a proposal as impossible does not mean that it is inconceivable. The existence of political debate shows that it is on the political agenda.

From Impossible to Not Impossible Changes

In reviewing proposals for reform, it is important to start from the historical present. Whatever else may be said of the British tax system, it is not a *tabula rasa*; it is a jungle rather than a Garden of Eden. At any given point in time, political assessments of proposals for reform can be made along a continuum ranging from impossible or extremely difficult through degrees of not impossible to no problem at all.

The replacement of the income tax by an expenditure tax is one example of a major revenue-neutral proposal for tax reform that has been dismissed as administratively impossible. It has also failed to find elected politicians prepared to embrace an idea that has had academic sponsors of repute. The proposal was promoted by Nicholas Kaldor of Cambridge (1955), and subsequently recommended by a committee headed by Professor James Meade (1978), a Nobel laureate. The underlying concept is simple: the base of taxation should no longer be income; instead, it should be expenditure.

Two leading advocates of the expenditure tax admit that 'the transitional problem is a serious one' (Kay and King, 1983: 87). They therefore recommend that the tax be adopted by a series of evolutionary steps, intended to mitigate some of the problems of transition. After considering difficulties of transition, they ask: 'Why do so many people believe, as we used to believe, that an expenditure tax might be fine in theory but could not work in practice?' (Kay and King, 1983:94). Two possible explanations were offered by the advocates, both of which were criticisms of critics rather than admissions of deficiencies in their proposals. Opponents of an expenditure tax ignored the alleged deficiencies of the established system, or were unwilling to think in terms of a root-and-branch change in the system.

Electoral politics can veto tax reforms as readily as can administrative objections. Many tax experts recommend repealing the relief from taxation of interest payments on a house mortgage. The argument is that this constitutes an unfair advantage to house-purchasers as against renters, who must pay rent from post-tax income, and that this is especially unfair in an era when house prices tend to rise faster than the cost of living. If tax relief were abolished, the resulting broadening of the tax base could raise an extra £5b in tax revenue or finance a cut in income tax rate of more than 3p in the pound. Administratively, it would be simpler to abolish tax relief on mortgages than to continue the present system.

The political argument against abolishing tax relief on mortgage payments is simple: 60 per cent of the electorate are now home-owners, most of whom are currently paying for their house through a mortgage. Any party proposing to abolish this tax allowance would be attacked for pushing up mortgage costs. Those who had already paid off their mortgage would also be adversely affected, for a prospective purchaser would not be able to pay so high a price if interest payments were not subsidized by tax relief. Recommendations to abolish tax relief on mortgages can thus be found in academic writings on public finance, but parties do not write the proposal into their election manifesto. For example, Jeff Rooker, the Labour Party housing spokesman, declared in a pre-election speech 'as long as we have an income tax system in the UK, mortgage tax relief will be available. I can't be more long-term than that' (*The Times*, 26 March, 1987).

In addition to ideas that are currently out of bounds, a variety of proposals for major changes in taxation remain in political limbo. The fact that they are often talked about indicates weaknesses in existing tax laws, and a degree of continuing interest in reform proposals. Yet ideas that remain indefinitely on the political agenda are ideas whose time has not yet – or may never – come (cf. Kingdon, 1984). They are best described as not impossible.

The introduction of a *local income tax* in place of rates on property is a very familiar idea in Britain; it was proposed at the time of local government reform in 1888. By the late nineteenth century, nearly every family had a money income; therefore, there was no need to rely exclusively upon taxes on tangible and impossible-to-conceal property. There is no doubt that a local income tax is administratively practicable, for it is in use in Scandinavia and West Germany, and in many American cities (Newton, 1980: 128ff.). Income tax is generally favoured because it reflects the ability of people to pay. In local government it has two other prominent features. An income tax can be levied according to the place of work rather than residence, thus making those who work in a city but live in a suburb contribute to city revenue. Revenue from such a tax can also be used to finance the repeal of rates.

Dissatisfaction with existing sources of local authority revenue led the 1974 Labour government to establish a wide-ranging inquiry into local government finance under Sir Frank Layfield (Cmnd 6453, 1976). It recommended, among other things, the adoption of a local income tax, collected through the PAYE system. The Thatcher government too has shown dissatisfaction with the existing system of local government finance. In 1986 it published a review, *Paying for Local Government* (Cmnd 9714, 1986). It has followed the 1974 Labour government in rejecting a local income tax. It has been distinctive in proposing a community charge, that is, a poll tax on every adult resident in a local authority.

225

Political reasons veto the adoption of a local income tax in Britain. Party political concerns are evident in Conservative dislike of a tax that would be levied by inner-city Labour authorities on the earnings of middle-class office-workers who live in Conservative suburbs. Moreover, because Conservatives are anxious to keep local authority spending down, they do not want to give the authorities a new and broader tax base. Labour as well as Conservative Chancellors of the Exchequer have argued that a local income tax would reduce the power of the Treasury to manage the economy, by reducing its control of revenue. Hence, local income tax has remained for a century a not impossible reform rather than a reality.

Another proposal on the political agenda for many years is the *equalization of tax allowances without regard to marital status*. Under present law, a single person receives an allowance of £2,335 as a reduction in gross income; a married man receives an allowance approximately one-and-a-half times the single person's allowance of £3,655; and a married woman in work has a personal allowance of £2,335 added to that already received by her husband, giving a married couple a total allowance of £5,990. If both partners to a marriage are working, not only do they earn more money but also they enjoy a tax allowance that is nearly two-thirds greater than that of a couple in which only the husband works (Cmnd 9756, 1986).

The present system of personal allowances discriminates not only between sexes and between married and unmarried persons, but also between women according to their status as employed persons or housewives. In addition, its effect varies according to family earnings. Because the income of husband and wife are combined for tax assessment, a couple who are both school teachers could find themselves liable for taxation at above the standard rate, and the effective tax rate on the earnings of a woman with a husband already in higher tax brackets could average 40 per cent or more. There is actually a tax incentive for wealthy working couples to be divorced and continue to live together, for this would lower their total income tax bill (cf. Cmnd 8093, 1980).

The political logic of reform is straightforward: it is to hold harmless the effects of change, by altering allowances so that no one would be worse off, and some would be better off. This could

226

be achieved by leaving the allowance for the most advantaged group, the two-earner family, as it is at £5,990. To achieve equalization, the allowance for a couple where the husband is the only wage-earner would need to rise by almost two-thirds to £5,990. To become equal to half the allowance for a married couple, that for a single person would need to increase by more than one-quarter to £2,995.

Money is the big difficulty in introducing such a substantial change in personal allowances. Because no family would pay more and some would pay less, the Treasury would be worse off. Depending upon the speed with which a new set of allowances was phased in and the relationship of changes in allowances to other changes resulting from inflation, the cost to the Treasury could be up to £2.7b (Cmnd 9756, 1986: 13) – and this total could be further increased by other consequential adjustments. No Chancellor has yet seen fit to endorse so big a change.

Inequities are also created by the interaction of tax allowances and social security benefits, which creates a *poverty trap* for people on low wages. At present, a low wage earner may find that for each additional pound earned, 60 to 100 per cent of the increase is lost in taxation and the withdrawal of means-tested benefits. Such losses can happen when a household goes above the threshold at which it is liable to pay income tax and social security tax at a combined rate of 36 per cent, and concurrently begins to lose means-tested income supplements. In extreme cases the claw back (that is, the reduction in benefit for each additional pound earned) can cause a family caught in the poverty trap to lose more than a pound for every additional pound earned, until additional earnings rise sufficiently to lift the family out of the trap.

The road to reform is clear in principle: to integrate the calculation of taxes and social security benefits so that poor persons would not be subject to very high rates of income loss as long as they remained on below-average incomes. The technical method for doing this can be described as a Negative Income Tax, for it involves authorizing a tax credit to each taxpayer. If income fell below a certain point, then the credit would be paid out in cash. If income was greater than the tax credit, taxes would be due in the normal manner. The reform is not identified with one political party. Milton Friedman, a prominent rightwing economist, has been a proponent of it, and moves in this direction were made by both the Heath and Nixon administrations in the early 1970s (Cmnd 5116, 1972; Lenkowsky, 1986).

Getting rid of the poverty trap is immediately attractive politically as a measure of blame avoidance. But there are two major sets of problems in abolishing the poverty trap. The first is money. A simple way to end the trap would be a hold harmless measure that raised the threshold at which low-earners were subject to very high marginal rates of income loss. But doing this would also benefit the majority of low income-earners, who are *not* caught in the poverty trap. The total cost of such a broadbrush approach to reform is estimated at about £8b (Cmnd 9756, 1986), and most of the money lost to the fisc would not go to the 600,000 or so taxpayers whose marginal rate of loss is 50 per cent or higher (Kay and King, 1983: 106).

Secondly, because the problem is caused by the perverse and unintended consequences of separate actions by two ministries, its resolution necessarily requires co-ordinated action by the Inland Revenue and the Department of Health and Social Security. The former is responsible for taxing the poor as well as the wealthy, and the latter for paying income-related benefits to the poor. Each agency has its own staff, its own priorities and its own records. While all the details of a household's income, benefits and taxes are in the hands of government, they are *not in the same hand*. To link records about individuals would be a massive task of computerization, requiring a continuing and high volume of exchange of information between taxing and spending arms of government by mechanisms that government does not at present have.

In the fullness of time, the destabilizing effects of political inertia can introduce big net changes that politicians have not consciously chosen. When political circumstances change, vetoes can be reduced to obstacles, and proposals that have languished on the political agenda may suddenly appear compelling. The cause of change is usually not the discovery of new ideas about taxation, but political changes that make the costs of doing nothing much greater than a decision to act (Rose, 1972). For example, VAT was not introduced because it had suddenly been invented. Antecedents of the tax had been used in past centuries, and a turnover tax was adopted in Germany in 1918 and in France in 1920 (Aaron, 1981). Value added tax was adopted in Britain as a necessary condition of joining the European Community, a political imperative of the Prime Minister.

A study of 'rationality, ideology and politics' in the evaluation of proposals for new taxes concludes that politics matters most, and that political arguments usually weigh strongly against major change. The only changes that can be expected are strictly incremental changes in the rate and base of established taxes, and other elements of fringe tuning. Writing from the perspective of reformers, Robinson and Sandford (1983: 232) conclude that this is 'a pretty pitiful result from two decades of enthusiastic tax reform'. But from the perspective of the fisc, there was nothing pitiful, or even static, for in the period that Robinson and Sandford studied, the fisc gained a 1,200 per cent increase in revenue, primarily due to the effects of political inertia.

In Pursuit of More Revenue

Why should politicians want more revenue, when their political instincts tell them that taking money from citizens is unpopular? The answer is contained in the great identity: spending programmes are generally popular. Even 'government-averse' politicians such as Margaret Thatcher or Ronald Reagan face pressures to increase public expenditure. From 1979 to 1987, the Conservatives have presided over a public-spending increase of more than £65b. Under President Reagan, federal government spending has gone up by more than $400b; this anti-spending (*sic*) politician has introduced the first trillion dollar budget in Washington.

The most immediate pressures for revenue are those that require spending more money to keep things as they are. Inflation affects the cost of government as well as everything else in the economy. The relative price effect – that is, the tendency for the cost of producing labour-intensive public services to rise faster than capital-intensive manufactured goods – generates a further demand for revenue. The major open-ended entitlements of the welfare state – education, health and pensions – require spending to rise when there are more people to claim the benefits to which they are entitled. None of these pressures expand the coverage of public policies, or raise the level of benefits received. Improving benefits or providing them to more people further increases the government's need for money (OECD, 1985).

Insofar as political inertia produces a greater increase in spending commitments than in tax revenue, politicians are necessarily forced to seek additional revenue by all means necessary. Given political constraints upon intentionally increasing taxes, there are attractions in seeking to raise more money from non-tax sources of revenue. The fact that they are already in use means that such measures are administratively practicable, as well as authorized by statute. But the fact that each usually makes a relatively small contribution to the fisc means that such efforts to increase public revenue usually cannot go far before a political reaction is generated by suddenly altering their scale.

Economic Growth

In theory, the most profitable and politically painless way to raise more money for the fisc is through economic growth. While this causes an increase in tax revenue to the fisc, a higher rate of economic growth also causes an increase in earnings and in consumption to the ordinary taxpayer, for post-tax take-home pay rises as well as tax revenue. An increase of 1 per cent in the annual rate of economic growth adds £4b to the tax base; if it is distributed as is the present tax effort, this would provide £2.6b for the private sector, and £1.6b to the fisc, even allowing a little for fringe cuts in taxes. Moreover, the increase in revenue can compound in successive years to the benefit of all concerned. Hugh Heclo (1981: 397) aptly describes the multiple benefits of a high rate of economic growth as making possible 'policy without pain'.

In practice, the British economy has grown more slowly than politicians would like. In the three decades since 1951 the annual rate of growth has averaged 2.1 per cent a year, less than half that of major Western nations. Moreover, the rate of growth has been slowing down; it has averaged 1.3 per cent per annum in the years since the 1973 oil crisis (Rose and Karran, 1984). In some years, the British economy has actually contracted. The slowing down of the British economy increases the need for more revenue by pushing up public expenditure to assist the unemployed and others affected by a stagnant economy. Since unemployment simultaneously depresses revenue from such sources as income tax, national insurance and corporation tax, the pressure to increase public spending comes at a time when tax revenue cannot be expected to grow painlessly.

In the 1960s politicians confronted with low rates of economic growth tried to forecast their way out of this dilemma, preparing estimates of future growth rates that were historically un-justified. The forecasts were politically appealing, for they encouraged more spending without implying any need to increase taxes. Spending rose as much or more than forecast, but revenue did not, because forecasts proved to be excessively optimistic. The worldwide recession of the mid-1970s has reduced confidence in mathematically sophisticated forecasts of economic growth. Even with hindsight the models may not produce accurate descriptions of what is likely to happen in the economy (Posner, 1978). Moreover, politicians are now aware of the risks of over-indulging in optimistic forecasting, because of the inflationary hangover that is likely to follow.

The attempt of supply-side economists in the Reagan administration to generate more revenue by 'painless' forecasts was sufficient to legitimate a major tax cut in 1981. But it was not sufficient to produce the revenue required to meet spending commitments (cf. Roberts, 1984; Stein, 1984). The immediate result was pressure to raise taxes when the policy was seen to fail. The medium-term consequence has been a deficit ap-proaching $200b a year in the American federal government – and a caution for politicians elsewhere against relying upon growth that may not occur.

Borrowing

Borrowing is a normal practice in financing any large organiza-tion, in order to deal with uncertainties and unevenness that inevitably arise in cash flow. Rather than budget for a revenue surplus large enough to cover every contingency, an organiza-tion may borrow. This logic implies that revenue surpluses as

231

well as deficits will occur. In fact, this is not the case. For decades the budget of British government has normally been in deficit.

A second reason for borrowing is that the money can be spent in ways that will increase future revenue sufficiently to meet the cost of the loans. Capital investment is a classic reason for borrowing; money invested in building houses may be repaid by future rent. Keynesian economists argue that in times of recession a fiscal deficit can generate increased public revenue by increasing consumer demand and economic growth. The same logic suggests that in boom times a government should run a budget surplus in order to reduce inflation. In fact, contemporary governments have not consistently followed Keynesian prescriptions, borrowing at times when the stimulus of a deficit was not required by Keynesian thinking (Saunders and Klau, 1985, tables 1, 19; Rose and Peters, 1978: 135ff.).

Since the experience of inflation in the mid-1970s, the Treasury has been concerned with the potential inflationary effects of increased borrowing, especially that public borrowing to finance current consumption might crowd out funds needed to finance investment in economic growth. These points, which are particularly stressed by monetarists such as Milton Friedman, are today accepted much more widely; classic Keynesian prescriptions do not generate as much confidence among policy-makers as they once did.

Credit – the ability of government to borrow money for current spending – is an important resource of government. But it is also a finite resource. This fact of life has repeatedly confronted governments prone to borrowing. In 1967 and again in 1976, Labour governments went to the International Monetary Fund for loans to help refinance a national economy becoming unstable because of the budget imbalance between spending and taxing.

The election in 1979 of a Conservative government under Margaret Thatcher, who entered office an ardent monetarist, has made the restriction of borrowing a central goal of government, taking priority before reductions in tax rates (Walters, 1986; Riddell, 1983). The government has brought the public sector borrowing requirement (PSBR) down to much lower levels than in most OECD nations, and inflation has followed the worldwide trend downwards. Since expenditure has remained high and the economy has only grown intermittently, this leaves limited scope for tax cuts. By contrast, the Reagan administration has been willing to finance tax cuts by borrowing.

Whilst the low PSBR of the Thatcher government in no sense defines a ceiling for raising revenue by borrowing, a constraint is imposed by the fact that money is borrowed against future tax revenues. The more money borrowed in the past, the greater the weight of debt interest payments generated by political inertia. Each year the government must borrow more money to pay the additional interest required to finance last year's borrowing.

As annual deficits accumulate from year to year, the cost of the interest on the debt tends to rise. In 1974, interest on the debt accounted for 11 per cent of public expenditure and 4 per cent of the British national product. By 1986 it accounted for £17.5b, a larger proportion of the budget than any other programmes except social security, defence and health (Cf. Table 2.3). Debt interest payments have become more than treble the annual public sector borrowing requirement. If the PSBR and interest rates rose rapidly, debt interest payments could become the second biggest expenditure item in the budget.

Charges

Whereas taxation offers nothing specific in return for money paid, user charges and fees offer something for something, that is, a specific benefit in return for a payment to a public agency. Charging for public services appears attractive to market-oriented politicians, for it makes those who benefit from a public facility pay for them. Even if the charge does not cover the full cost of providing the service, it does at least introduce a market signal of demand, which is relevant to decisions about pro-gramme expenditure (Seldon, 1977). In the absence of any charge, non-market means must be used to estimate the amount of public services that should be supplied. Charges are usually opposed by Socialists, who argue that public services should be available to citizens as of right, without regard to what they would or could pay. While economists recognize advantages in market signals, the external benefits of publicly provided services are such that economic justifications can often be advanced for providing public services without charge, or at a subsidy (cf. Judge, 1980).

The great bulk of public programmes are conducted on the principle that the recipients cannot or should not pay for them. By definition, no charges can be made for collective goods, such as defence and law and order, from which individuals cannot be excluded. In theory, charges could be made for all private goods and services; those who did not want to pay for these services (or claim a means-tested grant to pay for them) could be excluded. Services for which, in principle, it would be possible to make charges include education and health, and many local government services, such as recreation and rubbish collection. However, on grounds of political principle, these are usually provided free of charge.

Notwithstanding the principle of free public services, charges may incidentally be made for a variety of private goods provided by government. The charges may involve marginal benefits, as in the case of the national health service, or as a primary condition of use, as in council house rents, public transport or attendance at opera and ballet. But the revenue generated is usually insufficient to finance the cost of the service.

All nationalized industries make charges for their services. But since these industries normally are in competition with private-sector companies, with foreign firms or, in energy, with other nationalized industries, their prices cannot be raised without a risk of losing customers and aggregate revenue. This is particularly the case for those industries that run at a loss, or are intensely competitive. Pushing up charges in industries that more than cover their revenue can attract political criticism; the oppostion can argue that government is using quasi-monopoly powers to push up prices.

The political obstacles to increasing prices for public services are similar to those for increasing taxes. In the case of raising prices for such basic products as electricity, any substantial increase will visibly push up the cost of living. The imposition of a charge where none existed before will mobilize maximum opposition, for an issue of principle is raised, as well as a question of money. This can be seen in the opposition to museum charges, which have raised relatively small sums but breached the principle of free (that is, open without charge) museums. Opposition to introducing a charge where none has been made before explains why charges made in other countries, for example, tolls for the use of motorways, are not introduced by politicians who prefer to minimize political costs.

Privatization

Selling assets is another source of revenue. The motive for doing so may be commercial, as when the government grants a lease on Crown property to a private developer on terms that would be comparable to those charged by a private landowner. The motive may also be ideological: the Thatcher government's sale of publicly owned corporations, such as British Telecom, was stimulated by a belief in the advantage to society of private ownership, just as the nationalization measures of Labour governments have reflected a belief in the social superiority of public ownership. From a public-finance perspective, selling assets is also significant as a source of revenue (cf. Heald, 1985; Steel and Heald, 1985).

Until the mid-1970s, asset sales were not a significant source of revenue, for neither Conservative nor Labour governments wanted to sell public assets, and there was little that could be rented or leased to generate annual revenue. Since then, asset sales have been important in two very different ways, as an annual source of revenue from the sale of oil, and as a non-recurring source of revenue through the sale of capital assets, such as shares in nationalized industries.

The boom in *oil prices* turned the government's ownership of North Sea oil from a minor asset into a bonanza. While the oil fields are expensive to exploit, the rise in oil prices made them economically attractive. In turn, this increased the revenue that the government could extract, not only through taxation but also by leasing oil exploitation rights or selling oil through state-owned enterprises. Oil revenues grew rapidly with increased extraction in the late 1970s, and were further boosted by the second big oil price increase. By 1980, oil revenues were generating £6.2b of revenue for the government; of this, the government claimed four-fifths as taxes, and one-fifth from the sale of exploitation rights and the oil itself. By 1985, before the slump in world oil prices, total revenues had more than doubled.

The sharp fall in world oil prices in 1986 shows that revenue from market activities is vulnerable to fluctuations in the market. A drop in oil prices by a third to a half costs the Treasury billions of pounds in revenue from oil sales and taxes. The amount of revenue is further destabilized by the fact that oil is priced in dollars. Changes in the sterling–dollar relationship also alter revenue independent of the world price of oil.

By contrast, revenue generated by *privatization*, that is, the once-for-all sale of assets, is certain in the current year, but it is not renewable, for the asset is gone forever. One object of the privatization sales of the Thatcher government has been to remove government from many market activities. Another consequence has been to generate billions of pounds of revenue that, for one year only, can be used to offset expenditure in the budget.

In its first term of office, the Thatcher government generated only symbolic sums of revenue from privatization sales. In 1980 it raised £405m; in 1981, £494m; and in 1983, £488m. Except for oil-related activities, only the sale of Cable and Wireless shares netted more than £100m (Cmnd 9702–II, 1986: table 2.23). In its second term of office, the Thatcher government realized £1.1b in fiscal year 1983/4 from the sale of shares in British Petroleum, Britoil, and Cable and Wireless, and the following year a total of £2.0b, principally from the sale of British Telecommunications; Jaguar Motor Cars was also sold. Revenue has since been as much as an additional £4.7b in each of the three following financial years from sales of such assets as the British Gas Corporation, and British Airways.

The crucial feature of privatization through asset sales is that it cannot be sustained indefinitely, for assets will no longer be there to sell. The bulk of marketable public assets are due to have been sold by 1990. As long as it is in public ownership an enterprise such as British Gas could contribute a portion of its revenue annually to the fisc, but once in private hands it ceases to do so. The fisc has the capital gain from privatization proceeds, but if this is used to finance current expenditure, it is not an investment generating a continuing stream of income. The nationalized industries remaining in public ownership, for instance British Rail and the National Coal Board, will be loss-making corporations that annually take money from the fisc.

Budgetary Cannibalism

Budgetary cannibalism is the final way in which government may finance increased expenditure; the term refers to the practice of cutting back spending on some programmes to feed money to allocate to other programmes. Even when the total available for public spending remains constant, significant reallocations can be made between programmes. Strictly speaking, budgetary cannibalism does not provide additional revenue, but it does provide more money to spend on some programmes, albeit at the cost of cutting back on others (Tarschys, 1985).

In an era of budgetary expansion, cannibalism was not necessary; discrimination between programmes was expressed by some growing faster than others. Yet even in this period, after discounting the effects of inflation, a few programmes, such as defence and agriculture, did show a reduction in spending in volume terms.

Since the fiscal stress of the mid-1970s, government spending in volume terms has contracted for a number of programmes. Under both Labour and Conservative governments, spending has decreased in volume terms for housing, environmental services, transport and agriculture. It has decreased under Labour for defence, education, industry and trade as well, and under the Conservatives for libraries and museums, and school meals and welfare foods (Rose, 1984a: table 7.1; Robinson, 1986).

Budgetary cannibalism is more likely to be forced upon a government than to result from a positive decision. Pressures to spend more on some programmes arise from statutory and contractual commitments, such as to pensioners, the unemployed, and those due interest on loans to government. When bills must be paid and there is no scope for raising more tax revenue or raising more money from non-tax sources, then the only way to meet these claims is by cutting back expenditure on programmes for which spending is not mandatory.

A Cost–Benefit Analysis for Citizens

Taxation is the cost that citizens pay for receiving the benefits of government. Citizens do not purchase public benefits by paying taxes earmarked for particular public services, as one might purchase goods in a shop. Even in the case of social security, national insurance contributions are just that, contributions toward the cost of benefits. They are not sufficient to finance inflation-proofed benefits, and income-maintenance grants can be received by persons who have not paid contributions regularly.

Citizenship is an all-or-nothing proposition.[3] A person does not select which benefits and which taxes are desirable; benefits *and* costs must be accepted as a package. While the enjoyment of public benefits is optional – a person is not compelled to use the national health service, send children to a state school or live in a council house – the payment of taxes is mandatory.

As preceding chapters have shown, comparison of what citizens pay and what they get from government is *not* the basis for collective decision by the mass public. The entries in an analytic cost–benefit analysis are the result of a long process of many decisions made in the distant and near past. Individuals who do not like the aggregate result have no choice but to accept this legacy, or to emigrate from Britain. Acceptance is normal.

Costs and Benefits

Nearly nine-tenths of all families receive in a year at least one public benefit of major importance to family members: a pension, hospital care, education, subsidized public transport or council housing, unemployment benefit, etc. (Table 9.2). Some of these benefits are of daily importance, such as housing, public transport or a pensioner's income, and some benefits are invoked only intermittently in case of need, such as medical treatment or claiming an unemployment benefit. Even the small fraction not receiving any benefits at one point can expect to claim benefits when they are raising children, in sickness, and in old age. Most families benefit from public services in several ways. Even though no one programme is regularly used by more than two-fifths of families, the benefits are sufficiently widespread so that the average family will rely upon 2.3 benefits in a year. Just as everybody pays for the programme of the welfare state, so virtually everybody benefits.

If people had to provide such benefits for themselves rather than have them financed by the fisc, a family would need to save or spend thousands of pounds a year additional to its current household expenditure. Whether expenditure on health, education or pensions is financed by taxes, by private expenditure or by a combination of the two, in a modern money economy these

Table 9.2 Households Receiving a Major State Welfare Benefit

	Receive (as % total hosueholds)
Dependent on public transport	38
Pensions	36
Regular treatment, doctor	35
Education	34
Housing	30
Hospital care, past year	29
Unemployment benefit	23
Personal social services	5
All families, at least one benefit	89

Source: Calculated from a Gallup Poll survey, reported in the *Daily Telegraph*, 3 April, 1984.

services must be organized and paid for. However the bills are paid, these services will claim from one-sixth to one-third of the national product (cf. OECD, 1985).

The taxes levied to finance social benefits tend to be proportional rather than progressive in incidence. The proportion of earnings or gross cash income paid in tax is much the same for the average wage earner and for the well-to-do person. Even when taxes are progressive, there are strict limits to the potential for redistribution, since the immediate effect of progressive taxation is simply to reduce the gross income of those with above-average earnings. Taxation does not, by itself, increase the income of persons with below-average earnings.

The redistributive element in the budget arises from public expenditure on cash-transfer payments (such as pensions, unemployment benefits, etc.) and benefits in kind (such as education, the health service, etc.) Nearly the whole of redistribution occurs through cash-transfer payments. The provision of benefits in kind is only slightly redistributive – and sometimes favours those in higher income brackets. While low income groups tend to consume more health services and housing subsidies, high income groups tend to consume more education, and benefit more from rail travel subsidies (*Economic Trends*, No. 386, 1985: 113; see also Le Grand and Robinson, 1984).

239

The circulation of money between the public and private sector is to the benefit of both, inasmuch as cash-transfer payments put money in the hands of individuals who can decide how they want to spend it. The provision of health and education not only benefits the recipients of these services; it also provides jobs for millions of people. The existence of these double-sided benefits explains the breadth and depth of support for programmes of contemporary big government. This qualifies but does not deny the fundamental requirement of the great identity: money spent from the public purse, whether on consumption or transfer payments, must be matched by money raised in revenue.

Take-Home Pay as a Constraint

For generations experts in politics and public finance have specu-lated about the limits to public expenditure and taxation (cf. Larkey *et al.*, 1981). A half-century ago it was argued that the maximum that government could levy in taxation would be 25 per cent of the national product. In the postwar era, every industrial nation has gone well above that figure (Table 2.2). Britain today is average in the proportion of the national product taken in taxes.

Questions about the 'right' size of government are political, not technical. In debates, politicians on the left and right disagree about the ideal level of taxing and spending. In office, however, politicians tend to accept those commitments sustained by political inertia, making fewer changes to taxing and spending than their rhetoric implies (Rose, 1984a).

Take-home pay is a constraint upon politicians, for no elected government wants to raise taxes to such a level that the result is a fall in earnings. The Labour Party is not so enamoured of public expenditure that it promises trade union members a reduction in take-home pay as a condition of expanding the public sector. Nor do union leaders want to tell their members that they should accept less cash in hand for their work because the fisc needs more money to finance more public spending. The goal of politicians is to neutralize the effects of higher taxation by having take-home pay rise along with public expenditure. Even if take-home pay does not rise, politicians do not want blame for a fall in take-home pay.

As long as there is growth in the economy, it is possible for both public expenditure and take-home pay (that is, the post-tax pre-transfer earnings of the average worker) to increase.[4] A growth rate of 2.5 per cent in the economy could finance a 2.5 per cent growth in public expenditure and a 2.5 per cent growth in take-home pay. Even if the fisc received a disproportionate amount– say 60 or 80 pence of each pound added to the national product – no one need be worse off in take-home pay, and some house-holds would be better off because of increases in public benefits.

In a bad year, the economy can actually contract. While economic growth, however small, remains the norm in Britain, contraction happens more often than the Chancellor would like. When the economy contracts, take-home pay could rise if spending and taxes were cut drastically. But in a depression, there are strong political and economic arguments to increase public spending. This may temporarily force a reduction in take-home pay. In a very bad year, public expenditure can account for the whole of the fiscal dividend of growth and then some, forcing a real reduction in take-home pay, directly through higher taxes and indirectly through the tax of inflation. For example, an increase of 5 per cent in public expenditure (a sum equivalent to 2 per cent of the national product) requires 2 per cent growth in the economy, if it is to be financed painlessly. If the economy grows by only 1 per cent, take-home pay is likely to be reduced in consequence.

In decades of affluence after the Second World War, there was no problem in increasing both public revenue and take-home pay. From 1948 to 1960, when tax effort was decreasing, the average industrial worker's earnings rose by 36 per cent in real purchasing power terms. From 1960 to 1973, when tax effort increased in an effort to promote growth through public expenditure, take-home pay rose by 27 per cent. But since the onset of world recession in 1973, British governments have recurringly faced difficulties in maintaining take-home pay.

Since 1974 take-home pay has been as likely to fall as to rise from one year to the next (Table 9.3). It fell steadily from 1973 to 1977. After an abrupt rise in the election year of 1979, it fell again until the year of the 1983 election. Take-home pay has thus fallen in seven years, and risen in five. A decrease is not the result of party policy, for it has happened under both Conservative and

241

Labour governments. The cumulative effect of these ups and downs is that in a period of more than a decade, the value of take-home pay rose by only 3.8 per cent.

The frequent decline in take-home pay is not forced by contraction in the economy, for the economy has been growing in most years under review, and has cumulatively grown by 14.8 per cent since 1973. In three years in which the economy grew, 1976, 1977 and 1982, take-home pay fell, as well as falling in years when the economy contracted.

Take-home pay has been under pressure to decline because taxation has been rising faster than growth in the economy as a whole. While the rate of tax increase has not been steady, for the Wilson–Callaghan government initially favoured financing public expenditure by increased borrowing, the overall pattern is clear: in a slow-growth economy, increases in taxation often require a cut in take-home pay.

At no point did British government announce that it had decided to embark upon a policy of squeezing take-home pay. Nor at any time did an opposition party promise that, if elected, it would deliver cuts in take-home pay. The different patterns of change described in Table 9.3 were an unintended consequence of other decisions, most of which were taken by governments in the past. A fall in take-home pay becomes an unintended (and unwanted) outcome of forces of inertia that push up taxing and spending at a higher rate than can be financed by the painless mechanism of economic growth (Rose and Karran, 1984).

If Forced to Choose . . .

The average voter, like the average politician, has little difficulty in stating a preference about the political economy – more of everything, that is, more economic growth, more public benefits and more take-home pay. Such a choice is easy to make because it is based upon happy assumptions; it does not recognize any constraints.

But if government is forced to choose between two alternatives, each involving something deemed desirable (more public benefits or lower taxes) and something deemed undesirable (higher taxes or lower public benefits), what would voters want?

Table 9.3 The Consequences for Take-home Pay of Low Economic Growth and Increased Taxation

Year	National Product	Total Taxes (1973 = 100)	Take-home Pay
1948	47.9	49.0	58.0
1949	49.3	51.0	57.6
1950	50.9	49.4	58.7
1951	52.7	49.2	58.9
1952	52.6	49.3	61.8
1953	55.0	49.3	64.5
1954	57.1	49.9	67.5
1955	59.3	51.6	70.8
1956	60.3	51.7	71.9
1957	61.5	53.5	72.7
1958	61.5	55.7	71.6
1959	63.9	57.4	75.5
1960	66.9	58.1	78.9
1961	69.2	62.8	79.0
1962	69.8	66.0	78.4
1963	72.6	66.6	81.5
1964	76.4	68.9	83.3
1965	78.3	74.5	84.0
1966	79.9	79.2	83.3
1967	82.0	86.2	84.7
1968	85.4	91.5	84.9
1969	86.6	97.5	85.9
1970	88.5	103.3	89.0
1971	90.9	99.5	90.3
1972	93.0	98.5	97.7
1973	100.0	100.0	100.0
1974	99.0	105.7	98.4
1975	98.5	108.9	94.4
1976	102.0	109.4	92.2
1977	103.3	109.1	91.9
1978	106.8	111.9	98.2
1979	108.3	115.5	101.5
1980	106.8	121.1	99.7
1981	105.4	128.1	96.0
1982	107.2	131.6	95.7
1983	108.8	135.1	99.0
1984	110.6	138.5	102.4
1985	114.8	143.0	103.8

Source: Take-home pay as calculated by the Inland Revenue: the average earnings of a male manual worker less income tax and national insurance contributions. All figures calculated after deflation to constant value sums.

Many politicians think that they know the answer. Margaret Thatcher has frequently announced the desirability of reducing taxes, and Chancellor Nigel Lawson has told the House of Commons:

> We need to continue the process of reducing the burden of taxation, not just as a social service but as a moral duty and an essential means of improving our national economic performance. (House of Commons *Debates*, 3 June 1986)

Thatcherites welcome the fact that tax cuts imply tight constraints on public expenditure, for cutting public expenditure is regarded as desirable too.

Labour and Alliance MPs do not speak in praise of raising taxes, but their continued advocacy of programmes requiring an increase in public expenditure necessarily requires more tax revenue. In its 1983 election manifesto Labour raised the relevant question but gave only half the answer to the question it posed:

> Where will the money come from? Some of it will come from those oil revenues now pouring down the drain. Some of it will come from the billions we waste on the dole queues. Some of it will come from the billions now being allowed to be exported in investment abroad. Yes, and some of it will be *borrowed*.

Since then, the Labour Party has been ready to contemplate tax increases, subject to two conditions. The total sum of money raised would be strictly limited, and tax increases would be directed at a small minority on high incomes. Neil Kinnock justified thus Labour's rejection of the Conservative goal of cutting taxes:

> If it is feasible to operate the programme that we want for regeneration and reunification of this country without charging extra taxes, we would be delighted. I do not see any virtue in charging taxes for their own sake.
>
> But what we have got to do is be honest with people and say if you want these bills met, for the defence of our country for the security of our people, for ensuring a decent anti-crime and disorder regime; if you want to ensure that we can

generate jobs, care properly for the health service, see children are being looked after properly in schools, there is no way at the same time we can put an extra quid in your pocket. (BBC TV, *This Week Next Week*, 11 January 1987)

Since the 1979 election the Gallup Poll has monitored public opinion about priorities for taxing and spending by asking voters to choose which of three alternatives comes closest to their own views: i) taxes being cut, even if it means some reduction in government services, such as health, education and welfare; ii) things should be left as they are; iii) government services such as health, education and welfare should be extended, even if it means some increases in taxes.

When the question was asked after five years of a Labour government in 1979, the electorate divided into three approximately equal groups: one favoured maintaining the status quo, another favoured cutting taxes and services and a third favoured raising both (Table 9.4). The first term of the Thatcher government concentrated rhetorical attention upon cutting taxes and expenditure, albeit this was not achieved. The opposition called for more spending.

The Conservatives have won re-election, but Mrs Thatcher's priorities have failed to win the hearts and minds of most voters. In 1983 nearly half of the electorate declared a preference for higher taxes and spending, and less than one-quarter supported the inclination of the Prime Minister. By March 1984 a majority favoured higher taxes and spending, in direct opposition to the Prime Minister's views. By May 1987 three-fifths endorsed higher taxes and spending, as against 12 per cent favouring cuts in taxes and spending. Whereas in 1979 the median Gallup Poll respondent favoured leaving taxes as they are, since then those favouring higher taxes to finance increased public spending have become a majority (see also Heald and Wybrow, 1986: 124ff.; Rose and McAllister, 1986; 147ff.).

The Gallup Poll question does not call attention to two other circumstances in which taxes and public spending could rise. In a more favourable economic climate, an increase in taxes and in spending could go along with an increase in take-home pay. In unfavourable economic conditions, take-home pay could fall as taxes rose without any increase in the provision of public benefits.

Table 9.4 Popular Attitudes Towards Taxes and Social Spending

	May 1979	Mar. 1983	Mar. 1986	Oct. 1986
	(% endorsing)[a]			
Cut both taxes and social spending	34	23	14	12
Keep things as they are	25	22	25	21
Increase both social spending and taxes	34	49	54	61

a. Don't knows, not shown above, make each column add to 100 per cent.
Source: Gallup Political Index for month indicated.

Whereas an opinion survey can only ask voters to choose between hypothetical alternatives, the government of the day is responsible for what is done. The choice open to British government in the 1990s is like the horns of a dilemma. Political inertia has generated substantial and popular spending commitments. But the economy has not grown at a rate that can painlessly finance growing spending commitments. Thus politicians are now often forced to decide between two unpalatable alternatives: squeezing popular spending programmes, or seeing increased taxes threaten a cut in take-home pay.

No politician would describe the alternatives facing Britain today as a rational choice, let alone an attractive choice. But from the perspective of the *longue durée*, the inheritors of British government are not free to decide what they would like to do. They must cope with the consequences, taxes and all, of what has been produced by the forces of political inertia.

Notes

1   To facilitate comparison with the use of the index for OECD nations, the British taxes have been grouped according to OECD categories, which are very similar to those used in British national income accounts. The use of a more highly differentiated set of tax categories (cf. Rose and Karran, 1983: App. 1) would increase still more the distance that the tax system has moved since 1948.

2 Evaluation by the criterion of Pareto optimality – that no one be worse off and someone be better off – is usually tantamount to an endorsement of the status quo, for it allows any individual or group to veto a change in tax law. This is not a political theory normal in Westminster or Washington; it is the political theory of the old Polish Sjem (Groth, 1972).

3 Strictly speaking, residence in the United Kingdom is the basis of taxation. A British subject can avoid paying British taxes by taking up residence abroad, and a resident alien is deemed liable for payment of taxes, and eligible for most public benefits.

4 Transfer income is not included here, for many who pay taxes to finance such payments are not concurrently in receipt of benefits.

Appendix: List of Sources

1 Data on Current Taxes

All the statistical information on tax revenues was taken from the *United Kingdom Accounts*, compiled on an annual basis by the Central Statistical Office. This source was used in preference to separate publications by the Inland Revenue and the Customs and Excise Office as it is comprehensive and contains details of all taxes levied in Britain. Moreover, it is historically consistent, allowing for the extraction of a reliable time series since 1948.

The names, definitions and means of assigning revenues into different categories have altered over time; new taxes have been introduced and others repealed since 1948. Consequently, information relating to the taxes is grouped into continuing taxes (those levied throughout the period 1948–85); new taxes (those levied in 1985 but introduced after 1948); repealed taxes (those levied in 1948 but repealed before 1985); and introduced and repealed taxes (those introduced after 1948 but repealed before 1985). For the continuing and new taxes, guidance on identification is given below from the most recent (1986) set of National Accounts, along with details of the sources from which data for the earlier years was obtained. All the details are for tax revenues collected in 1985 and relate to table and line entries in *United Kingdom National Accounts, 1986* (London: HMSO, 1986) compiled by the Central Statistical Office. For taxes repealed, information and identification is given for the last full year in which the tax was levied.

APPENDIX: LIST OF SOURCES

Continuing Taxes

Tax Category	1985 Value £m	National Accounts Entry
Income tax	35,448	Table 7.2, lines 1, 2
National insurance	21,468	Table 7.2, line 22
		Table 7.5, lines 1, 5, 6
Local authority rates	13,580	Table 8.2, line 11
Hydrocarbon oil duty	6,260	Table 7.2, line 13
Tobacco duties	4,342	Table 7.2, line 12
Vehicle licences	2,389	Table 7.2, line 21
Wine and spirits duties	2,212	Table 7.2, line 11
Beer duty	1,935	Table 7.2, line 10
Customs and protective duties	1,304	Table 7.2, lines 14, 19
Stamp duty	1,160	Table 7.2, line 26

New Taxes Introduced Since 1948

Tax Category	1985 Value £m	First Full Year	National Accounts Entries
Value added tax (VAT)	20,962	1974	Table 7.2, line 16
Corporation tax	9,128	1967	Table 7.2, line 6
Petroleum revenue tax (PRT)	7,369	1978	Table 7.2, line 4
National Health Service	2,019	1958	Table 7.2, line 32
Capital gains	1,209	1967	Table 9.6, line 35

Repealed Taxes since 1948

Tax Category	Last Year Value £m	Last Full Year	National Accounts Entries
Purchase tax	1,389	1972	*National Income and Expenditure, 1981, table 7.2, line 13*
Profits/excess profits	466	1965	*National Income and Expenditure, 1970, table 37, lines 3, 4*
Entertainment tax	2	1960	*National Income and Expenditure, 1965, table 36, line 13*

Introduced and Repealed Since 1948

Tax Category	First Full Year	Last Year Value £m	Last Full Year	National Accounts Entries
Selective employment tax	1967	449	1972	*National Income and Expenditure, 1981,* table 7.2.

Residual Taxes

There are some taxes which only raise a minor amount of revenue. Moreover, when a tax is discontinued small amounts of revenue may continue to be received for several years; conversely, new taxes may raise a minor amount when they are introduced mid-way through a calendar year. There are some taxes listed under a general categoric heading, such as death duties, for which form and legislation has altered. All those types of taxes are aggregated under the general heading of residual taxes, including overspill relief, death duties, temporary import charge, European Community levies, car tax, gas levy, television contractors' payments, Northern Ireland rates, sugar levy, transport levy, television advertisements payments, capital transfer tax, development land tax, London Regional Transport levy, European Coal and Steel Community levy, redundancy fund contributions and special banking tax.

Tax Category	1985 Value £m	National Accounts Entries
Residual taxes	3,380	*National Accounts, 1986,* table 7.2, lines 8, 15, 17, 18, 23, 24, 25, 27, 28, 29, 33, table 9.6, lines 33, 34, 37

2 Previous Tax Data

Data on taxation for earlier years is taken from the following sources:

1948–53: *National Income and Expenditure, 1957* (London: HMSO), tables 31–3, 36–40, pp. 29–38.

1954–61: *National Income and Expenditure, 1965* (London: HMSO), tables 36, 37, 39–41, pp. 42–9.

1962–9: *National Income and Expenditure, 1970* (London: HMSO), tables 37–9, 41, pp. 42–9.

1970–80: *National Income and Expenditure, 1981* (London: HMSO), tables 7.2–7.6, 8.2, 8.3, 9.7, pp. 48–68.

1981: *National Income and Expenditure, 1982* (London: HMSO), tables 7.2–7.6, 8.2, 8.3, 9.7, p. 48–68.

1982: *National Income and Expenditure, 1983* (London: HMSO), tables 7.2–7.4, 8.2, 8.3, 9.6, pp. 44–60.

1983: *United Kingdom National Accounts, 1984* (London: HMSO) tables 7.2–7.5, 8.2, 8.3, 9.6, pp. 56–74.

1984: *United Kingdom National Accounts, 1985* (London: HMSO), tables 7.2–7.5, 8.2, 8.3, 9.6, pp. 56–74.

3 Other Data Sources

Tax Rate and Base Levels

Information on tax rates and bases is obtained from the following publications: *Report of HM Customs and Excise* (published annually as a Command paper); *Report of the Board of Inland Revenue* (published annually as a Command paper); *Annual Abstract of Statistics* (published annually by HMSO); *Inland Revenue Statistics* (published annually by HMSO).

Additional unpublished information was provided by both the Board of Inland Revenue and HM Customs and Excise.

Budget Tax Changes

Information on the number and content and value in £ millions of tax changes introduced by Chancellors of the Exchequer in their budgets is as reported by the Treasury on Budget Day and printed in the *Financial Times*.

International Tax Comparisons

Comparative cross-national tax and spending data was obtained from the following publications: *Revenue Statistics of OECD Member Countries* (published annually by OECD) and *OECD National Accounts Statistics*, Vols 1 and 2 (published annually by OECD).

References

Aaron, Henry, ed. (1981) *The Value-Added Tax: Lessons from Europe* (Washington, DC: Brookings Institution).

Alt, James E. (1979) *The Politics of Economic Decline* (Cambridge: Cambridge University Press).

Alt, James E. (1983) 'The evolution of tax structures', *Public Choice*, 41, 1, 181–222.

Anson, Sir William R. (1908) *The Law and Custom of the Constitution*, 3rd edn, 3 vols (Oxford: Clarendon Press).

Ardant, Gabriel (1975) 'Financial policy and economic infrastructure of modern states and nations', in Charles Tilly, ed., *The Formation of National States in Western Europe* (Princeton: Princeton University Press), 164–242.

Aristotle (1972 edn) *The Politics* (London: Heinemann).

Atkinson, A. B., and Stern, N. H. (1980) 'Taxation and incentives in the United Kingdom', *Lloyds Bank Review*, April.

Atkinson, A. B., and Stiglitz, J. E. (1980) *Lectures on Public Economics* (Maidenhead: McGraw-Hill).

Bachrach, Peter, and Baratz, Morton (1970) *Power and Poverty: Theory and Practice* (New York: Oxford University Press).

Barnett, Joel (1982) *Inside the Treasury* (London: Deutsch).

Binney, J. E. D. (1958) *British Public Finance and Administration, 1774–1792* (Oxford: Clarendon Press).

Braun, Rudolf (1975) 'Taxation, socio-political structure and state building', in Charles Tilly, ed., *The Formation of National States in Europe* (Princeton: Princeton University Press), 243–327.

Braybrooke, D., and Lindblom, C. E. (1963) *A Strategy of Decision* (New York: Free Press).

Brennan, Geoffrey, and Buchanan, James M. (1980) *The Power to Tax* (New York: Cambridge University Press).

Breton, A. (1974) *The Economic Theory of Representative Government* (London: Macmillan).

Brown, C. V. (1983) *Taxation and the Incentive to Work*, 2nd edn (Oxford: Oxford University Press).

Brown, C. V., and Jackson, P. M. (1978) *Public Sector Economics* (Oxford: Martin Robertson).

Buchanan, J. M., and Wagner, R. E. (1977) *Democracy in Deficit: The Political Legacy of Lord Keynes* (New York: Academic Press).

Bulmer, Martin (1986) *Neighbours: The Work of Philip Abrams* (Cambridge: Cambridge University Press).

253

Bunbury, Sir Henry (1957) *Lloyd George's Ambulance Wagon* (London: Methuen).

Butler, D. E., and Stokes, D. (1974) *Political Change in Britain*, 2nd edn (London: Macmillan).

Butterworths UK Tax Guide, 1984–85, 3rd edn (London: Butterworth).

Caiden, Naomi, and Wildavsky, Aaron (1980) *Planning and Budgeting in Poor Countries* (New Brunswick, NJ: Transaction Books).

Castles, F. G., ed. (1982) *The Impact of Parties* (London: Sage).

Chester, Sir Norman (1981) *The English Administrative System 1780–1870* (Oxford: Clarendon Press).

Clarke, Sir Richard (1973) 'The long-term planning of taxation', in B. Crick and W. A. Robson, eds, *Taxation Policy* (Harmondsworth: Penguin), 15–70.

Cm. 5 (1986) *77th Report of the Commissioners of Her Majesty's Customs and Excise* (London: HMSO).

Cm. 14 (1986) *Her Majesty's Treasury: Autumn Statement 1986* (London: HMSO).

Cmnd 1432 (1961) *Control of Public Expenditure* (The Plowden Report) (London: HMSO).

Cmnd 5116 (1972) *Proposals for a Tax-Credit System* (London: HMSO).

Cmnd 6543 (1976) *Local Government Finance* (Layfield Committee)

Cmnd 8093 (1980) *The Taxation of Husband and Wife* (London: HMSO).

Cmnd 8160 (1981) *123rd Report of the Commissioners of Her Majesty's Inland Revenue* (London: HMSO)

Cmnd 8822 (1983) *Keith Committee on Enforcement Powers of the Revenue Departments*, 2 vols (London: HMSO).

Cmnd 9576 (1985) *127th Report of the Commissioners of Her Majesty's Inland Revenue, 1984* (London: HMSO).

Cmnd 9655 (1985) *76th Report of the Commissioners of Her Majesty's Customs and Excise* (London: HMSO).

Cmnd 9702 (1986) *The Government's Expenditure Plans 1986/7 to 1988/9*, 2 vols (London: HMSO).

Cmnd 9714 (1986) *Paying for Local Government* (London: HMSO).

Cmnd 9756 (1986) *The Reform of Personal Taxation* (London: HMSO).

Cmnd 9831 (1986) *Inland Revenue, Report for the Year Ended 31st December 1985* (London: HMSO).

Cochrane, D., and Orcutt, G. (1949) 'Application of least squares regression to relationships containing autocorrelated error terms', *Journal of American Statistical Association*, 44.

Crecine, J. P. (1971) 'Defence budgeting: organizational adaptation to environmental constraints', in R. F. Byrne *et al.*, *Studies in Budgeting* (Amsterdam: North-Holland).

Dahl, R. A. (1957) 'The concept of power', *Behavioral Science*, 2, 201–15.

Davis, O., Dempster, M. A. H., and Wildavsky, A. (1966) 'A theory of the budgetary process', *American Political Science Review*, 60, 529–47.

Dempster, M. A. H., and Wildavsky, A. (1979) 'On change: or, there is no magic size for an increment', *Political Studies*, 27, 371–89.

Deutsch, K. W. (1963) *The Nerves of Government* (New York: Free Press).

Dilnot, A., and Morris, N. (1981) 'What do we know about the black economy?', *Fiscal Studies*, 2, 1, 58–73.

Donoughue, Lord (1986) 'The conduct of British economic policy', in R. Hodder-Williams and J. Ceaser, eds, *Politics in Britain and the United States* (Durham, NC: Duke University Press), 119–41.

Dowell, S. (1888) *A History of Taxation and Taxes in England* (London: Longman).

Downs, Anthony (1957) *An Economic theory of Democracy* (New York: Harper).

Economic Progress Report (1983) 'Making a budget', No. 153 (January), 1–5.

Economic Trends (1985) 'The effects of taxes and benefits on household income 1984', No. 386 (London: HMSO), 99–115.

Feldstein, Martin (1976) 'On the Theory of tax reform', *Journal of Public Economics*, 6, 1–2, 77–104.

Furnham, Adrian, and Lewis, A. (1986) *The Economic Mind* (Brighton: Wheatsheaf).

Gallup Political Index, monthly (London: Gallup Poll Ltd).

Godwin, M., Hardwick, P., and Sandford, C. (1983) 'PAYE: costs v. benefits', *Accountancy*, 94 (November), 107–12.

Good, David A. (1980) *The Politics of Anticipation: Making Canadian Federal Tax Policy* (Ottawa: Carleton University School of Public Administration).

Goode, Richard (1984) *Governmental Finance in Developing Countries* (Washington, DC: Brookings Institution).

Grazia, Raeffele de (1980) 'Clandestine employment', *International Labour Review*, 119, 5, 549–63.

Groth, A. J. (1972) *People's Poland* (San Francisco: Chandler).

Gurr, T. R. (1970) *Why Men Rebel* (Princeton: Princeton University Press).

Hadenius, Axel (1985) 'Citizens strike a balance: discontent with taxes, content with spending', *Journal of Public Policy*, 5, 3, 349–64.

Harris, Kenneth (1985) 'The evolution of a strategy: interview with Nigel Lawson', *Observer*, 17 March.

Heald, David (1983) *Public Expenditure* (Oxford: Martin Robertson).

Heald, David (1985) 'Will the privatization of public enterprises solve the problem of control?', *Public Administration*, 63, 1, 7–22.

Heald, Gordon, and Wybrow, Robert J. (1986) *The Gallup Survey of Britain* (London: Croom Helm).

Heclo, Hugh (1981) 'Toward a new welfare state?', in P. Flora and A. J. Heidenheimer, eds, *The Development of Welfare States in Western Europe and America* (New Brunswick, NJ: Transaction Books), 383–406.

Heclo, H. and Wildavsky, A. (1981) *The Private Government of Public Money*, 2nd edn (London: Macmillan).

Hinrichs, Harley (1966) *A General Theory of Tax Structure Change During Economic Development* (Cambridge, Mass.: Harvard University Law School).

Hogwood, B. W., and Peters, B. Guy (1983) *Policy Dynamics* (Brighton: Wheatsheaf).

Hogg, Sarah (1985) 'Conjuring up the money mandarins', *The Times*, 14 March.

Hood, C. C. (1976) *The Limits of Administration* (London: Wiley).

Hood, C. C., Huby, M., and Dunsire, A. (1984) 'Bureaucrats and budgeting benefits', *Journal of Public Policy*, 4, 3, 163–80.

Hood, C. C. (1985) 'British tax structure development as administrative adaptation', *Policy Sciences*, 18, 1, 3–32.

Huhne, Christopher (1986) 'Indulging the baser instincts for high minded motives', *Guardian*, 18 December.

Inland Revenue (1985) *Inland Revenue Statistics 1985* (London: HMSO).

International Monetary Fund (1983) *Government Finance Statistics Yearbook*, Vol. 7 (Washington, DC: International Monetary Fund).

Jones, G. W., and Stewart, J. D. (1983) *The Case for Local Government* (London: Allen & Unwin).

Johnston, Sir Alexander (1965) *The Inland Revenue* (London: Allen & Unwin).

Johnston, J. (1974) *Econometric Methods* (London: McGraw-Hill).

Judge, Ken, ed. (1980) *Pricing the Social Services* (London: Macmillan).

Kaldor, Nicholas (1955) *An Expenditure Tax* (London: Allen & Unwin).

Karran, Terence (1985) 'The determinants of taxation in Britain', *Journal of Public Policy*, 5, 3, 365–86.

Karran, Terence (1985a) *The Determinants of Taxation in Britain: An Empirical Test*, University of Strathclyde Studies in Public Policy No. 141 (Glasgow: University of Strathclyde).

Kay, J. A. (1986) 'Tax reform in context: a strategy for the 1990s', *Fiscal Studies*, 7, 4, 1–17.

Kay, J. A., and King, M. A. (1983) *The British Tax System*, 3rd edn (Oxford: Oxford University Press).

Kerr, Clark (1983) *The Future of Industrial Societies: Convergence or Continuing Diversity?* (Cambridge, Mass.: Harvard University Press).

Kingdon, John W. (1984) *Agendas, Alternatives and Public Policies* (Boston: Little, Brown).

Larkey, Patrick D., Stolp, Chandler, and Winer, Mark (1981) 'Theorizing about the growth of government', *Journal of Public Policy*, 1, 2, 157–220.

Lee, Eugene C. (1986) 'Let the voter decide? The case of the 1981 rates referendum proposal', in Eugene Lee and Harold Wolman, *Urban Economic Development and Local Democracy* (London: Public Finance Foundation).

LeGrand, Julian, and Robinson, Ray (1983) *The Economics of Social Problems*, 2nd edn (London: Macmillan).

Lenkowsky, Leslie (1986) *Politics, Economics and Welfare Reform* (Lanham, Md: University Press of America/American Enterprise Institute).

Lewis, Alan (1982) *The Psychology of Taxation* (Oxford: Blackwell).

Leys, Colin (1983) *Politics in Britain* (London: Heinemann).

Lindbeck, Assar (1976) 'Stabilization policy in open economies with endogenous politicians', *American Economic Review*, 66, 2.

Lindblom, C. E. (1965) *The Intelligence of Democracy* (New York: Free Press).

Lipsey, David (1983) 'The making of the budget', *Sunday Times*, 13 March.

Lowell, A. Lawrence (1912) *The Government of England*, 2nd edn, 2 vols (London: Macmillan).

Mayhew, David (1974) *Congress: The Electoral Connection* (New Haven, Conn.: Yale University Press).

Meade, James E., Committee (1978) *The Structure and Reform of Direct Taxation* (London: Allen & Unwin).

Mosley, Paul (1984) *The Making of Economic Policy* (Brighton: Wheatsheaf).

Mosley, Paul (1985) 'When is a policy instrument not an instrument? Fiscal marksmanship in Britain, 1951–84', *Journal of Public Policy*, 5, 1, 69–86.

Mueller, Dennis C. (1979) *Public Choice* (Cambridge: Cambridge University Press).

Musgrave, Richard A. (1969) *Fiscal Systems* (New Haven: Yale University Press).

Musgrave, R. A., and Musgrave, P. (1980) *Public Finance in Theory and Practice* (New York: McGraw-Hill).

Newton, K. (1980) *Balancing the Books: Financial Problems of Local Government in West Europe* (London: Sage).

Newton, K., and Karran, T. J. (1985) *The Politics of Local Expenditure* (London: Macmillan).

Neustadt, Richard E., and May, Ernest (1986) *Thinking in Time* (New York: Free Press).

Niskanen, W. A. (1971) *Bureaucracy and Representative Government* (Chicago: Aldine).

Nordhaus, William (1975) 'The political business cycle', *Journal of Political Economy*, 85, 169–90.

O'Connor, James (1973) *The Fiscal Crisis of the State* (New York: St Martin's Press).

OECD (1971) *National Accounts, 1950–1968* (Paris: OECD).

OECD (1980) *The Tax/Benefit Position of Selected Income Groups* (Paris: OECD).

OECD (1981) *Income Tax Schedules: Distribution of Taxpayers and Revenues* (Paris: OECD).

OECD (1981a) *Long-Term Trends in Tax Revenues of OECD Member Countries, 1955–1980* (Paris: OECD).

OECD (1984) *Tax Expenditures: A Review of the Issues and Country Practices* (Paris: OECD).

OECD (1984a) *Revenue Statistics of OECD Member Countries, 1965–1983* (Paris: OECD).

OECD (1985) *Social Expenditure: 1960–1990* (Paris; OECD).

OECD (1986) *Revenue Statistics of OECD Member Countries 1965–1985* (Paris: OECD).

OECD (1986a) *Personal Income Tax Systems under Changing Economic Conditions* (Paris: OECD).

Parry, Geraint, and Morriss, Peter (1974) 'When is a decision not a decision?', in I. Crewe, ed., *Elites in Western Democracies* (London: Croom Helm), 317–36.

Parry, Richard (1985) 'Britain: stable aggregates, changing composition', in R. Rose, *Public Employment in Western Nations* (Cambridge: Cambridge University Press), 54–96.

Peacock, Alan (1981) 'Fiscal theory and the market for tax reform', in K. W. Roskamp and F. Forte, eds, *Reforms of Tax Systems* (Detroit: Wayne State University Press), 11–21.

Peacock, A., and Wiseman, J. (1961) *The Growth of Public Expenditure in the United Kingdom* (Princeton: Princeton University Press).

Pechman, Joseph, ed. (1985) *The Promise of Tax Reform* (Englewood Cliffs, NJ: Prentice-Hall).

Peretz, Paul (1982) 'There was no tax revolt!' *Politics and Society*, 11, 2, 231–49.

Pliatzky, Leo (1982) *Getting and Spending* (Oxford: Blackwell).

Posner, Michael, ed. (1978) *Demand Management* (London: Heinemann).

Prest, A. R., and Barr, N. A. (1979) *Public Finance in Theory and Practice*, 6th edn (London: Weidenfeld and Nicolson).

Public Accounts Committee (1986) *Arrears of Work at Tax Office*, 47th Report, 1985/6, House of Commons Paper No. 350 (London: HMSO).

Radian, Alex (1980) *Resource Mobilization in Poor Countries: Implementing Tax Policies* (New Brunswick, NJ: Transaction Books).

Riddell, Peter (1983) *The Thatcher Government* (Oxford: Martin Robertson).

Roberts, Paul K. (1984) *The Supply-Side Revolution* (Cambridge, Mass.: Harvard University Press).

Robinson, Ray (1986) 'Restructuring the welfare state: an analysis of public expenditure 1979/80–1984/5', *Journal of Social Policy*, 15, 1, 1–22.

Robinson, Ann, and Sandford, Cedric (1983) *Tax Policy-Making in the United Kingdom* (London: Heinemann).

Rose, Richard (1972) 'The market for policy indicators', in A. Shonfield and S. Shaw, eds, *Social Indicators and Social Policy* (London: Heinemann), 119–41.

Rose, Richard (1974) *The Problem of Party Government* (London: Macmillan).

Rose, Richard (1974a) 'Coping with urban change', in R. Rose, ed., *The Management of Urban Change in Britain and Germany* (London: Sage), 3–26.

Rose, Richard (1976) 'On the priorities of government', *European Journal of Political Research*, 4, 3, 247–89.

REFERENCES

Rose, Richard (1980) 'Misperceiving public expenditure: feelings about "Cuts"', in C. Levine and I. Rubin, eds, *Fiscal Stress and Public Policy* (London: Sage), 203–30.

Rose, Richard (1984) *Understanding Big Government* (London: Sage).

Rose, Richard (1984a) *Do Parties Make a Difference?* 2nd edn (London: Macmillan).

Rose, Richard (1985) 'Maximizing tax revenue while minimizing political costs', *Journal of Public Policy*, 5, 3, 289–320.

Rose, Richard (1985a) *How Exceptional Is American Government?*, University of Strathclyde Studies in Public Policy No. 150 (Glasgow: University of Strathclyde).

Rose, Richard (1985b) 'The programme approach to the growth of government', *British Journal of Political Science*, 15, 1, 1–28.

Rose, Richard (1985c) *Politics in England: Persistence and Change*, 4th edn (London: Faber).

Rose, Richard (1985d) 'Getting by in three economies', in J. E. Lane, ed., *State and Market* (London: Sage), 103–41.

Rose, Richard (1986) 'Law as a resource of public policy', *Parliamentary Affairs*, 39, 3, 297–314.

Rose, Richard (1986b) 'The dynamics of the welfare mix in Britain', in R. Rose and R. Shiratori, eds, *The Welfare State East and West* (New York: Oxford University Press), 80–102.

Rose, Richard (1986e) 'Common goals but different roles: the state's contribution to the welfare mix', in R. Rose and R. Shiratori, eds, *The Welfare State East and West* (New York: Oxford University Press), 13–39.

Rose, Richard (1987) *Ministers and Ministries: A Functional Analysis* (Oxford: Clarendon Press).

Rose, Richard (1987a) 'Steering the ship of state: one tiller but two pairs of hands', *British Journal of Political Science*, 17, 4.

Rose, Richard (forthcoming) 'Giving direction to civil servants: signals from law, expertise, the market and the electorate', in J. E. Lane, ed., *Bureaucracy and Public Choice* (London: Sage).

Rose, Richard, and Karran, Terence (1983) *Increasing Taxes, Stable Taxes or Both?*, University of Strathclyde Studies in Public Policy No. 116 (Glasgow: University of Strathclyde).

Rose, Richard, and Karran, Terence (1984) 'Inertia or incrementalism? A long-term view of the growth of government', in A. J. Groth and L. L. Wade, eds, *Comparative Resource Allocation* (Beverly Hills: Sage) 43–71.

Rose, Richard, and McAllister, Ian (1986) *Voters Begin to Choose* (London: Sage).

Rose, Richard, and Page, E. C. (1982) 'Chronic instability in fiscal systems', in Rose and Page, eds, *Fiscal Stress in Cities* (Cambridge: Cambridge University Press), 195–245.

Rose, Richard, and Peters, B. Guy (1978) *Can Government Go Bankrupt?* (New York: Basic Books).

Roskamp, Karl, and Forte, Francesco, eds (1981) *Reforms of Tax Systems* (Detroit: Wayne State University Press).

Sandford, Cedric (1973) *Hidden Costs of Taxation* (London: Institute for Fiscal Studies).

Sandford, Cedric, Godwin, M., Hardwick, P., and Butterworth, I. (1981) *Costs and Benefits of VAT* (London: Heinemann).

Sandford, Cedric (1983) 'The costs of paying tax', *Accountancy*, 97, June, 108–11.

Sarlvik, Bo, and Crewe, Ivor (1983) *Decade of Dealignment* (Cambridge: Cambridge University Press).

Saunders, Peter, and Klau, Friedrich (1985) 'The role of the public sector', *OECD Economic Studies*, No. 4, 5–239.

Sbragia, Alberta (1986) 'Capital markets and central–local politics in Britain', *British Journal of Political Science*, 16, 3, 311–40.

Schattschneider, E. E. (1960) *The Semi-Sovereign People* (New York: Holt, Rinehart & Winston).

Sears, David O., and Citrin, Jack (1982) *Tax Revolt: Something for Nothing in California* (Cambridge, Mass.: Harvard University Press).

Seldon, Arthur (1977) *Charge* (London: Institute of Economic Affairs).

Sharkansky, Ira (1970) *The Routines of Politics* (New York: Van Nostrand Reinhold).

Simon, Herbert (1952) 'A behavioral model of rational choice', *Quarterly Journal of Economics* 69, 1, 99–118.

Skidelsky, Robert J. (1970) *Politicians and the Slump* (Harmondsworth: Penguin).

Smith, G. (1980) *Something to Declare: 1000 Years of Customs and Excise* (London: Harrap).

Smith, Stephen (1986) *Britain's Shadow Economy* (Oxford: Clarendon Press).

Social Trends, 16 (1986) (London: Central Statistical Office, HMSO).

Steel, David, and Heald, David (1985) 'The privatization of public enterprises, 1979–83', in P. Jackson, ed., *Implementing Government Policy Initiatives: The Thatcher Administration 1979–83* (London: RIPA), 69–91.

Stein, Herbert (1984) *Presidential Economics* (New York: Simon & Schuster).

Stockman, David (1986) *The Triumph of Politics* (New York: Harper & Row).

Surrey, Stanley (1973) *Pathways to Tax Reform: The Concept of Tax Expenditures* (Cambridge, Mass.: Harvard University Press).

Surrey, Stanley, and McDaniel, Paul (1985) *Tax Expenditure* (Cambridge, Mass.: Harvard University Press).

Tanzi, Vito (1980) *Inflation and the Personal Income Tax* (Cambridge: Cambridge University Press).

Tarschys, Daniel (1985) 'Curbing public expenditure: current trends', *Journal of Public Policy*, 5, 1, 23–68.

Taverne, Dick (1986) 'The select vs. the universal: the SDP approach to welfare', *New Statesman*, 26 September.

Tinbergen, Jan (1952) *On the Theory of Economic Policy* (Amsterdam: North-Holland).

Titmuss, Richard M. (1970) *The Gift Relationship* (London: Allen & Unwin).

Treasury (1984) *Financial Statement and Budget Report 1984–85* (London: HMSO).

Wallis, K. F., Andrews, M. J., Bell, D. N. F., Fisher, P. G., and Whitley, J. D. (1984) *Models of the UK Economy* (Oxford: Oxford University Press).

Walters, Alan (1986) *Britain's Economic Renaissance: Margaret Thatcher's Reforms 1979–84* (New York: Oxford University Press).

Weaver, Kent (1986) 'The politics of blame avoidance', *Journal of Public Policy*, 6, 4.

Webber, Carolyn, and Wildavsky, Aaron (1986) *A History of Taxation and Expenditure in the Western World* (New York: Simon & Schuster).

Whiteley, Paul (1986) *Political Control of the Macro-Economy* (London: Sage).

Wildavsky, Aaron (1975) *Budgeting: A Comparative Theory of Budgetary Processes* (Boston: Little, Brown).

Wildavsky, Aaron (1980) *How to Limit Government Spending* (Berkeley: University of California Press).

Wildavsky, Aaron (1984) *The Politics of the Budgetary Process*, 4th edn (Boston: Little, Brown).

Wildavsky, Aaron (1985) 'Keeping kosher: the epistemology of tax expenditures', *Journal of Public Policy*, 5, 3, 401–11.

Wilensky, Harold (1986) *The New Corporatism: Centralization and the Welfare State*, Contemporary Political Sociology Series 06–020 (London: Sage).

Willmott, Peter (1986) *Social Networks, Informal Care and Public Policy*, Research Report No. 655 (London: Policy Studies Institute).

Witte, John (1985) *The Politics and Development of the Federal Income Tax* (Madison: University of Wisconsin Press).

Index

(Because so many entries refer to taxation, this word is normally omitted below).

H. Ferenczi Selem Verlag und Imprimatur purchase contact over
bitte wenden sich an verlag-informationen, contact Imaus & Imaus
Verlag GmbH, Kaulbachstraße 28, 80539 München, Germany